THE FIST THAT SHOOK THE WORLD

THE CINEMA OF BRUCE LEE

THE FIST THAT SHOOK THE WORLD

THE CINEMA OF BRUCE LEE

By Lou Gaul

MIDNIGHT MARQUEE PRESS, INC.
BALTIMORE, MARYLAND

ISBN 1-887664-12-2
Library of Congress Catalog Card Number 97-070784
Manufactured in the United States of America
Printed by Kirby Lithographic Company, Arlington, VA
First Printing by Midnight Marquee Press, Inc., April 1997

To my Mother,
who always taught that through hard work all things are possible;
to my Father,
who always told me that education opens any door;
and to my Wife,
whose caring and support provides daily inspiration.
With love, always.

TABLE OF CONTENTS

FOREWORD

Why a book about Bruce Lee?

Why now?

Those are fair questions, especially from people who have steadfastly considered the so-called "chop socky" pictures nothing more than a way for exhibitors to attract action-starved—not to mention popcorn-hungry—patrons to their theaters. Defending the martial arts genre neither interests nor excites me.

Bruce Lee, however, does excite me, something he has done ever since I first saw him in the early 1970s. Watching audiences respond to him with unrestrained cheers during the battles and respectful silence during the build-ups transformed the viewing experience into something ranging from a rousing sporting event to an uplifting religious revival meeting.

Quite simply, there has never been anyone like him on screen.

Ever.

In a world of copies, Bruce Lee remains a striking original. Certainly filmdom has had its traditional action heroes, from straight-shooting John Wayne to wisecracking Bruce Willis, but no such actor ever brought his personal history to his art and displayed it in such a totally raw, emotionally intriguing, completely unforgettable manner.

Lee willingly did what few screen artists ever do: He exposed his personal demons, focused on them, and produced a blazing show of strength, power that he seemed to rip from within the darkest depths of his psyche. The hateful prejudice he faced, the hard-won respect he fought to achieve, the closed "white" world he sought to conquer, and the intense passion he possessed for the martial arts all surface in his four major films, *Fists of Fury*, *The Chinese Connection*, *Return of the Dragon*, and *Enter the Dragon*. (For the sake of clarity, all of Bruce Lee's films will be referred to by their American distribution titles in this text.)

Those who feel these pictures are mere simplistic revenge tales that glisten only due to Lee's magnificent physical artistry should scratch the surface, look deeper, and study the images. I hope this book will help people do exactly that.

Although not pretending to touch on every element in Lee's body of work, I have toiled to identify the major themes, symbols, and motivations in his oeuvre. I do it with the deepest respect for Bruce Lee, his family, and the legacy he left behind.

However, my intention was never to be an advocate trying to transform doubters of Lee's cinematic power into true believers. Shame on those who don't already appreciate his incredible and indelible impact on entertainment.

Lee displayed the majesty of the martial arts to people everywhere and, to put it mildly, the world has never been the same. When we see a child play a video game (be it *Mortal Kombat* or any similar title), when we see Mel Gibson using an Asian fighting style in the *Lethal Weapon* series, when we see a self-defense academy in every American town, when we see the blazing action in a John Woo or Ringo Lam film, or when we see Chuck Norris karate kicking villains on the CBS hit *Walker, Texas Ranger*, it all goes directly back to Bruce Lee, who—sadly—never lived to see his international impact.

And returning to those who deride his body of cinematic work, I suggest enjoying the sense of excitement, adventure, and discovery Bruce Lee still provides almost a quarter of a century after his death.

Like James Dean (the symbol of rebellious youth) and Marilyn Monroe (the symbol of sexual possibilities), Bruce Lee—the symbol of the common man's fighting spirit in an oppressive world—has become a screen icon for present and future generations. His passion radiates off the screen.

Before starting to read, you may want some idea of how Lee's four films rank in terms of quality and impact. Here's how I list them:

Number 1: *Return of the Dragon*. Lee staged the fights in all of his films, but this is his only official directorial effort. As such, it provides more insights into the action-filmmaker than any of his other works. We see his broad brand of humor, his intense love of working people, and perhaps most importantly, his inspired sense of style in staging fight sequences. Most notable, of course, is his hard-hitting choreography for the climactic battle between him and Chuck Norris. Lee intended the one-on-one fight to be the best hand-to-hand scene ever captured on celluloid. He succeeded.

Number 2: *Enter the Dragon*. Sure John Saxon gets too much screen time and the main villain is lifted directly out of a James Bond adventure, but Lee was at the peak of his physical powers and strained to do the best job possible. He knew the stakes were high. Lee had long waited to break into the American market and viewed *Enter the Dragon* as the perfect opportunity. His screen character may be cold, but the passion Lee brings to the fight sequences—particularly the intense underground fortress battle involving 50 opponents—melts that frosty exterior.

Number 3: *The Chinese Connection*. For his second starring role, Lee was willing to expose his emotional side, something he would never do again on screen. How many action superstars would be willing to cry and leap on top of the casket of a loved one? Although taking a great risk by going to such lengths with the emotional level, Lee pulls it off and in the process infuses the picture with a heartfelt undercurrent. Lee also punctuates it with some terrific combat scenes, though the final battle with the evil Japanese school owner lacks raw power, much like his climactic battle with Han in *Enter the Dragon* seems slightly disappointing compared to the earlier fight scenes.

Number 4: *Fists of Fury*. Though a noble first effort, the film takes far too long—almost 45 minutes—before allowing Lee to snap into action. Once the fighting starts, however, *Fists of Fury* assumes a nasty, almost horror film-like edge in terms of the gore level, and it's the only Lee picture where the best battles occur at night, with the moonlight suggesting the dark side of the character that surfaces when he begins mortal combat. One can't help admiring the rawness of this work, which still possesses a violent shock value and provides a frightening jolt.

Stefan Hammond and Mike Wilkins note in *Sex and Zen & A Bullet in the Head: The Essential Guide to Hong Kong's Mind-Bending Films* (1996) that:

> "What Elvis Presley was to rock 'n' roll, Bruce
> Lee was to celluloid kung fu."

Years before George Lucas introduced The Force to audiences, Bruce Lee displayed The Fist. It was one that truly shook the world.

INTRODUCTION

"To express yourself in freedom, you must
die to everything of yesterday. From the 'old,'
you derive security; from the 'new,' you gain
the flow."

—Bruce Lee [1]

When Clive James appeared on NBC's *Today Show* to discuss his 1993 book, *Fame in the 20th Century*, Bryant Gumbel asked the Australian author to name the two people with the most recognizable faces in the world.

"Muhammad Ali," James said as the TV host nodded in agreement. He then paused, adding, "and Bruce Lee."

The second name stunned the normally controlled Gumbel. He stared briefly at James, who quickly explained that on a worldwide basis, Lee—an Asian-American martial artist and motion picture star—ranked right behind history's greatest boxer in terms of international recognition, despite having only four complete motion pictures featuring him in starring roles. For Lee's American fans, the interchange was a defining moment. Suddenly, a figure, one whose body of work was thoughtlessly dismissed by the vast majority of the country, was named the second most recognized person on the planet, an achievement that can only be imagined by today's highly paid action stars.

Steven Seagal, Chuck Norris, Jackie Chan, and Jean-Claude Van Damme— as well as other obviously less talented martial arts performers—are all pretenders to the throne.

There remains only one king of cinematic kung fu: Bruce Lee. He still holds that position more than two decades after his passing.

In his short, meteoric film career, Lee, who died under seemingly mysterious circumstances at the age of 32, expressed himself by breaking down traditions in the martial arts and by shattering barriers of prejudice in Hollywood, a place which he termed "like a magic kingdom... beyond everyone's reach." [2] The fight against racial hatred ranked as the toughest battle of his life, the one that most damaged his spirit. After vowing to become a motion picture star, Lee focused on big-screen success despite the words of warning from knowledgeable, well-meaning friends and students like screenwriter Stirling Silliphant,

13

who recalled: "He said he'd be the biggest star in the world, bigger than (James) Coburn or (Steve) McQueen. I said, 'No way. You're a Chinese in a white man's world.' Then, he went out and did it."[3]

At the time of Lee's death, Italian producer Carlo Ponti was preparing a film deal that would have made the Chinese-American martial artist the highest paid actor in the world.[4] Even without the Ponti deal, Lee, whom the *Village Voice* dubbed "the Burt Reynolds of the Orient"[5] at the time (a fitting title since Lee, like Reynolds, could easily alter from a macho presence to a comedic characterization), was the first Chinese-American to achieve superstar status.[6]

Through his body of work—*Fists of Fury, The Chinese Connection, Return of the Dragon,* and *Enter the Dragon*—Lee forever changed the image of the martial arts—and of the Chinese—in the minds of Americans. But he went far beyond this limited goal. He became a potent image of the hero; even, in the minds of some, a demi-god with near supernatural powers; an image of self-perfection through self-discipline; a fearless rebel against a corrupt social order.[7] "Bruce was more than just a single success story," said Sterling Silliphant. "He represented a whole race finally accepted in films."

But Lee's appeal transcended color barriers and socio-economic lines. In *Saturday Night Fever* (1977), director John Badham placed a Lee poster in a prominent frame position as John Travolta, playing hipster-wanna-be Tony Manero, dresses in front of a mirror. Travolta's street-wise character, who works as a hardware-store clerk, only comes to life when performing dazzling dance routines within the confines of a disco's dance floor; likewise, Lee's characters explode when on a battlefield but either blend into the background (as in *Fists of Fury*) or stands out because of his bumbling (as in *Return of the Dragon*) when interacting in everyday situations.

Lee's screen persona is also exploited in director Robert Milligan's *Bloodbrothers* (1978) when Richard Gere takes his younger brother to see *Enter the Dragon* as a special treat and a means of escaping a bleak blue-collar existence. Thirty seconds of the cavern scene are shown, and the action clearly touches the boy, taking him to a fantasy world in which a smaller man conquers incredible odds through a daring combination of martial arts expertise and animal ferocity.

Lee's savage fighting—with its elements of deadly danger and seething passion—certainly stirred a viewer's blood. His physical force went beyond a mere screen image and touched his fans in a way very few performers ever have or will.

An incredibly sordid assortment of rip-off films attempted to squeeze profits out of Lee's screen appeal after the actor's untimely death. Pictures with titles such as *Bruce Lee—His Last Game of Death, Bruce Lee and I,* and *The Way of the Dragon: The Story of Bruce Lee* flooded theaters, and at one time, plans were announced for *Ilsa Meets Bruce Lee in the Devil's Triangle.*

Lee devoted his life to learning, developing, teaching, and expanding his art.

Fortunately, it never went before the cameras. Ilsa, played by Dyanne Thorne, previously appeared in *Ilsa—Shewolf of the SS* (1974), *Ilsa—Harem Keeper of the Oil Sheiks* (1976), and *Man Eaters* (1978), all directed by Don Edmonds. The busty character's specialty was wearing Nazi uniforms and torturing naked men and women. Thorne also starred in *Wanda the Wicked Warden* (1979), directed by Jess Franco. She played an Ilsa-like character named Greta the Torturer.

Such exploitative cinematic fare simply tarnished the name of Bruce Lee, who devoted his life to learning, developing, teaching, and expanding his art.

15

From the old masters of gung fu (the Cantonese spelling, which Lee always preferred to the Westernized kung fu), the martial artist learned the basic principles of the "art" of self defense and then added his own style, naming it "Jeet Kune Do." Armed with an incredible physical prowess, he arrived on the screen ready to do battle with the massive social forces that had held him and millions of Chinese in bondage.

His screen antics also fueled the sales of kung fu films worldwide. As Chinese producer Run Run Shaw told *Time* magazine: "American people always love action. Hollywood made lots of money with cowboys until Italians made cowboy pictures with more action (a reference to Sergio Leone's 'spaghetti' westerns *A Fistful of Dollars*, *For A Few Dollars More,* and *The Good, the Bad and the Ugly*, all with Clint Eastwood). Next (from England) came James Bond. Now from Hong Kong comes Kung Fu."[8]

Lee's cinematic nicknames—The Fist That Shook the World, The Fastest Fist in the East, The Little Dragon, The King of Kung Fu, and The Man with the Golden Punch[9]—attested to more than just his physical feats. In his first three Hong Kong pictures (as opposed to the American-financed *Enter the Dragon*), Lee struck a blow for poor common folks, with the force of his fist truly shaking the world as he won the hearts of Asians, blacks (especially in American cities),[10] and Arabs, as well as some Caucasians,[11] as an indestructible hero. To blacks, Chicanos, and Chinese, he was a hero because he succeeded. In Third World countries, he was the first hero they ever had.[12] He became the first Chinese screen hero celebrated by an international audience.[13]

"I think Bruce is a great exploitation actor, like (Clint) Eastwood, (John) Wayne, etc. They believe what they do at the moment they are doing it, no matter how outrageous; these actors are worth their weight in gold," observed Fred Weintraub, producer of *Enter the Dragon*.

What made Lee worth even more than Eastwood and Wayne types, however, was his genuine victory against the Hollywood establishment, which believed so strongly in the prejudice of the American public that it prevented Lee from becoming a major TV personality. As one ABC-TV executive said during the casting for *Kung Fu*: "You can not make a star out of a 5-foot-6 Chinese actor."[14] He had to leave the U.S. and go back to his parents' homeland—Hong Kong—in order to be revered in America, the country of his birth. (Lee wasn't the only superstar rejected by Hollywood. Executives at Universal Pictures once dismissed action-great Clint Eastwood because his Adam's apple was too big, a physical trait which made them feel that the actor would never be accepted as a leading man.)

Self-defense experts John Corcoran and Emil Farkas have credited Lee with having more impact on the fighting arts than "all the other martial artists in the world put together."[15] Praise for his legendary physical abilities is endless, with James Coburn, his second celebrity student (after Steve McQueen),

Lee's screen antics fueled the sales of kung fu films worldwide.

declaring that Lee was "the most perfect physical specimen I have ever seen"[16] and "the Nijinsky of the martial arts."[17] Lee's wife, Linda, who often worked as his partner when he developed new fighting techniques, termed him "the Galileo of the martial arts."[18] According to screenwriter Joe Hyams, who wrote about his dealings with Lee in *Zen in the Martial Arts*, the Chinese-American man was a "legend" in the martial arts before stepping before a camera.

Even folksinger Phil Ochs, a man more prone to soft ballads than hard punches, became a Lee devotee after experiencing the power of his performance with a Philippines audience in September 1972. Ochs called Lee's physique "the science of the body taken to its highest form; and violence (in his films), no matter how outrageous, is always strangely purifying."[19]

In a 1982 issue of the martial arts fanzine, *The Jade Screen*, Alex Ben Block attributed some of Lee's rise to being in the right place at the right time. Block told interviewer Gary Kohatsu:

> "I think where timing came into play (in terms of Lee's success) was that America made a move toward China at the same time. It was the end of the Vietnam war, and there was a great feeling that we didn't understand the

17

Lee's rise to worldwide motion picture stardom remains the stuff of which legends are made.

Orient, and now it was time to begin learning about it. There was an openness on the part of Americans of all nationalities, races, whatever, to begin to see what there was to learn about these people in the Orient.

"We just got the hell kicked out of us by the North Vietnamese, and (President Richard) Nixon had gone into China, and we saw a civilization that was working for them. And I think Bruce Lee came along at the right time in that way.

"As for the movie thing, I think he was responsible. He had crossover appeal, meaning he was an Oriental (but) he could play to American audiences, to many different races, and be successful... A lot of other movies made were either so badly made or so stupid that people couldn't identify, and that's why after Bruce Lee died, the martial arts genre never succeeded anywhere near the dimensions people expected. When Bruce Lee lit the fuse, everybody was waiting for the explosion creating a new genre which would stay with us for years, and that never really happened."

Lee saw movies as a "combination of commercial creativity and creative commerce" and recognized that gung fu films represented a limited genre with only one asset—gung fu—going for them and everything else against them.[20] He adhered to the genre's one aesthetic principle (if the gung fu is lousy—or if there's not enough of it—the movie fails), and then bravely battled to expand it.

First, with *Fists of Fury* and *The Chinese Connection*, he attempted to be involved with improving the writing and staging the action. With *Return of the Dragon*, he shattered the Hong Kong film studio tradition of only using contract players and wrote, directed, co-produced, and starred in the project. All three films contain simplistic plots, but elements of racial and sexual stereotyping lurk beneath the surface, giving them—as well as *Enter the Dragon*—a subtext that deserves study.

The following book will pinpoint many of the elements of prejudice throughout Lee's career, the use of prejudice as a theme in his films, sexual elements in the pictures, critical overviews, and scene readings. For clarification, the text is divided into a number of sections, with the cumulative effect of presenting a picture of a gifted, driven genius whose sheer audacity, unyielding principles, and stern stubbornness made him not only a martial artist but, in the grand sense, a cinematic artist as well.

Lee once said:

> "To generate great power, you must first totally relax and gather your strength, and then concentrate your mind and all of your strength on hitting your target."

His target—at first a seemingly impossible one—was worldwide motion picture stardom.

His rise to it remains the stuff of which legends are made.

CHAPTER ONE
BIRTH OF THE DRAGON

Born in San Francisco's Chinese Hospital on November 27, 1940, Lee, whose Chinese name was Lee Jun Fan (which means Return to San Francisco; the name was later changed to Lee Yuen Kam because the Chinese characters in the name were similar to his late grandfather's), was the son of a Cantonese Opera Company star (Lee Hoi Chuen, a Buddhist) and his wife (Grace, a Catholic). Lee, dubbed "Bruce" by one of the hospital nurses, had two brothers (Peter and Robert) and two sisters (Agnes and Phoebe).[21]

As a star in the Chinese Opera (which was like America's vaudeville, as opposed to the much more serious Peking Opera), Lee Hoi Chuen was performing in New York's Chinatown 3,000 miles away when Bruce was born. Three months after his son's birth, Lee Hoi Chuen took his family back to Hong Kong. At six months of age, the infant Lee was carried into a scene of *Tears of San Francisco*. He returned to the screen from the age of six to 18, making 20 films under the name of Lee Siu Loong—The Little Dragon.[22] He received that nickname because he was born in the year of the Dragon at the hour of the Dragon.[23]

At six, he appeared in a Cantonese tearjerker, *The Birth of Mankind*, in which he turned into a pickpocket and was run over by a truck. The film flopped, but two years later, he was cast with E Chow Shui, the great Cantonese film comedian of the 1940s, in *Kid Cheung*, which established him as a child performer and created the fighter persona which he would continue through his adult career. In it, he played a youngster who physically challenged other boys.[24] His father, who practiced t'ai-chi ch'uan[25] and died in 1965 shortly before his 64th birthday, was less than happy with Bruce's endeavors as a child performer and, through the years, urged his son to concentrate on a more "stable" career than acting.[26] As a youngster, Lee had planned to become a doctor.[27]

The most famous of his youth films were: *The Birth of Mankind* (1946), *Kid Cheung* (1950), *Blame It On Father*, *A Myriad Homes*, *A Mother's Tears*, *In the Face of Demolition* (all in 1953), *Orphan's Song*, *An Orphan's Tragedy*, *We Owe It to Our Children*, *Love* (all in 1955), *Too Late For Divorce* (1956), *The Thunderstorm,* and *The Orphan* (both 1957).[28] Because of the indifferent treatment given to Cantonese films, most of his early pictures no longer exist.

As he entered his teen years, Lee was described by one Golden Harvest executive as a "thug."[29] His brother Robert recalled that Bruce "loved to fight" and said his brother claimed to average "two fights per day" as a youth.[30] Because of Lee's nervous energy, his brother Peter said the family nicknamed him "Never Sit Down."[31]

According to his sister Agnes, Lee's number of battles escalated through the years. She observed:

> "As a teenager, he began to get into more and more fights for no reason at all. And if he didn't win, he was furious! He always considered himself a winner, and losing even occasionally was unbearable to him."[32]

Although Lee's family resided in the fairly prosperous section at 218 Nathan Road in Kowloon, his father allowed many people to stay with the family (including some Cantonese servants, a young boy whom the family had adopted, and a couple of other relatives), for a total of 16 people.[33] The over-crowded conditions and lack of supervision, especially from his father (who had been injured during a Japanese bombing raid on Hong Kong in December, 1941), caused Lee to roam the streets and become a gang leader by the time he was in the 11th grade.

At age 13, he decided to formally learn to defend himself and began to practice wing chun, close-quarter street fighting.[34] He studied under Yip Man, a Chinese immigrant from the Kwantung Province who brought wing chun (which means beautiful springtime) from behind the Bamboo Curtain.[35] As legend goes, the form, which stresses simple, direct movements designed for females and those with small frames, was founded by a Buddhist nun, Yim Wing Chun, at some time between the 16th and 17th centuries. She eliminated most of the katas (or movements—some kung fu systems require memorizing more than 100 katas; wing chun has only three)[36] and stressed speed as opposed to strength.[37]

For three years, Lee attended school at the exclusive St. Francis Xavier College, run by an old German missionary and ex-boxer, Brother Edward, in Kowloon. Brother Edward loved self defense and encouraged Lee to pursue the art form.[38] Lee became the school boxing champion, and he and his fellow students especially enjoyed the intense competition between themselves and the British students at the nearby King George V School. In the afternoon, he and the other Chinese students would participate in name calling with the British youths, a situation that resulted in numerous fights in which the youngster experimented with the principles of wing chun and boxing.[39]

Lee also appreciated what martial arts exercising did for his body. His favorite ploy to interest girls was to ask them to "feel my muscles."[40] He applied the physical moves of wing chun to dancing, at which he became extremely adept, and in 1958 was named the top contestant in a Crown Colony cha-cha championship.

But his street fighting continued to cause trouble at home. After *The Orphan*, Run Run Shaw, owner of Shaw Studios, wanted Lee to sign a long-term contract. Lee convinced his parents to let him drop out of school (where he had the equivalent of a 10th-grade education) and accept the offer. Although his mother believed her son had the talent, she worried about the young man's fights. When the authorities officially complained about his ever-worsening behavior, his mother Grace declined Shaw's offer and sent her son, via steamship, back to San Francisco. He had just $100 in his pocket.[41]

It marked the start of a voyage which would alter the course of Lee's entire life.

CHAPTER 2
RETURN TO AMERICA

With a background in Hong Kong movies, Lee, upon arriving in San Francisco in 1958, briefly considered applying for film work, but he believed America to be a racist society, one which either actively discriminated against Chinese or blatantly ignored them.

Lee observed:

> "When I went back to the States, I said, 'Here I am, a Chinese, not prejudiced or anything, just realistic thinking.' How many times in (Hollywood) films is a Chinese required? And when it is required, it is always branded as the typical tung, dung, tung, tung, tung, with the little pigtail in the back... You know the type. So I said the hell with it."[42]

Lee's analysis of the prejudiced view of the Chinese was extremely astute. The cliché of the "yellow menace" had prowled through Western cinema from silent days. Some German-made films—Robert Reinert's *Opium* and Fritz Lang's *Der Spinnen*—contained a distinct anti-Chinese sentiment at a time suspiciously close to when that country lost its Chinese concessions.

The chorus was taken up at the end of World War I in Hollywood, when Chinese immigration raised the spectre of a very basic chauvinistic fear. A flood of films appeared in which the ultimate horror was revealed as being a mixed marriage, something that had to be avoided even if death provided the only alternative. (Lee faced that old prejudice when he asked Linda Emery, a Caucasian whose mother strongly objected to her daughter's relationship outside her race, to be his wife.) Serials like *The Yellow Menace* and titles like *Mandarin's Gold* and *The Yellow Arm* streamed out of the studios. Lon Chaney appeared as Yen Sin in *Shadows*, and Constance Talmadge was granted a last-minute reprieve in *East is West*, because, in the last reel, she is revealed to be white.

The anti-Chinese image continued through Warner Oland's 1929 Fu Manchu in *The Mysterious Dr. Fu Manchu* to British actor Christopher Lee's sanguine interpretation of this shady manipulator of men in 1966's *Brides of Fu Manchu*.[43]

Anticipating such prejudice, Lee dashed any thoughts of a film career; instead, he considered teaching the martial arts.[44] He briefly worked as a dance instructor in San Francisco[45] before leaving for a job as a busboy-waiter at Ruby Chow's, a Chinese restaurant in Seattle, Washington, where he resided.

Lee, who was unhappy about going from being a member of a prosperous Hong Kong family to working at a restaurant, continued as a waiter while earning a diploma at Edison Vocational High School, and then enrolled as a philosophy student at Washington University. There, he met a young American medical student, Linda Emery, of Swedish origin. The woman, whose father died when she was four, felt attracted to Lee's authoritative manner.[46] They were introduced through Linda's Chinese girlfriend, who studied the martial arts with Lee. The couple married in 1964 and had two children, Brandon and Shannon.

While at Washington University, Lee was a member of the Armed Forces Reserve but was classified 4-F in 1963 for an undescended testicle.[47]

Lee had been developing his own martial arts philosophy, which he called Jeet Kune Do, which translated means "way of the stopping fist" or "way of the intercepting fist."[48] He improved on the wing chun style, which forms the nucleus of Jeet Kune Do,[49] saying that attack offers the best form of defense, and rejecting the conventional 1-2 sequence of block and counter attack in favor of simultaneously blocking and punching.[50]

As he would later scoff at the traditions of the movie moguls in Hong Kong, Lee readily attacked the traditional styles of martial arts masters, an outspoken stance that earned him many enemies. Lee, who listened to the complex rhythmical patterns of Indian music on stereo headphones when seeking inspiration for new self-defense movements,[51] believed that "efficiency" is anything that scores and that belts, given to reward levels of martial arts achievement, were "only to hold pants up."[52] (That "pants up" quote was borrowed by screenwriter Robert Mark Kamen for *The Karate Kid*, in which Noriyuki "Pat" Morita, when questioned by student Ralph Macchio about the teacher's belt ranking, jokes about the unimportance of traditional ranking by saying his waist band came from "J. C. Penney's.")

In the front of his Los Angeles dojo (gym), he even erected a miniature tombstone, complete with flowers and the words:

"In memory of a once fluid man, crammed
and disturbed by the classical mess."[53]

The difference between Lee's Jeet Kune Do, described as "a devastating amalgam of speed, power, and deception,"[54] and the classical forms has been likened to the difference between pre-1800 British formation fights and Vietnam guerrilla warfare.[55]

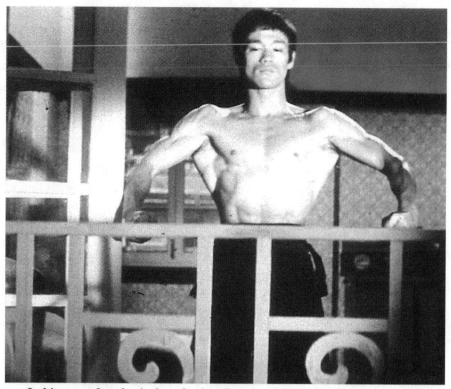

In his quest for physical perfection, Lee drove himself with a vengeance.

Linda Lee, in her book, *Bruce Lee: The Man Only I Knew*, described her husband as:

> "Never orthodox—he was always the
> innovator; the skeptic; the iconoclast. Right
> from the beginning, for example, he set his
> face against the kind of rankings (belts, from
> white to black) that exist in karate."[56]

While in Seattle, Lee opened his first studio—The Jun Fan Gung-Fu Institute—in a basement of the city's Chinatown section[57] and, in 1963, he planned to open a chain of the schools to earn a living.[58] He also earned the wrath of competing martial arts instructors, because he taught non-Asians the Oriental art form and defense techniques.[59]

Lee, realizing that he should adapt his martial arts ability to make a place in the world,[60] used his quick wit and startling physical abilities to interest people and proved somewhat successful at the task. By 1964, however, he realized that Seattle was too unsophisticated for the martial arts school chain concept and moved to Oakland, California, where he hoped the facilities would find a

27

more open-minded—and financially able—following. According to his first student and assistant instructor, Jesse Glover, Lee did not consider himself a good teacher, because he was so caught up in his own development and had little patience and time for slow learners.[61]

For Jeet Kune Do, Lee preferred kicks from the waist down,[62] although he displayed higher, flashier kicking movements in his films. When asked about his reasons for the low kicks, Lee slyly referred to the prejudice with which many Americans viewed his countrymen: "Kung fu is very sneaky. You know the Chinese, they always hit low."

In his quest for physical perfection, Lee drove himself with a vengeance. He was reported to have had his sweat glands removed from under his arm to make him look better[63] and vigorously exercised each day—many times on apparatus of his own design—for a minimum of two hours. (He was the fore-runner of other performers who altered their physiques for different screen images. Robert De Niro gained 60 pounds to play Jake LaMotta in 1980's *Raging Bull*, Mariel Hemingway had breast implants to portray slain *Playboy* Playmate Dorothy Stratten in 1983's *Star 80*, Ben Kingsley lost 20 pounds to resemble 1982's *Gandhi*, and Christopher Reeve—under the guidance of David Prowse, best known as Darth Vader in *Star Wars*—added 20 pounds of muscle to star as the Man of Steel in 1978's *Superman—The Movie*.)

In 1970, while experimenting with a 125-pound weight, he severely injured his back and was told he damaged a sacral nerve and would never be able to perform his kicks again. He stayed in bed for three months (a time his wife described as watching her spouse "enduring great mental and physical pain, stress, and financial problems") and waited six months before beginning light exercise.

During the recovery period, he compiled the notes which became the basis for his book, *Jeet Kune Do*. Through his drive to regain his physical abilities, Lee devoted himself to returning to peak form and succeeded[64] and never ceased in his quest for improvement and perfection. At the time of his death in 1973, he was striving to improve his finger thrusts. Pieces of wood that contained deep impressions of his fingers were found in his Hong Kong home.[65]

Embarrassed by his English,[66] Lee dedicated himself to eliminating or drastically reducing his thick accent. (With the exception of *Enter the Dragon*, all of his films were dubbed.) Los Angeles Lakers star Kareem Abdul-Jabbar, the former UCLA basketball star who studied Jeet Kune Do under Lee during his junior year, recalled that Lee was furious when he accidentally slipped into a Chinese accent and the student noticed the mistake. Jabbar said:

> "He was a funny guy, very proud. I
> remember one time when we were talking,
> having a rapid discussion about something,

and all of a sudden, he slipped into a Chinese
accent sort of thing. He pronounced this word
incorrectly—I don't remember what it was—
and I laughed. He got really mad, and before
it could go any further, I had to grab him and
hug him. He was very human behind all that
invincibility, and he didn't want anybody to
see him in his moments of weakness."[67]

While giving a demonstration to promote his school at the 1964 International Karate Championships in Long Beach, California, Lee was spotted by hair stylist Jay Sebring (who was killed by the Charles Manson family in the infamous Sharon Tate slayings).[68] A few months from that night, Sebring, who became a Lee student, would mention the Chinese-American's name to producer William Dozier, who was then preparing a show entitled *Number One Son*, based on Charlie Chan's offspring. It would mark the start of Lee's cinematic career as an adult and the beginning of the fierce prejudice he would face—and endure—while he remained in Hollywood.

30

CHAPTER 3
THE FIGHT FOR STARDOM BEGINS

A TV version of the popular radio show, *The Green Hornet,* from the 1930s and 1940s, first created by George W. Trendle (who also created *The Lone Ranger*), was launched in the wake of the success of *Batman*, which was also produced by William Dozier and starred Adam West and Burt Ward as two caped crime fighters. (*The Green Hornet* was telecast on ABC, Fridays, 7:30 to 8 p.m., from Sept. 9, 1966 to July 14, 1967.)

In the familiar plot outline, Brit Reid (Van Williams), a crusading editor and publisher of *The Daily Sentinel*, fought crime in the secret guise of The Green Hornet. Only his faithful manservant Kato (Lee) and District Attorney F.P. Scanlon (Walter Brooke) knew Reid's secret identity.

Some changes were made in adapting *The Green Hornet* to television and to the 1960s. In addition to the newspaper, Brit owned a TV station. The evil he fought often involved organized crime (not the bizarre villains of *Batman*) and his contemporary crime-fighting gadgetry included The Black Beauty, a customized 1966 Chrysler Imperial, rebuilt—for $50,000—by Hollywood designer Dean Jeffries.[69]

Lee's involvement in *The Green Hornet* really started when Dozier considered him for a starring role in *Number One Son*, a series which he had begun planning in 1961.[70] Ross Martin, who starred as Robert Conrad's secret service partner Artemus Gordon in TV's *The Wild Wild West* (CBS; 1965-1970), signed to star as Charlie Chan.[71]

Lee cynically commented on his participation in *Number One Son*, saying of the prejudiced way in which Hollywood producers saw Asians:

> "Naturally, I was signed to play Charlie Chan's Number One Son. I mean, that's what Chinese actors do for a living in Hollywood, isn't it? Charlie himself is always played by a round-eye wearing six pounds of make-up."

Lee signed for $1,800 a week, which he considered "a fortune," in February, 1965.[72]

But *Number One Son*, because of Lee's nationality, never developed into a series. Screenwriter Lorenzo Semple, Jr., who penned the screenplays for the remake of *King Kong, Never Say Never Again,* and the 1966 pilot episode of *Batman*, said of the proposed program:

> "I had been hacking around writing horrible pilots, which didn't sell, for producer William Dozier. Then, Bill made a deal with ABC to do a Charlie Chan series called *Number One Son*. I wrote the script in Spain, where I was living at the time. The network liked it, except they said, 'There's only one thing wrong. We've decided that we don't want anything with a Chinaman in it.' They felt rather guilty, so they told Bill: 'If you like, you and Lorenzo can do *Batman*.' Bill came to see me in Madrid and was pretty embarrassed."[73]

Dozier later came back to Lee with the Kato role, and 20th Century-Fox, which owned the series, put the actor on retainer. The report on Lee's camera test for the studio reads: "When Lee punched, the whole process only used up three frames. In a second, 24 frames of film will be used. Bruce only used an eighth of a second to give a punch."[74]

After Lee's death, 20th Century-Fox released a compilation of *Green Hornet* episodes as a feature film titled *Bruce Lee: The Green Hornet*, and began it—to the delight of Lee's fans—with his original screen test for the Kato role. The dialogue of that screen test is as follows:

> **Tester** (off screen): "Now Bruce, just look into the camera lens right here and tell us your name, your age, and where you were born."
> **Lee**: "My last name is Lee, Bruce Lee. I was born in San Francisco in 1940. I am 24 right now."
> **Tester**: "And you worked in motion pictures in Hong Kong?"
> **Lee**: "Yes, since I was around six years old."
> **Tester**: "And when did you leave Hong Kong?"
> **Lee**: "1959, when I was 18."

Tester: "That's right... I understand you just had a baby boy."

Lee: "Yeah." (laughter)

Tester: "And you've lost sleep over it, have you?"

Lee: "Three nights." (laughter)

Tester: "And tell the crew what time they shoot pictures in Hong Kong."

Lee: "Well, it's mostly in the morning, because it's kind of noisy in Hong Kong, you know. There's around three million people there, so every time they have a picture it's mostly, say, around 12 a.m. to 5 a.m. in the morning."

Tester: "And you went to college in the United States?"

Lee: "Yes."

Tester: "And what did you study?"

Lee: "Oh, philosophy."

Tester: "Now, you told me earlier today that karate and jujitsu are not the most powerful or the best method of Oriental fighting. What is the most powerful and best form?"

Lee: "Well, it's bad to say the 'best,' but in my opinion, I think that gung fu is pretty good."

Tester: "Would you tell us a little bit about gung fu?"

Lee: "Well, gung fu originated in China. It is the ancestor of karate and jujitsu. It is more of a complete system, and it's more fluid. By that, I mean more flowing. There is more continuity of movement instead of one movement, then two movements, and then stop."

Tester: "Look right into the camera lens and explain the principle of the glass of water as it applies to gung fu."

Lee: "Well, (of) gung fu, the best example would be a glass of water. Why? Because water is the softest substance in the world, but yet it can penetrate the hardest rock or anything—granite, you name it. Uh, water is also insubstantial. By that, I mean you cannot grasp hold of it. You cannot punch it and hurt it. So every gung fu man is trying to be soft like water and flexible and adapt himself to the opponent."

Tester: "What's the difference between a gung fu punch and a karate punch?"

Lee: "Well, a karate punch is like an iron bar, whack! A gung fu punch is like an iron chain with an iron ball attached to the iron and it goes whang! And it hurts inside."

Tester: "OK. Now we're going to cut, and in just a second, we'll have you stand up and show us some gung fu and some movement."

Lee: "OK."

Tester: "Now look directly into the camera, Bruce. Directly at it. And now give me a three-quarter this way. And hold it. And give me a profile that way, all the way. Good. Hold it. Now come back to a profile on the other side. Hold that. Give me a three quarter on that side, and then give me right into the camera again. All right. Now the camera will pull back and first show me the movement in the classical Chinese theater."

Lee: "Classical Chinese theater?"

Tester: "Well, you know. What we talked about in the office. How they walk and how they start moving."

Lee: "Well, you know, in Chinese Opera they have the warrior and then the scholar. The way the warrior walks would be something like this (demonstrating). Walking this way, straight, come out, bend, straight, and then walk out again. An ordinary scholar would be just like a female. A weakling—90 pounds and Charles Atlas. (laughter) He'll be just walking, you know, like a girl. Real shoulder up and everything."

Tester: "So by the way they walk, you can tell who they are?"

Lee: "Right. What character they represent."

Tester: "Now, show us some gung fu movements."

Lee: "Well, it's hard to show it alone, but I will do my best."

Tester: "All right. Maybe we can find a fellow to walk in."

Lee: "Yeah, that would be fine."

Tester: "OK."

Lee (after a volunteer has been found): "Although accidents DO happen (teasing the volunteer). There are various kinds of strikes. It depends on where you hit and what weapon you use. To the eye, you would use the fingers. (Does a finger jab and then says to the cowering victim), 'Don't worry, I won't hurt you.' To the eyes. Straight to the face. From the waist..."

Tester: "Let's move this gentleman around so you're doing it more into the camera, OK?"

Lee: "And then there is (a) bent-arm strike using the waist again into a back fist."

Tester: "Let's have you back off just a ways. (laughter from crew) OK. Go ahead."

Lee: "And then, of course, gung fu is very sneaky. You know the Chinese. They always hit low, come high, go back to the groin."

Tester: "Now turn around the other way, would you Bruce?"

Lee: "OK."

Volunteer: "These are just natural reactions" (explaining his flinching throughout the demonstration).

Tester: "Right into the camera. Show us again."

Lee: "All right. There is the finger jab, there is the punch, there is the backfist, and then low. Of course, then they use the legs. Straight to the groin or come up. Or, if I could back up a little and then come back."

Tester: "All right."

Lee (to volunteer): "You look kind of worried."

Tester: "He has nothing to worry about. Now, once again show us how a gung fu man would very cooly handle it and walk away. Now Bruce, so that we can clearly see what you are doing this time, show me now the difference between jujitsu, which is long and involved, and gung fu, which is very quick."

Van Williams and Bruce Lee on the set of *The Green Hornet*.

Lee: "Now, for instance, you will read in a book and magazines that when somebody grabs you, you will first do *this* and then *this* and then and then—thousands of steps before you do a single thing. Of course, these types of magazines would teach you to be feared by your enemies and (be) admired by your friends. But in gung fu, it always involves a very fast motion, like, for instance, a guy grabbing your hand. It's not the idea to do so many steps (stomps his foot to demonstrate). Stamp him right on the instep. He'll let go."

Lee (continuing): "Same thing in striking and in everything. It has to be based on a very minimum motion, so that everything would be directly expressed in one motion. And he's gone. Doing it graceful, not going, 'Ahhhhhhh!'"

Bruce Lee, during the filming of *The Green Hornet*, maintained the integrity of his gung fu. Here Lee is seen in the episode, "May the Best Man Lose."

During those months prior to shooting *The Green Hornet*, Lee, who received $1,800 in option money, moved to Los Angeles to be closer to the dojo, opened his third studio at 628 College St. in Los Angeles,[75] and spent a month studying dramatics under coach Jeff Corey.[76] That marked his only formal acting training.

Mindful of the demise of *Number One Son* and aware of the previous treatment of Chinese characters by Hollywood, Lee said of his hiring for *The Green Hornet*:

> "You know why I got the job? Because the hero's name was Brit Reid, and I was the only Chinese guy in all of California who could pronounce Brit Reid, that's why."[77]

According to Silliphant, Lee "would never play the chop-chop pigtail coolie" and termed his battle to obtain work in Hollywood as a "really grim fight against prejudice."[78]

During the 26 episodes of *The Green Hornet*, Lee maintained the integrity of his gung fu, which he refused to allow to be put in a bad light. As in his upcoming Hong Kong films, he avoided participating in long, unrealistic hand-to-hand battles when a few swift, well-placed blows would suffice. He also declined to inhibit the speed of his blows, instead having the cameramen use slow motion to capture the fast, fluid movements, a method which would be adapted by the *Kung Fu* series.[79] Lee also refused a lucrative deal proposed by businessmen who planned to open a franchise of Kato Self-Defense Schools. He felt without personal control, his Jeet Kune Do philosophy would be prostituted.

While shooting *The Green Hornet*, he became friendly with assistant producer Charles Fitzsimon. During a lunch together, Fitzsimon suggested that Lee could earn a small fortune by giving private lessons for $50 or more an hour rather than charging $22 a month to students at his dojo. Bruce—who would eventually raise his rates to $250 an hour and was once flown to Switzerland by Roman Polanski for special lessons—mentioned the idea to his student and hair stylist, Jay Sebring. The famous beautician connected Lee with Steve McQueen (who Lee described as a "fighter") and James Coburn (who Lee termed "a philosopher"), his first and second celebrity students. His reputation and contacts with powerful people in the entertainment industry grew from that point.

After one season and a $1 million loss, ABC opted to drop *The Green Hornet*, which the producers claimed could have been more popular and profitable if the network expanded it from 30 to 60 minutes. The show, however, turned into a smash overseas, especially in the Philippines, Singapore, and Hong Kong. The series proved so influential in Hong Kong that the day after an episode in which Kato used a nunchaku (a weapon made from two pieces of wood, each about one-foot long and linked to each other at one end by chains or string), teenage boys began carrying the flashy weapon on the streets.

As of this writing, none of the 26 episodes of *The Green Hornet* has been released on videotape or laser disc. They have also been unavailable for airing on either cable, syndicated, or network television for years.

The Green Hornet aired on ABC Friday nights from 7:30 p.m. until 8:00 p.m. The show's theme song was an updated arrangement of Rimsky-Korsakov's "Flight of the Bumble Bee" performed by Al Hirt. According to *The Green Hornet Book*, the episode titles and air dates are:

"The Silent Gun" —premiere September 9, 1966
"Give 'Em Enough Rope" —September 16, 1966
"Programmed for Death"—September 23, 1966
"Crime Wave"—September 30, 1966

Adam West, Bruce Lee, and Van Williams. Lee and Williams would appear on a two-part *Batman* starring West.

"The Frog is a Deadly Weapon"—October 7, 1966
"Eat, Drink and Be Dead"—October 14, 1966
"Beautiful Dreamer, Part One"—October 21, 1966
"Beautiful Dreamer, Part Two"—October 28, 1966
"The Ray is for Killing"—November 11, 1966
"The Preying Mantis" (pitting Lee's Kato against a Chinatown kung-fu gang)—November 18, 1966
"The Hunters and The Hunted"—November 25, 1966
"Deadline for Death"—December 2, 1966
"The Secret of the Sally Bell"—December 9, 1966
"Freeway to Death"—December 16, 1966

"May the Best Man Lose"—December 23, 1966
"Seek, Stalk and Destroy"—January 6, 1967
"Corpse of the Year, Part One"—January 13, 1967
"Corpse of the Year, Part Two"—January 20, 1967
"Bad Bet on A 459—Silent"—February 3, 1967
"Ace in the Hole"—February 10, 1967
"Trouble for Prince Charming"—February 17, 1967
"Alias the Scarf"—February 24, 1967
"Hornet, Save Thyself"—March 3, 1967
"Invasion from Outer Space, Part One"—March 10, 1967
"Invasion from Outer Space, Part Two"—March 17, 1967
"The Hornet and The Firefly"—March 24, 1967

The Green Hornet and Kato also appeared in a two-part *Batman*—"A Piece of the Action" and "Batman's Satisfaction"—which teamed them with the Caped Crusader (Adam West) and Robin (Burt Ward). The plot involved capturing a stamp thief named Colonel Gumm and is reportedly best remembered for having Kato and Robin reach a stand-off in a battle with each other.

Recognizing that *The Green Hornet* might earn back its losses and perhaps a profit overseas, 20th Century-Fox sent Lee and his family on a Hong Kong publicity tour. During that time, the man received his first taste of mass adulation as he was greeted by cheering crowds at the airport and mobbed at every site he visited. Lee, who was viewed as a local boy who made good in America, appeared on talk shows to give gung fu demonstrations.[80] Even when back in the U.S., he received daily calls from Hong Kong disc jockeys who talked to him on the air. When one inquired whether he would return to Hong Kong to appear in a motion picture, Lee said he would, provided the price was right. Producer Raymond Chow, who broke away from the powerful studio owned by Run Run Shaw, was informed of the broadcast and began plans to bring Lee back.

Lee, however, was much more interested in continuing his American entertainment career.

In 1968, he made guest appearances on *Ironside*, *Blondie,* and *Batman*, and a year later, his friend and student, screenwriter Stirling Silliphant, created a special character for Lee in the film *Marlowe*. Based on the Raymond Chandler novel, *The Little Sister*, the film features James Garner as hard-boiled dick Philip Marlowe and was directed by Paul Bogart. *Marlowe*, in which Lee plays a heavy named Winslow Wong, flopped during its initial release, but was reissued by MGM three years later, after Lee came to fame in his Chinese pictures. Silliphant, who has been credited with doing more for Lee's career than any other person,[81] said:

James Garner and Bruce Lee in *Marlowe*.

> "Two of the best sequences had Bruce in
> them. I wrote him into [them]. In one, he came
> in and tore up Garner's office. In the other, he
> met Garner on the roof of the Occidental build-
> ing and took a header, kicking and screaming
> off into space."

Based on Lee's inspiration, Silliphant, when commissioned to write the
fourth episode of the 1971 TV series, *Longstreet*, starring James Franciscus as
a blind insurance investigator, titled it *The Way of the Intercepting Fist* as a
tribute to Lee's Jeet Kune Do. He also wrote Lee into the episode to play an
antique dealer as well as Franciscus' self-defense instructor, a role for which he
received more fan mail than the series' star.[82] (Silliphant, who met Lee in the
middle of 1968, also used him as the off-camera fighting coach for *A Walk In
Spring Rain*. The 1969 production, filmed in Tennessee, features Ingrid Bergman
as a college lecturer's wife who during a mountain vacation falls in love with a
local man, played by Anthony Quinn.)[83]

Extremely pleased with Lee's work in *Longstreet*, Paramount Pictures flew him back from Hong Kong to appear in three more episodes, which were done in the one month production lag between *Fists of Fury* and *The Chinese Connection*.

Throughout these same years, Silliphant, Coburn (who had studied with Lee for three years),[84] and Lee planned to combine their talents on a project entitled *The Silent Flute*. The writer and actor put up $12,000 each in 1969 and hired a screenwriter, whose script Silliphant termed "mostly science fiction and screwing." The three teamed—meeting every Monday, Wednesday, and Friday without fail from four to six p.m.—to pen their own script.

The trio developed a tale with Lee playing five roles and dominating the story, which concerned a young student's evolution through the martial arts, his problems of ego, his newfound courage in facing death, and his spiritual rebirth.[85] Coburn, then a box-office name due to the successful *Flint* spy series (1966's *Our Man Flint* and 1967's *In Like Flint*, which, like *Enter the Dragon*, were inspired by the James Bond series), was to provide the marquee value. In three months, Silliphant polished the script and sent it to Warner Bros., which agreed to back the production if it could be filmed in India, where the company had "blocked rupees" (funds earned in the country but which could not be withdrawn).

While Lee and Coburn scouted for locations in India, friction developed between them. The American star objected to Lee's flashy displays and stunts, which attracted crowds; Lee couldn't understand why, at hotels like the Taj Mahal in Bombay, Coburn received the lavish suites and best attention, while he and Silliphant were allotted merely average rooms. Silliphant recalled:

> "Bruce came to me one evening and said, 'I'm the star, not him.' For the first time, I realized my guru wasn't just a great martial artist; he was also an actor filled with ego. I didn't respect him any less. I just saw him more realistically. He said then he'd be the biggest star in the world, bigger than Coburn or McQueen. I said, 'No way. You're a Chinese in a white man's world.' Then, he went out and did it."[86]

Coburn, out of "artistic conviction" and because India lacked "the kind of 'no place' look" the project required,[87] decided against doing the picture in that country, although Lee thought the project, which stressed many of the philosophical aspects of the martial arts, should be done at any cost. When Coburn informed Warner Bros. of his decision, the studio dropped all plans for *The*

Silent Flute. (At the time of his accidental death on the set of *The Crow* on March 31, 1993, Lee's 28-year-old son Brandon was considering the possibility of mounting a version of *The Silent Flute* as a tribute to his father.)

A few months later, Silliphant signed to write a script for Irwin Allen at 20th Century-Fox, and as part of the deal, received a commitment from the studio to film *The Silent Flute.* But by that time, Lee had established himself as a star in Hong Kong, while Coburn's career had lost its luster. When Silliphant reached Lee with the news of the approval, the Asian-American actor said: "Why should I carry Coburn on my shoulders?"[88] A few years later, producer Sandy Howard resurrected the project, retitled it *Circle of Iron*, and cast David Carradine in the lead. Released in 1979, the film was a critical and commercial disaster.

While considering *The Silent Flute*, Warner Bros. was also contemplating a new series, *Kung Fu*, which was initially conceived as a feature film by writers Ed Spielman (who speaks Mandarin Chinese and had studied Oriental philosophy and fighting techniques for a decade) and Howard Friedlander.[89] Originally titled *The Warrior*, the project concerned a Shaolin master who finds himself exiled in the American West after killing a member of the Chinese Imperial House. (Ironically, Lee was also developing an unrelated idea about a Shaolin priest roaming the old West.) Fred Weintraub, who later produced *Enter the Dragon*, attempted to convince Warner Bros. to do it as a feature project for Bruce Lee, but during a change in management regimes at the studio, the big-screen version was dropped.[90]

The plot, however, formed the basis for *Kung Fu*, a series that Lee desperately wanted to helm and which would have changed the course of his life. Even while filming *Fists of Fury* in Hong Kong, he still planned to return to Hollywood for *The Warrior—Kung Fu*, and bragged to the local press that he had the role. Lee said:

> "Warner Bros. has full confidence in me and wants to have things done as planned. I was a little worried because a series like this means all kinds of work, like 365 days a year. But finally I said, 'I'm gonna do the series one way or the other—damn the torpedoes, full speed ahead.' I decided to take the plunge."[91]

In talking to reporters, Lee recognized the inherent racism in America and pointedly observed:

> "What's holding things up now (for his *Kung Fu* signing) is that a lot of people are

sitting around in Hollywood, trying to decide if the American television audience is ready for an Oriental hero. We could get some really peculiar reactions from places like the Deep South."

But Warner Bros. apparently never seriously considered Lee. As Weintraub has said of his negotiations:

"I approached Warner's to do it as a feature, and they said, 'Not on your life. You just can't have a Chinese hero.' I then gave the script to a guy who was running Warner's television and told him that it would make a perfect thing for TV and that I had Bruce set to play the part. We brought the idea to ABC. They loved the script but said a Chinese actor could never do it. So they hired David Carradine. That's when Bruce got upset and left for Hong Kong, because he felt he couldn't make it here."[92]

Tom Kuhn, head of Warner Bros. television, said Lee was never a probable candidate for the role.

"We didn't think Bruce could be a weekly television star, which is different from doing one-shot features," he said. "Although we knew he wanted it, Bruce Lee was never seriously considered."

According to Kuhn, Warner Bros., ABC, and the casting agents felt that Lee's English was not accent-free enough, that his name couldn't carry a show, and that he lacked experience.[93]

As Lee's wife Linda has noted:

"I doubt if they ever really tried to rationalize their ideas; they obviously just didn't see him as the right heavyweight material. Probably it just never occurred to them that a Chinese could become a hero in a white man's world."[94]

After accepting the loss of the role, Lee pointedly commented: "I guess they weren't ready for a Hopalong Wong."[95]

Even with David Carradine—a trained dancer who had the "kind of dignity and lyricism" the network wanted—in the lead, ABC was very skeptical of the show's chance for success. Producer Jerry Thorpe, who found the script in the studio archive and revived the project, said ABC initially felt:

> "That it would be too esoteric, that it
> would attract a buff or a cult audience, not a
> mass audience. They were afraid it was too
> intellectual for young people."

ABC agreed to shoot it as a movie of the week. Due to positive reviews, the network approved three trial segments as a mid-season replacement.[96] The show did break through to a mass audience, with a successful run beginning in October 1972 and ending in June 1975.[97] (Brandon Lee appeared with Carradine in the 1986 made-for-television vehicle, *Kung Fu: The Movie*, and Carradine still plays the role in the syndicated series, *Kung Fu: The Legend Continues*.)

The series, described as a philosophical Western, concerned a Buddhist monk—born of Chinese and American parents (inserted to explain Carradine's participation)—who was raised in a Shaolin Temple and forced to flee China after killing a member of the Chinese royal family. Each week, American bounty hunters, law men, or outlaws tangled with the main character, Cain, who used a form of Shaolin boxing, and felt the sting of his soft style. Thematically, the series, like most television shows, reinforced middle-class attitudes: If you are kind to others and reserve your strength and ability, you will be rewarded and good will prevail because the orderly way is always right.

This is the opposite of the Bruce Lee Hong Kong gung fu films, in which strength and ability must be displayed. There is no reward in gung fu films except the satisfaction of revenge and the opportunity to earn the respect of others who witness the performance of superhuman agility.[98]

After the insult of losing *Kung Fu*, Lee once again focused his talents on breaking into either television or films despite the rampant prejudice, which kept him off the screen. Thanks to Lee's interviews on Hong Kong radio shows due to the success of *The Green Hornet*, Raymond Chow of Golden Harvest, whose first release was *The Invisible Eight* in January 1971, signed him to a two-film contract, which called for him to earn $7,500 per picture. Run Run Shaw had only offered Lee $2,000 per film and a long-term contract. When Lee asked for more details, Hong Kong movie mogul Shaw cabled: "Just tell him to come back and everything will be all right." Lee considered that response a patronizing insult.[99] The Shaw Brothers didn't lament the losing of

Invincible [King] Boxer, released in America as *Five Fingers of Death*, created a demand for Hong Kong films and opened the way for Bruce Lee's success.

Lee because the studio had David Chiang under contract and felt his star status was strong enough to carry the company.

The Chinese film companies often create publicity releases and photographs of pictures being considered for production and distribute them to the press for publication. If the public shows enough interest, the pictures are then produced. If the Shaw Brothers had conducted such a test with Bruce Lee, their studio might have discovered enough interest in his talents to warrant a more lucrative contract.

In terms of the Hong Kong market, Lee's timing was perfect. In 1966, facing dwindling domestic box-office returns and a growing threat from television (much as U.S. motion picture studios faced in the 1950s), the major studios in the Hong Kong film industry set themselves the target of breaking into the American market within five years. It took them six. The breakthrough occurred at the Cannes film market in 1972, when martial arts movies from both the Shaw Brothers and their chief rival, the Cathay Organization, stole the thunder from the latest American pornography, represented by pictures such as *Deep Throat* and *The Devil in Miss Jones*.

Later that year, Warner Bros. purchased the Shaw Brothers' film *Invincible Boxer* (released in Britain as *King Boxer* and in America as *Five Fingers of Death*) and watched the $300,000 picture out-gross its own costly, sophisticated productions, especially among black American audiences.[100] In the U.S. alone, it earned $3.8 million.[101] National General Pictures, which has since folded, had purchased the rights for the first two Bruce Lee pictures six months before the U.S. release of *Five Fingers of Death*.[102]

After the kung fu boom started, Chinese producers began escalating the European price of their hard-hitting pictures from $5,000 to as much as $250,000.[103]

In her book, *The Martial Arts Films*, Marilyn D. Mintz notes the universal appeal of the Hong Kong products:

"The essential aspect that differentiates the martial arts film from all other film is the emphasis on fighting ability. The appeal is primordial—the individual against great odds, having to rely on his own spiritual and physical capabilities to survive and endure. Bruce Lee personified a dynamic, universally recognizable hero. His technique and magnetism, as well as his film sense, helped establish the Chinese martial arts film in the West as an exciting style that provides extraordinary possibilities in movement. The overwhelming international acceptance of the films came at a time of increasing East-West understanding and cultural exchange."[104]

But Lee, who was called a "Messiah" for the Chinese of Hong Kong,[105] still sought stardom on American television, even though Robert Lee said his brother, at this point, considered dropping out of show business to become a bodyguard after the demise of *The Green Hornet* and *Longstreet*.[106] After completing *Fists of Fury*, he returned to California to film three more episodes of *Longstreet* (he was added as a background character, since the episodes had been written before the introductory show). In October 1971, Warner Bros., which had deprived him of *Kung Fu*, suddenly approached Lee with a "flattering" and "inviting" offer. In her book, Linda Lee details the points of the contract proposal as:

1) $25,000 for which Warner Bros. would receive exclusive rights to Lee's TV services in order to develop a project for him.

2) If a pilot was developed, the following fees would be applicable against the $25,000: a) 30-minute pilot, $10,000; b) 60-minute pilot, $12,500; c) 90-minute pilot, $15,000; d) 120-minute pilot, $17,500. If the pilot fell through, the $25,000 might be applied toward a feature deal.

3) Series prices if pilot was accepted: a) 30-minute show, $3,000 per original telecast (scale residuals); b) 60-minute show, $4,000 per original telecast (scale residuals).

Lee consulted with Coburn about the contract, and the American actor warned him about television "chewing up geniuses."[107] Lee, however, still considered permanently returning to the U.S. to pursue a TV deal until later in October 1971, when he attended the premiere of *The Big Boss* (the title of *Fists of Fury* outside the U.S.) and witnessed the incredible audience response.

The viewers clapped, cheered, and gave the picture—and its star—a standing ovation. Lee was mobbed and found it impossible to leave the theater.[108] Scalpers would soon get $45 for a $2 ticket in Singapore.[109] Sensing a bigger career might await him on the silver screen in theaters across the globe, Lee dropped any ideas of doing an American TV series and set his sights on taking the Hong Kong film industry by storm.

He ended up conquering the cinematic world.

KARATE/ KUNG-FU!

The new screen excitement that gives you the biggest kick of your life!

Bruce Lee

every limb of his body is a lethal weapon in

"Fists of Fury"

National General Pictures presents Bruce Lee in "FISTS OF FURY" • Produced by Raymond Chow
Screenplay and Direction by Lo Wei • Color • A National General Pictures Release

CHAPTER 4
THE *FURY* EXPLODES

"In terms of martial arts films, Bruce Lee
made the only ones which I thought were even
watchable."—Steven Seagal, in a personal
interview with the author on April 3, 1988

Fists of Fury (100 minutes), a $100,000 production that began filming in
July 1971, was set in Bangkok, Thailand, and shot in Pak Chong, a location so
remote that Lee lost 10 pounds because of the lack of meat in his diet.[110] The
picture immediately established the persona Lee would maintain throughout
his screen career: That of the outsider.

In his essay, "Puritanism Revisited: An Analysis of the Contemporary
Screen-Image Western," Peter Homans describes a classical Western hero as:

"...first of all, a transcendent figure, origi-
nating beyond the town. Classically, he rides
into the town from nowhere; even if he is the
marshal, his identity is in some way dissoci-
ated from the people he must save. We know
nothing of any past activities, relationships,
future plans or ambitions. Indeed, the hero is
himself often quite ambiguous about these."[111]

Using that definition, the Lee screen persona certainly fits into the
cinematic mold of the vintage Western hero. (Interestingly, Clint Eastwood,
famous for his Man With No Name appearances in Sergio Leone's 1964 fron-
tier epic, *A Fistful of Dollars*, and its two sequels, 1965's *For A Few Dollars
More* and 1966's *The Good, the Bad and the Ugly*, acquired the rights to the
Chinese film *Sword of Vengeance* and at one time planned to do a Western
version of the tale.)[112]

Fists of Fury (originally titled *King of the Boxers* and then changed to *The
Big Boss* for the Mandarin market and *Fists of Glory* in other parts of the world)
also established the following patterns which weave throughout Lee's projects:

•The use of a simplistic story;

•The inability of official authorities to control social ills (all cured through the physical prowess of Lee's characters);

•The lack of either parents or trustworthy/competent older members of society to guide younger people;

•The almost total absence of children (which might be interpreted as Lee's characters surviving in dying societies with bleak futures);

•The theme of Westernized capitalistic elements as corrupting influences;

•The triumph of an individual character—always played by Lee—over the evil forces;

•The predominant use of women as either mother figures, housekeepers, or prostitutes.

The intense mistrust and hatred for the Japanese does not surface until *The Chinese Connection*.

In the following critical visual reading of *Fists of Fury* (100 minutes) as well as Lee's other major films (*The Chinese Connection*, 106 minutes; *Return of the Dragon*, 91 minutes; and *Enter the Dragon*, 99 minutes), these and other elements will be pinpointed and discussed.

In the first shot of *Fists of Fury*, written and directed by Lo Wei, Cheng (Bruce Lee) is viewed walking off a dock, respectfully following behind senior uncle (Tu Chia Ching), a poor farmer. The shot immediately establishes the young newcomer as an outsider entering a new society. (The dock scene parallels Lee's own experience, having been sent—by his mother—from Hong Kong, via boat, to San Francisco in 1958 to establish himself in America.) The second line of dialogue sounds like a warning Lee might have heard from his family, who feared that his fighting would lead him to prison, in the late '50s.

Uncle: "Life here is very different from back home, so be careful. Don't get into any fights, Cheng. You remember your promise (made to his mother). You are on your own from now on."

Immediately upon arriving, Cheng and his uncle stop for rice cakes at a refreshment stand (operated by Nora Miao, who would later star opposite him in *Return of the Dragon*) and encounter four local toughs, all dressed in

Tony Liu and Bruce Lee rehearse a fight scene for *Fists of Fury*. **Lee felt many fights in prior Mandarin films were unrealistic.**

Westernized outfits (open-collar shirts and slacks, with the leader wearing a loud red shirt and smoking) in contrast to Lee's traditional Chinese working garb. As Lee rises to aid the girl as she is harrassed, his uncle warns, "Don't meddle," and the older man continues to enjoy his cold drink despite the hostility. When the girl threatens to call the police, the thugs laugh (a contempt for the law expressed by both the heroes and the villains in all of Lee's pictures).

After stealing rice cakes from and slapping a young boy, the four are challenged by Chen (James Tien, a popular Hong Kong martial arts actor), Cheng's cousin, who has apparently come to meet the boat. Chen defeats the four—with no help from Cheng—but the workmanlike battle lacks snap and spark, with the punches appearing to have little impact as the four adversaries immediately rise after each blow. The unreality of similar fights in other Mandarin films made Lee realize that their style required drastic changes. He observed:

> "They (the fights) were terrible. Everybody always fighting the same way and fighting all the time. They were unrealistic, always a lot of overacting. I introduced some new elements, some subtlety, like when I kicked, I really kicked."[113]

53

Bruce Lee's Cheng still believes in traditional values, which he will find have little place in this tough new environment.

Following his triumph over the toughs, Chen takes Cheng and the uncle back to his house, where Cheng again shows his respect for the older man by courteously bowing and moving aside so the uncle may enter first. These brief but telling shots reveal that Cheng still believes in the uncle's traditional values, which he will find have little place in this tough new environment. During a discussion with the brothers and cousins, the uncle informs them about the homeland and about his friends who have decided to chase younger women. "A woman can be a blessing or a ruin to a man," he says, suggesting Cheng's later adventures with a benevolent female family member and a local prostitute.

At the gathering, the sole female, Chow Mei (Maria Yi), who dresses traditionally and wears little girl-style pigtails, is sent for a gallon of rice wine and dispenses it to the young men as they listen. Cheng appears uncomfortable

when the man discusses sex in front of Mei and sits apart from the group, looks bored in the background, and then smiles awkwardly as Mei glances at him.

Chen has obtained a position for Cheng at the local ice factory, a drug-distribution front. Cheng stands outside the factory gate with his uncle, again entering from the outside and respectfully walking behind his older relative.

Cheng (Lee) clasps the jade locket his mother gave him when he promised not to fight, with the chain symbolizing social restriction.

The loud, jarring sounds of the machinery sawing the thick ice blocks sharply contrast to the sounds of the laughter of the men in the preceding scene. The first words the manager (Chin San) says to Cheng are: "Just try to get along. No fights." The line immediately establishes that the manager, who represents the owner Boss Mi (Han Ying Chieh), wants to maintain the status quo and for Cheng to conform to the rules.

During its filming, *Fists of Fury* encountered some serious production problems. When half of the production was originally completed, producer Raymond Chow was unhappy with the footage, fired the first director, and hired Lo Wei, who, like Chow, was also a former Shaw Brothers employee. Lee also was permitted to rewrite the script, but he and Lo Wei agreed on very little. Those problems may account for the schizophrenic nature of *Fists of Fury*, which, for its first half, concentrates predominately on Chen, who is viewed as a noble father figure out to protect his family members and friends and follow the rules of normal society. Only after Chen's death does Lee's Cheng dominate the story—and the action.

In the next scenes, Chen guides a friend out of an illegal gambling den after the man's wife—who waits outside crying helplessly (the women in Lee's pictures never effect a change by themselves)—implores Chen to bring out her spouse. Chen fetches the man, who has lost his money in an illegal game, and graciously extends a loan to be returned at any future date. After the incident, five thugs follow Chen and Cheng, and Chen tells his new friend, "Don't get into it." Cheng clasps the jade locket his mother gave him when he promised not to fight, with the chain symbolizing social restriction (mother-family-rule). Whenever Cheng is emotionally propelled to fight, he touches the jade and withdraws.[114]

During the street brawl, Cheng avoids the action except for knocking out two adversaries with quick punches, which provides a preview of the upcoming battles. He attributes the move to "a few tricks from back home."

The next morning, the uncle, after a final lecture to Cheng on the uselessness of fighting, leaves for home, and Mei, again in her mother role, scrubs clothes on rocks as the Boss' villainous son (Tony Liu), who wears a Westernized purple shirt with an open collar, boldly approaches her. She calls for Cheng and cowers in his arms as Liu's character, who plans to give Mei to his lecherous father as a gift (emphasizing the idea of women as objects), walks away.

At the ice factory, the foreman (Chen Chao) wears black, waves a stick (the cousins joke that he resembles a "band leader," a reference to the way capitalists orchestrate the average working man), and walks on cases, which places him in a dominate position. When Cheng arrives slightly late, the foreman calls him a "dumb ox" and "stupid farmer" and attempts to push him out of the way, but he finds the young man unmovable. As the foreman attempts to move Cheng, the position of power changes in the frame as the newcomer moves to the dominant position, looking down on the suddenly vulnerable foreman.

The idea that Cheng, who travels to work alone (setting him outside the group), does not fit into the ice factory surroundings is immediately clear. The first piece of ice he handles alone crashes from the production line and splits open, revealing the drugs inside to two of the cousins, Wong and Chan. A second supervisor punches Cheng for pushing the ice with such force, and the outsider is quickly surrounded by relatives and co-workers determined to know why the newly hired employee was hit. The well-meaning but unfocused group members, however, are just as ineffectual at getting an answer to that simple question as they are in dealing with the Boss.

Bruce Lee's Cheng shares a quiet moment with Chow Mei (Maria Yi), who does domestic chores for her brothers and cousins.

After work, the manager summons the two witnesses, offers them a $1,000 bonus, a deal which he—complete with a straight face—terms "an offer you can't refuse," and informs Wong and Chan that there's "no profit in ice; in dope, plenty." The honest cousins, realizing their place in society, term themselves "country folk" and decline the proposal to become part of the narcotics operation and respectfully refuse the payoff. They are killed by hatchet and knife and deposited in ice blocks by the foreman and his henchmen.

Back at home, Chen allows Mei to serve the meal to the surviving cousins but tells her to save two portions, serving as the protective father figure in the group's communal existence. But Chen's paternal manner will prove no match for the villainy at hand. (The lack of Chen's effectiveness parallels the ineffectiveness of the older teacher, who attempts to follow a peaceful code after the vicious murder of a kung fu school's revered teacher, in *The Chinese Connection*, which will be detailed in the next chapter.)

The following day, the Boss (Han Ying Chieh, who also served as the picture's fight choreographer) shows lethal defense moves to his son and his bodyguards during a training exercise. Boss Mi says, laughing: "It's speed and keen senses. Stay alert and always relaxed. That's the secret."

During a conversation, the son, who procures "young chicks" for his father, requests 2,000 yen, a sum for which he will provide him with a girl—Mei—who he describes like "a little dove" and who, he claims, will make him "feel 20 again." *Fists of Fury* shows Boss Mi and his son as corrupt capitalists who put a price on everything and reduce women, whom the Boss shoots with darts and hooks on drugs, to products with dollar signs.

The final villain—like the Boss—in kung fu films is always an older man, a father figure who is clearly out of the mythological consideration of Cronus (a dethroned titan) or Seth (a son of Adam). Cronus is usually pictured as a bent old man with a scythe in one hand. In the other, he holds a snake that bites its own tail. The story of Cronus' swallowing his children symbolizes the idea that time creates and then destroys what it has created, just like these kung fu villains destroy. Seth, who was usually represented by the head of a strange-looking animal that may have been a cross between a donkey and a pig, was in constant warfare with his brother, Osiris, who represented the principle of goodness. Seth killed his sibling.

The kung fu hero is as clearly a mythical extension of Zeus or Horus. Zeus, the king of the gods and supreme ruler of men in Greek mythology, was especially associated with justice and punished the wicked and rewarded the good. Horus, the ancient god of light and heaven, was the first Egyptian god recognized as a national god and worshipped in both Lower and Upper Egypt. A life-giving god who held the ankh (the symbol of life) in his right hand, Horus was pictured as either a falcon or a human with a falcon's head.

Such mythical patterns also reflect universal psychological conflicts. The father figure is always rich (a worthwhile symbolic adversary for a ghetto hero), lecherous (a dirty old man), and quite skillful. There is some implication that he may be a self-made ghetto figure who has profited by a betrayal of his origins, a terrible father who, like Cronus, has gobbled up his children and must be destroyed by the last of those children.[115] When Cheng faces the Boss at the climax of *Fists*, all of his male cousins—including the boy (the only child character, and a very minor one at that, in any Lee picture) who sold rice pies in the opening scene—have been slaughtered by the Boss' minions.

Chen and another cousin leave the ice factory to visit the Boss, who receives a neck massage from a servant girl as he talks with the two visitors seeking the whereabouts of Wong and Chan. Suspicious of the Boss' explanation, Chen threatens to contact the authorities, a declaration proving him to be an unsophisticated participant in dealing with criminals.

"The police will laugh at you," the Boss says, suggesting the control the rich have over the authorities. Upon hearing the threat, the Boss orders his men into action. Although Chen and his cohort fight back, neither proves a match for the professional henchmen. The villains use a hatchet and knife (both thrown at the victims), as they did with Wong and Chan, to kill them. The extended

Bruce Lee as Cheng turns the weapons of his enemies against them during the ice-house battle..

fight sequence abounds with poorly filmed action, a stark contrast to Cheng's later scenes, which Lee choreographed.

At the house, Mei (a worried mother figure) cries while leaning against a pole, a contrast to the men who, although concerned, retire to bed. In the morning, the bubbly, heavyset cousin (Chin Ti, a stock comic figure in all three of Lee's Hong Kong pictures) briefly assumes the leadership post, sending Cheng to look for the two in the dock area and the others to various locations. When Cheng returns to the ice factory, he immediately stands apart from the group, stoically staring up as the foreman and manager attempt to explain the situation. A fight ensues, with the manager summoning the Boss' armed goon squad to end the battle. The workers, during another extended fight sequence lacking power, appear on the brink of victory, when some goons, armed with various weapons, arrive in a bus and give them a fierce beating until one makes the mistake of hitting Cheng and ripping off his mother's locket.

Until this point 45 minutes into *Fists of Fury*, Lee has been a shy, dull, and reticent character. But when he attacks, his whole body works in harmony and conveys the intensity so strongly that it becomes almost sexual. Kung fu then serves not only for resolving thematic conflicts, but also for evaluating one's personal value. The degree of a person's proficiency in the martial arts actually renders his value in the society. Lee is also a lone, individual hero (a point reinforced by the shot of him outside the group when he returns from the dock on which he initially entered). Although proclaiming he is on the "people's side," Lee, visually, is never on the "people's side."

This film and his others obviously belittle the impact of any collective action, with almost all of the group battles being shown as rampant and fruitless. When Lee steps onto the battleground, he waves his colleagues aside and takes on the enemies by himself. Lee always fights alone. The visual rhetoric usually corresponds to his individual heroism. Lee is seldom in the same frame with his siblings. Rather than integrating with the mass, he gets separate, privileged shots.[116]

This initial Bruce Lee battle also set standards for hand-to-hand combat scenes with neither the weaponry nor trick effects (many via trampoline) on which Chinese films had relied. Lee convinced Lo Wei to eliminate such unrealistic elements and focus on the pure physicality of his art.[117] Until *Fists of Fury*, Chinese movies had tried to emulate the Japanese samurai (warrior) movies by emphasizing the use of weapons. (Lee, however, respected and studied the Japanese samurai films in which the fighting was kept within "the realm of reality.")[118]

In this one innovative film, Lee reduced the Asian fantasies and emphasized Western realism. Lee believed the fewer camera tricks the better. Long shots were used often and cuts were reduced, so audiences could tell they were watching genuine kung fu instead of camera deceptions. Lee's choreography thus transmitted a sense of fidelity that impressed Western as well as Eastern audiences.[119]

As the Italians did for the gunfight, so the Chinese established a new visual rhetoric for the presentation of hand-to-hand combat on film; their distinctive, unprecedented fight scenes were clearly a prime factor in the genre's international success, and it was inevitable that their influence would endure in the popular cinema of most countries. Chinese fights are hyperbolic, and the hero and his colleagues normally face overwhelming odds.[120]

As Lee said:

> "All the time before, Chinese flicks were, you know, kind of unrealistic. Really, I mean, overacting. A lot of jumping around. All in all, it's not real, you know what I mean. So I came back home to Hong Kong and I introduced some new elements to it, like when I kick, I really kick and all that."[121]

Lee's pre-eminence in martial arts movies sprang from his ability to give dramatic body to the philosophies that inform the various disciplines; his inventiveness as an actor matches his fighting expertise. His provocative fighting stance—legs apart, knees bent, hands on thighs—seems to carry a sexual charge, confirmed by the transported expression and yelp of delight that accompany each connecting blow. In this and all his future pictures, he demoralizes his opponents with glares of withering contempt, and underlines each move or hiatus with a cacophonous repertoire, used more in later films, of animal-like screeches, wails, and barks. His supreme contempt is to treat the bout as a joke (something he carries to a rousing extreme in the fights with the Japanese school leader and Russian karate expert in *The Chinese Connection*), but even the most comic casual gesture can be inflected with a vicious intensity. Maintaining fully conscious control, he achieves the dream transmutation of the body into pure will, and the dramatic devices serve to demonstrate the process.[122]

The factory fight scene marks Cheng's major turning point. The *Fists of Fury* plot, like plots of many other Chinese films, deals with a lower-class figure who contains his kung fu skill at first and attempts to be a respectable working-class resident. He allows others—in this case his relatives—to fight the initial battles because he has vowed to follow the acceptable code of behavior. His resolve disappears when his family is attacked and destroyed, and he sees that being a good worker and loyal citizen has ruined him.[123] He has tried to follow the advice his uncle first gave him on the dock, but following the traditional course—the law of the establishment that protects the status quo—will not work in this corrupt land.

Cheng's first opponent approaches him with a knife, which he kicks out of his hand and follows with a sidekick to the mouth. (Because of his kicking speed and combinations, Hong Kong fans dubbed Lee "the man with three legs.") From here, Lee dominates the center of the frame as all of the other men stand back and simply watch and clap for him. In a flurry of solid kicks and punches, Cheng then uses his combat skills to disarm and disable the other thugs, who soon stumble away and retreat on a company bus.

It's a solo performance, a dance of death-defying moves that redefined action cinema.

But unlike Chen, whose goodness assumed saintly proportions, Cheng proves a more human hero. When the manager summons him to the office, Cheng accepts a promotion to foreman, naively believing that he can make a difference at the factory and—symbolically—in society. But the job initially confines him, almost as much as his mother's locket did, as he attempts to once again adjust to a society which will try to control him by corrupting him.

Also lured away from their main concern—finding out what happened to their four cousins—are the co-workers who, selfishly believing they will get a better deal with Cheng as foreman, lift him up on their shoulders and celebrate.

Cheng is introduced to foreign liquor by one of The Boss' prostitutes (Malalene).

While the men celebrate, Mei, in addition to serving as the mother who cares for them (seen removing clothes from a line), also serves as their collective conscience, reminding the smiling men that their relatives remain missing.

In contrast to Mei are the prostitutes, whom the manager hires to make Cheng forget about his loved ones. To celebrate the promotion, the supervisors feed the unworldly Cheng a fancy dinner and ply him with expensive Hennessey cognac (a French liquor representing a corrupting European influence), which the unsophisticated man gulps instead of sips. They also give him a prostitute (Malalene), who wears a flashy red dress and her hair down (a distinct contrast to the good-girl Mei, who wears muted colors and traditional hair styles).

Cheng, obviously out of his league and in a world he doesn't comprehend, stands like a gentleman as he's introduced to the prostitutes. The film crosscuts from the fancy meal to the simple dinner at the house of Cheng's relatives.

The Lee hero is always promoted as an ascetic (practicing strict self-denial) hero, sexually repressed in a basically puritan society. His romantic rapport with the female protagonists always remains on a platonic plane—escalating to *Enter the Dragon*, in which his only contact with a female consists of conversations with a fellow spy. Sex is always the corrupting force that exists in the realm of decadence (the associations with the brothel, prostitutes, slave traffic in *Enter* and *Fists* and striptease dance in *The Chinese Connection*).[124]

Cheng passes out before any sexual contact can take place with the prostitute.

While intoxicated, Cheng prostitutes his own art by performing breaking demonstrations for the trollops and the Boss' henchmen. Cheng passes out before any sexual contact can take place with Malalene's character. Back at the house, Mei cries, obviously fearing for Cheng's safety, as Lo Wei cuts to a shot of the prostitute, who has quickly undressed and strokes the unconscious man's muscular chest. He is an outsider—a pure spirit as yet uncorrupted by the world—to her as much as to his cousins, men who lack the physical ability to break the social chains that bind and are slowly strangling them.

The cousins mistakenly assume that Cheng traveled to the police station to inquire about the missing men. Although the authorities are mentioned throughout *Fists of Fury*, they only arrive in the final seconds, just in time to clean up the carnage, which the Boss began and which Lee's Cheng, through violence, ends.

The next morning, Mei, who is carrying a basket of clothes (again reemphasizing her domestic role), spots a clearly uncomfortable Cheng exiting the brothel and cries when he runs away due to embarrassment. When informed that he went to dinner instead of to the police, the cousins accuse him of "selling out." None of the group comprehends the wealthy Boss' manipulation. When Cheng does visit the Boss' palatial home, he enters through a chained gate, a symbol of the man's hold on the workers. Lo Wei shoots the scene from above, allowing the pool—a symbol of both the water Cheng crossed to arrive in this new land and the Boss' wealth—to dominate the frame. Four trained German shepherds charge Cheng, who avoids them through a series of jumps that show him to be a force of nature. When one of the animals finally grabs the outsider, the Boss calls them off, saying "Be still," and the attack-trained canines obey as quickly as his human thugs.

During the conversation between the narcotics dealer and Cheng, a servant girl spills tea and the Boss blows a dart into her right breast, calling her a "little fool." The villain then says: "I treat my workers justly. I regard them as my family. I take care of them, look after them. Why, I even lend them money." These four sentences show the depth of his perversity and total disregard for the sanctity of the family. The Boss, who has his shoulders massaged by a girl young enough to be his granddaughter, presents himself in a paternal light, but even the unsophisticated Cheng recognizes the cruelty of the dart incident to punish a minor mistake of clumsiness.

But the wily Boss also recognizes Cheng's desire to succeed in the world, telling him: "You have a bright future, if you apply yourself." In that Western big-business tradition, to get along, you go along. The worldly Boss feels that Cheng is not "buying" the excuses, and the villain's son takes his father's mind off the problem by reminding him of Mei, the pure, innocent girl whom the Boss plans to rape and destroy later that evening.

Back at home, Cheng again tells his cousins the Boss' official explanation—that he's worried about the missing workers, but they scoff at the excuse and claim that the promotion, which escalated Cheng to a leadership position over the others, "went to his head," while Mei pleads for some compassion for the newcomer. That night, Cheng returns to the brothel to obtain information from the prostitute, who unsuccessfully attempts to seduce him and then tells him about the drugs in the blocks of ice and shows him her dart scars. After providing Cheng with the information, the prostitute is killed by a knife thrown by Boss Mi's son, and immediately after, Mei is abducted by the Boss' men as she removes bed covers from a clothes line, still another domestic chore.

At the ice factory, *Fists of Fury* alters in mood and texture and accelerates in energy, assuming an almost film noir atmosphere as Cheng, under the cover of night, discovers the bodies of his relatives and then faces Boss Mi's son and armed henchmen. Unlike the daylight factory fight with the thugs, this battle has a tone of finality. In that first major battle, Cheng merely disarmed his opponents and knocked them out; in this brutal exchange, he uses their weapons against the adversaries and kills them. His fighting has an intense, animalistic quality about it. At one point, Cheng picks up a saw and buries it in an opponent's skull, a series of frames cut from prints due to the amount of gore in the character's baptism of blood. Lee said:

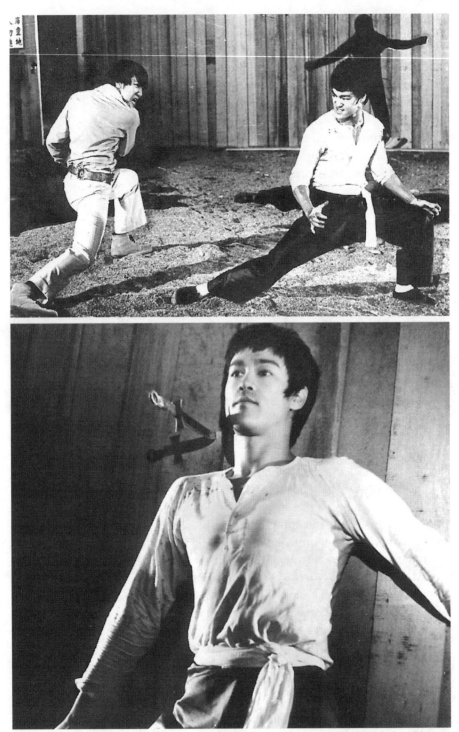

The Boss' son (Tony Liu) employs weapons but still proves no match for Cheng.

Thugs surround Cheng with a moving circle—trying to contain his wild spirit.

"When I fight, I come out the same—like an animal."

Rarely was that displayed more forcefully than in this battle, in which Cheng displays his taste for revenge and combat by tasting blood—a gesture Lee will repeat in *Enter the Dragon*—from a wound after Boss Mi's son slices him with a knife.

Once outside the ice house, the thugs surround him with a moving circle, trying to contain his wild spirit. But Cheng continually breaks out of the circle, each time dispatching adversaries until the only two remaining are he and Boss Mi's son, whom he slays with a power punch from his right fist that vibrates after the blow.

After the battle, Cheng, bloody and shaken, returns home, slips on a pool of blood, and discovers that his family members have all been slaughtered in their beds, a mass murder that might have been avoided had he remained at the residence. (In his Hong Kong career, Lee played two crying scenes, one at this point in *Fists* when discovering the bloody body of his young cousin—the film's symbol of innocence—and in *The Chinese Connection* when arriving at the funeral of his beloved teacher.)

Rather than contacting the police, Cheng waits until morning and sits by a river to contemplate his situation, options, and future. In a voice-over, he says:

Cheng readies himself for action at the mansion of The Big Boss.

"I dreamed of many good things happening for me here. Now, there's nothing. Everything is finished, gone. My uncle said there's a god who watches over us. Where was he last night?" He then vows that the evil ones will pay, "even if I die."

Cheng realizes his fate as a ghetto figure whose skill and agility are devoted not to social success—such as a job as foreman—but to the execution of his lethal talents to earn peer respect and destruction of his enemies. Cheng throws a blue bag, containing his bloody shirt from the previous night, and a few worldly possessions into the water, suggesting the finality of his upcoming actions. He is prepared to fulfill his destiny.

In his final confrontation with the Boss, Cheng, who unsuccessfully tries to warn the drug kingpin's henchmen against entering the fight, is the "animal" that Lee described. The Boss holds a cage with two parakeets and tosses it onto a tree branch. Cheng then throws a knife he used to kill the Boss' guards and frees the caged birds, symbolically communicating the type of freedom sought by his murdered family members.

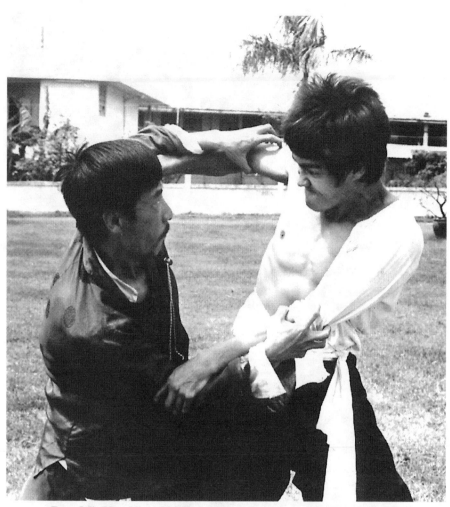

Boss Mi (Han Ying Chieh) is unprepared for the skills of Cheng.

Once the hand-to-hand combat begins, Cheng delivers his punches and bone-crushing triple kicks with perfect discipline (despite his wounds from the previous night), his eyes glaze over and bulge from his head, his lips curl, and his throat contracts with famous "kiai" (animal-like yells and squeals). Cheng defeats the Boss with a knife movement, the type the corrupt man had demonstrated for his evil son and hired killers in his first scene. Cheng kicks a thrown knife back at the Boss, and it penetrates his stomach. The villain is then knocked to the ground by his out-of-control opponent and, although dead, is viciously punched in the face nine times, once for each member of Cheng's family.

The hero seemingly acquired a heightened power at the moment of his greatest trial, like God-given strengths. Social, cultural, historical, political, and mythical issues are inextricably tangled in these final moments.[125]

Cheng seemingly acquired a heightened power at the moment of his greatest trial.

Fists of Fury begins a pattern in Lee's pictures of turning an opponent's expertise with weapons or style of fighting against him. In *The Chinese Connection*, he employs an enemy's Samurai sword as an instrument of death. In *Return of the Dragon*, he adapts Americanized boxing moves to defeat a United States champion. In *Enter the Dragon*, he impales an evil drug kingpin on a spear. And finally with the climactic confrontation in *Game of Death*, his character can only survive by meeting experts in various fighting styles and turning their own martial arts forms and weapons against them.

With the fight finished, Mei, who was freed from a locked room by one of the Boss' unhappy slaves and escaped a life as a prostitute thanks to Cheng, brings the police. Her final words to Cheng are: "Give up." Cheng, who strikes

a crucifixion pose before being handcuffed, is led away as a hero the fans of such a poverty-row[126] production could appreciate: A warrior who, despite his heroic violent actions, still ends up in the arms of the law because he dared to challenge the wealthy forces in society and conquer them.

Bruce Lee set standards for hand-to-hand combat scenes with neither the weaponry or trick effects that Chinese films had relied upon.

The following paragraphs will provide examples of additional visually intriguing, emotionally compelling, and intellectually interesting elements from *Fists of Fury*.

Six Sequences to Watch Closely in *Fists of Fury*

•The most gruesome scene in all of Lee's films does not involve the star. It occurs in the ice house when two cousins, who find drugs contained in a block of ice, are murdered with a knife and hatchet. Then, one is seen being cut apart at his midsection via a huge circular saw normally used to cut ice blocks but utilized here to slice a body so that it will fit into a metal ice container.

•Note while watching *Fists of Fury* how director Lo Wei moves Lee to the middle of the frame and keeps him there after the Boss' son and henchmen viciously kill James Tien's Chen, who had been the protector of his cousins and co-workers. Until that point, the kindly Chen always held the central frame position, with Lee usually behind him or to his left or right. Once Chen, whose goodness and sense of law and order proved no match for the Boss, is murdered, Lee immediately assumes the dominant frame position, signaling the shift of power accorded to Lee due to his lethal abilities, the only things the criminals understand and respect.

•Almost 45 minutes of screen time pass before Lee's character has his first real battle. Watch the first enemy who approaches him with a knife. With a lightning-fast forward movement, he kicks the weapon out of the man's hand and into the air. He employs the identical kick to dislodge the Samurai sword from the Japanese instructor's hands in *The Chinese Connection*.

•*Fists of Fury* is the first of the three films (*The Chinese Connection* and *Enter the Dragon* are the other two) that contain partial nudity but no love-making. That pattern is established with Lee's first starring-role film. A prostitute undresses in *Fists of Fury*, but Lee's drunken character has already fallen asleep and never touches her. (In *The Chinese Connection*, a Geisha dances for the Japanese villain and a Russian fighter, during which she removes her bottom garment and is viewed only from behind. Lee has no part in the scene. In *Enter the Dragon*, prostitutes undress for Jim Kelly and John Saxon, though all sexual activity occurs off camera. Again, Lee has no part in such scenes. *Return of the Dragon* does have a brief segment with Lee interacting in a non-sexual manner with a partially clothed prostitute, though the footage was deleted for American audiences.) In Lee's cinematic universe, time never existed for physical activities other than fights, during which the characters sometimes grunt, perspire, and shriek, which in some ways suggests the sex act.

•During the night ice-house battle, the Boss' son uses a knife against Lee's character, who has been splattered with the blood of his previous adversaries but until this point has not shed his own. The Boss' son manages to slice Lee's left upper arm, and the wounded man dabs his right fingers across the cut and tastes the blood, an action that alters the texture of the scene and seems to startle his opponent due to its animal-like quality. Lee will repeat the tasting action, notably at the end of *Enter the Dragon* during the deadly mirror-room battle with Han.

•Just before fighting the Boss, Lee faces the villain's knife-wielding henchmen, who he suggests keep away, saying, "It's not your fight." They still attack, and Lee, for the first time, has come armed and pulls two knives from sheaths strapped and hidden near his ankles. This contrasts previous scenes when he takes weapons away from opponents and then uses the instruments of death against the enemies. It shows the transformation of the character (something previously suggested by the blood tasting) from a dangerous fighter to a deadly animal-like killing machine.

unstoppable!
unbelievable!
unbeatable!

BRUCE LEE

the master of karate kung fu is back
to break you up, smash you down
and kick you apart with

"THE CHINESE CONNECTION"

National General Pictures presents Bruce Lee in "THE CHINESE CONNECTION"
Produced by Raymond Chow • Screenplay and Direction by Lo Wei
[R] RESTRICTED Color • A National General Pictures Release ©

CHAPTER 5
A SHATTERING
CONNECTION

"Bruce Lee was the kick-boxing star of the kung-fu movies that swept first the cinemas of the Far East, then the Chinatowns of the world's big cities, and finally everywhere that powerless people dreamed of paralyzing their oppressors with a sudden outburst of uncanny martial arts. Before Bruce Lee, the typical kung-fu movie had been just an endless succession of fight sequences. Bruce Lee revolutionized the form. As the first truly idealistic kung-fu star, he gave the audience something Charles Bronson couldn't, even with the most thoughtfully arranged wig. Bruce Lee was a philosopher. He fought crime out of his unshakable conviction that a pure life was possible. In a world that had come to be ruled by fear, he dared to dream."—Clive James in *Fame in the 20th Century* (Random House)

Fists of Fury could be considered a cinematic assault on the corruption of big business, as personified by the deceitful Boss, who represents the imperialistic oppressor, while Lee's second Hong Kong film—*The Chinese Connection*—proves a more ethnically oriented production and attacks the Japanese, long enemies of the Chinese. (*The Chinese Connection* was titled *Fists of Fury* outside of the English-speaking world. The name change resulted from a labeling mistake when the prints were shipped overseas.)

The two films share common elements, including:

> •Similar casts;
> •The same director-screenwriter (Lo Wei);

•A story in which most of Lee's loved ones (in *Fists*, his cousins; in *Chinese*, his fellow students) are slaughtered by his enemies;
•A climactic act of self-sacrifice.

But they vary in their visual scheme, with the first film showing its on-location, low-budget origins, while the second, filmed entirely within Golden Harvest Studios on a $200,000 budget,[127] boasts a stylistically controlled appearance. The two productions also vary greatly in another major respect: The second wastes very little time before allowing Lee to snap into action, rarely stops him throughout the story, and even ends with him frozen in air, preserved in a suicidal leap at armed authorities under orders of the Japanese.

Until Bruce Lee's films, no performers talked much about the strong anti-Japanese sentiment in Hong Kong. In ancient Chinese legend, the Japanese race was born when a Chinese emperor shipped his beautiful but errant daughter to Japan as a punishment. At that time, the Japanese islands were supposedly populated entirely by apes.

For centuries, China and Japan have perpetuated a hostile relationship between their countries, punctuated at numerous intervals by open warfare. Japan was one of the major imperialist powers responsible for the territorial carve-up of China at the turn of the century. And again, Japan humiliated China, Hong Kong, and the rest of the Far East during the last world war. A dependence on Japanese goods is neither forgotten nor forgiven by many Chinese. During a 1974 tour of Malaysia and Indonesia, the Japanese Prime Minister was stoned.[128]

Chinese leader Chou En Lai communicated this anti-Japanese sentiment in 1968 when he accused Japan of gross imperialism in Asia. Chinese communities took this message to heart—reversing the popularity of the Samurai movies shown in Hong Kong. The charge gathered momentum through the years, fueled perhaps by Lee's incredibly popular movies. For instance, the actor insisted his character challenge a Japanese karate academy rather than a Chinese kung-fu school in *The Chinese Connection*.

Lee spent his childhood in Hong Kong during the savage Japanese occupation. He once perched himself astride the wall of a verandah two stories above Nathan Road to shake his fist at a Japanese plane flying overhead.[129]

One writer summed up *The Chinese Connection* as being "the good yellows (Chinese) against the bad yellows (Japanese)." Most Chinese hark back to the glorious past of mainland China.[130]

Set in 1908 Shanghai at the Ching Wu School, *The Chinese Connection* (at one point titled *The School of Chivalry*) is based on an actual incident when the excellent Master Huo Yuan-Chia was poisoned and his most able student avenged the loss.[131] According to legend, the real story concerns a troupe of Japanese Bushido experts who traveled to Shanghai to challenge the legendary fighter,

76

Master Huo, a native of Hopei province. He was the Sijo (founder) of mi tsung-i (art of the labyrinth), a style of Chinese boxing that has no set form but which changes constantly and unexpectedly. The style prevents an opponent from having time to analyze it and build a defense.

At age 48, Master Huo was said to possess awesome strength, and no record exists of him ever having been bested. He made a habit of defeating foreigners (much as Lee would do on the screen), including a giant Russian and a British wrestler. Huo was a source of national pride, and, despite an illness, he accepted the challenge from the Japanese Bushido experts and, along with his senior students, severely beat them. Shortly after, a leading Japanese physician at the Shanghai hospital offered to cure the ailing master. Once inside the hospital, it is believed that Huo was poisoned, for he was not to emerge alive.[132]

The Chinese Connection opens at the funeral of the founder of the Ching Wu School. The ceremony is in progress when Chen Chen (Lee) enters (again establishing him as a character coming from the outside into a situation). Chen wears white (the color of Chinese mourning), while the other students all wear black, an effect that makes Lee stand out in the crowd—isolating him (an image repeated throughout his films)—and showing the depth of his sorrow. Chen actually tosses himself into the open grave and attempts to dig through the soil, an action that is stopped when Tien (Hwong Ching Hsin) hits the distraught student over the back of the head with a shovel.

The founder of the Ching Wu school obviously represents a father figure, and this opening funeral scene contains parallels with Lee's emotional actions at a memorial service for his own father. His brother, Robert, recalled:

> "In 1965, our dad passed away. Bruce was the last to come—he couldn't get a flight and didn't make the funeral. I picked him up at the airport. When we got to the funeral parlor, he walked on his knees all the way from the elevator to the cassock in front of the coffin. You see, to Chinese, to come late to your father's funeral is like being unfilial (not observing the obligations of a child to a parent). Bruce really wanted to gain my father's respect, and Dad was always really strict with us."[133]

Inside the school, Chen, now in black, rests under a sketching of Teacher, while Yuan Li-erh (Miao Ker Hsiu) tries to feed him (a domestic chore much like those performed by the female character in *Fists of Fury*). She also informs Chen that he must "think about the future," but the death has disturbed his

Bruce Lee as Chen reacts with obvious confusion over the strange death of his beloved teacher.

visions of a tranquil life, as if that would be possible in a land dominated by the Japanese. Chen is told that officials, all controlled by the powerful Japanese, ruled that Teacher died of pneumonia, an explanation accepted by all of the other students.

But Chen alone discards the official response, asking: "How could a healthy man die?" (Ironically, thousands of Lee's fans must have asked themselves the same question when the seemingly indestructible star died at age 32.) Chen is immediately obsessed with discovering the truth, while the other students and teachers suggest accepting the explanation and simply getting on with their lives.

At a post-burial ceremony, a speaker describes Teacher as "the greatest boxing instructor of all time. He stood for everything that's right." At that point, an effeminate Japanese interpreter (Wei Ping Ao) enters with two young warriors in Japanese garb and gives the Chinese kung fu men a sign—which reads SICK MEN OF ASIA—sent by Susuki (Riki Hashimoto), the leader of a rival Japanese karate school. The interpreter says:

Chen stands motionless as the Japanese interpreter (Wei Ping Ao) slaps him on the cheek.

"The Chinese are a race of weaklings. No comparison to Japanese. Just look at yourselves. You're pathetic, do you know that? Yes, I realized you'd all be here now, yet I do not look frightened, do I? Any one of you man enough to meet the challenge?"

If defeated, the two Japanese warriors offer to "eat" the words on the sign.

Chen (again dressed in white in contrast to the others in black) steps forward to meet the challenge but he is calmed by Tien, the Teacher's second in command, who follows the dead leader's credo that one must be prepared to fight but do everything to maintain peace. The older man naively believes that turning the cheek will result in a final victory and is following the deep-rooted Chinese cultural heritage that promotes respect and reverence for one's teacher.

Once stopped, Chen stands motionless as the effeminate interpreter slaps him on the cheek, asking: "Are you yellow or something, sick man of Asia?" Out of respect for Tien, Chen, who again stands alone, keeps his hands at his

Chen prepares for combat when his Chinese martial arts school is invaded by a Japanese boxing club.

side, although his broad facial contortions mirror his loss of face, growing angrier and hungrier for revenge.

At the Japanese school, the students can be heard grunting and groaning as they toss each other in traditional judo throws as Chen enters, holding the SICK MEN OF ASIA sign. He easily defeats the two Japanese karate men who insulted his school (the crisp moves of Lee are in sharp contrast to the less effective judo movements at the scene's opening). One of the losers orders the other students to "surround him," placing Lee in the same type of circular situation as in the ice factory battle with the Boss' henchmen in *Fists of Fury*. With the help of a nunchaku, which he makes magically appear while somersaulting across the thick floor mat, Chen, who uses the weapon to pound on his opponents' feet, stands victorious, having also defeated their full-bodied teacher, Yoshida (Feng Yi). Yoshida wears thick glasses, giving a visual stereotype that appears to be lifted out of a 1940s' Hollywood war movie.

Chen then addresses his enemies: "Now you listen to me. I'll only say it once. We are not sick men." When Lee delivered that line in Hong Kong theaters, the audiences "erupted from their seats."[134]

Chen delivers a kick to the back of the Japanese boxing teacher Yoshida (Feng Yi).

Through the violent solo action that climaxes with the two Japanese bullies eating the paper sign, Chen has set the wheels in motion for tragedy. The Japanese karate school leader instructs his students to attack the school (and not to return if they fail). As Chen walks through the streets, he encounters a burly guard who refuses to allow the Chinese man to enter Shanghai Park. Although a sign reads, "No Dogs and Chinese Allowed," the guard permits a Caucasian woman and her canine to pass but not Chen, who is told, "You're the wrong color, so beat it."

A young Japanese man, walking with two male and two female friends, agrees to escort Chen into the park if he "pretends" to be a dog. Chen viciously beats the three men and then jumps up and kicks the sign into small pieces. When the guard blows a police whistle, a crowd of Chinese onlookers, who previously made no attempt to help Chen (who continues to act alone), crowd around the young man and escort him away from the area.

The brief scene may be the most important sequence in Lee's body of work. For his poor fans, it summed up much of their pent-up hostility toward prejudiced treatment they had received throughout their lives. A writer, whose

A burly guard refuses Chen permission to enter Shanghai Park.

friend attended the Hong Kong premiere of *The Chinese Connection*, described
the response to the scene as:

> "Like striking up Dixie at a Ku Klux Klan
> rally. A mighty roar, deafening applause, and
> stamping of feet shook the theater. My West-
> ern friend scrunched lower in his seat,
> suddenly feeling very much like the foreigner
> in an alien land."[135]

The idea for the "No Dogs and Chinese Allowed" sign came from Kareem
Abdul-Jabbar during one of his many conversations with Lee. Jabbar recalled:

> "I was a history student, and I had studied
> the history of the Orient, Africa, and Asia. We
> talked about those things a lot—about the
> rights of the common man and things like that.
> We had a lot of philosophical discussions.

Chen fights the Japanese men who belittle him at Shanghai Park.

In fact, he used one thing we spoke about in one of his movies. During the British occupation of the southern parts of China, they had signs in a lot of restaurants that said, 'Dogs and Chinese Not Allowed.' That was something he didn't know about, and it surprised me. He put it in the movie."[136]

While Chen is involved in the park incident, the Japanese students invade the Chinese school, destroy the monument to Teacher, and demand that Chen be surrendered to them within three days. During this battle, *The Chinese Connection* differs from *Fists of Fury* in that the women fight beside the men and appear to be equals in terms of physical prowess. The students, however, take on the same characteristics as the cousins in *Fists* as they respect Chen's ability but resent his maverick actions. The fight at the school also totally lacks the raw, striking power of Lee's encounters.

After the Chinese students refuse to hand Chen over to the Japanese, who will kill him, Tien tells the revenge-seeker that he must vanish, saying: "For

Chen uses his fists to kill one of the men (Han Ying Chieh) who poisoned his teacher.

our sake, you must go tomorrow morning." Now, the students are placing him outside the group instead of banding around him to defeat their enemies. Chen—now totally isolated—must work alone.

That night Chen tells Yuan (who in a previous scene tried to convince him to eat a meal and who in this scene has just packed for him, reinforcing her domestic position) that he returned to Shanghai to ask her "to become my wife," which the young woman desires. Chen: "I have been rather a failure, haven't I?" He then tells her to go to bed, without the slightest hint of sexual contact or even desire, two elements that have no place in his obsessive quest for revenge.

After she leaves, Chen discovers that Teacher had been poisoned via tainted baked goods by two chefs (Huang Chung Hsun, who would later play Lee's uncle in *Return of the Dragon*; and Han Ying Chieh, who portrayed the Boss in *Fists of Fury* and who served as fight choreographer for both films). He slays the duo with his bare hands, killing Hsun's villain with the same vibrating punch he used on the Boss' son in *Fists of Fury* and Chieh's character, with multiple punches to the solar plexus, as he shouts, "Why did you kill my Teacher?"

Lee's image fills the screen with the face of a man—his features contorted, eyes staring—who appears to be wrestling with a power almost beyond his

Chen and Yuan (Miao Ker Hsiu) share a rare, tender moment.

own control. Chen is a virtuous, diligent, chaste, and loyal fighter whose duty is to avenge the victims of oppressors, who are customarily either Japanese or traitors employed by or employing Japanese.[137] Although his vengeance will claim the lives of the guilty parties, it will do nothing to change the status quo ensuring the iron-fisted rule of the Japanese.

Chen transforms his revenge into a public display by hanging the two bodies from a post on the center of the international settlement. To escape the law, Chen hides in a cemetery (hinting at the bleak end he will meet), and Yuan finds him eating—with his face snarled in an animalistic fashion—freshly cooked meat over an open fire at their old meeting place. This scene provides Lee with the only romantic sequence of his career. During their conversation, Chen even mentions "all the plans," which is reminiscent of his riverside thoughts before the final confrontation in *Fists of Fury* when he realized that his plans—his dreams—would never come true. Although expressing his "love," Chen makes it clear that her life would be in danger if they marry.

During the cemetery conversation, they say:

Yuan: "Do you remember all the plans that we used to have?"

Chen: "I do."

Yuan: "The ideas we used to have for the school. The way we said we would keep it going. The family we said we would have. What did we decide on? A little girl—a boy, too. And then, while you were out teaching every day at your own school, I'd do the house-work, and I'd come around and collect you here, and we'd go and bring the kids home from school. And now, what will happen? Will any of it come true?"

Chen: "I'm sure it will."

Yuan (now in a close-up, screen left): "If you go on like this, you know, it might never happen."

Chen (now in a close-up, screen right): "Don't think that. Of course, it will work out."

Yuan: "Do you really love me?"

Chen: "Of course, I do. You mean more to me than anyone."

Yuan: "Do I?"

Chen gently kisses her twice and then they embrace and kiss as the fire— for the first time—is heard crackling in the background (a Hollywoodized ro- mantic touch). As they embrace, she whispers: "So will you please tell me now about your plans?" Chen rises and walks away.

Yuan: "Why don't you speak?"

Chen (with his back to her): "I'll tell you this much, I'm taking you away with me."

Yuan: "Where to?"

Chen: "Somewhere. Somewhere where they'll never find us. Somewhere we'll be safe."

The conversation clearly establishes Chen as the strong male leader, with Yuan as the willing follower. Most of Yuan's lines end in question marks, as she clearly waits for answers—direction—from Chen. Even though she trains at the kung fu school with the men, she longs for a domestic existence ("I'd do the housework") and children ("a little girl—a boy, too"). But the romance is ill-fated, as Yuan identifies a name for Chen and provides information about those responsible for his Teacher's death. As the name is spoken, the music abruptly changes from romantic violins to piercing percussion beats.

Lo Wei appears to have had very little interest in this lone romantic interlude. He directed it while listening to the dog races on the radio.[138] According to Linda Lee, one of her husband's biggest regrets was that he never had the proper opportunity to express his sexuality more in films.[139]

At the Japanese school, the effeminate interpreter, who links the Japanese with weakness, suggests to Yoshida and Susuki that they should allow the authorities—symbolically society—to do their dirty work and track down Chen. "You may be one of Japan's best friends," Susuki tells the interpreter after the suggestion, which links the Japanese and corruption.

The murder investigation is handled by a Chinese inspector (played by director Lo Wei), who shows his contempt for the Chinese school by wearing his black hat and smoking a cigar (which he discards on the floor) inside the Spartan facility. The inspector says:

> "This is no simple affair. You know how strong the Japanese are, especially here in the settlement. I'm only doing my duty as a policeman. Don't you see that?"

Obviously, the inspector has surrendered his pride to the powerful Japanese and now acts as their stooge, prepared to blindly carry out their bidding. (Interestingly, some of Lee's fans accused him of acting as a British "stooge" in *Enter the Dragon*, which will be discussed.) If Chen is not handed over for the murder of the two cooks, the Japanese consul has demanded that the Chinese school be permanently closed.

At the Japanese school, a full-bodied stripper dances for Susuki and the Russian fighter Petrov (Robert Baker), who has been imported to the facility. The fighter's effeminate interpreter pulls off the dancer's panties. In an intoxicated state, he burbles, "Goodness me, what a time we're having!" The interpreter proves a sloppy drunk, allowing the liquor to fall out of his mouth as he talks. Susuki and the Russian laugh at his antics, and then Susuki jokingly commands that if the interpreter wants to leave, he must "go out like a Chinese—on your hands and knees."

Once outside, the interpreter kicks a rickshaw, displaying his contempt and disregard for the poor Chinese man who operates it. Wearing a different outfit to shield his identity, Chen impersonates the driver and takes the interpreter into an alley. After seeing Chen's demonstration of raw power as he lifts the rickshaw (a rare example of a trick effect in a Lee film) with the intoxicated rider still inside, the undisciplined man begs for "pity," provides information,

87

Japanese karate students surround Chen.

and then—although permitted to live—attacks the Chinese fighter from behind. After dispatching the adversary, Chen hangs him from the street post as a way of publicly announcing to the citizenry that justice will be done.

At the Japanese school, the inspector and two assistant officers have their hats off, a sign of respect and fear. Susuki accuses the Chinese policeman of "protecting" Chen, because they are of the same race. Susuki stands, giving him a position of power in the frame, as the inspector sits and nervously smokes a cigarette, as opposed to wearing his hat and calmly puffing as he did at the Chinese school. He also discards the cigarette in an ashtray, unlike at the Chinese school, where he callously tossed it on the floor.

Outside the Japanese school, Chen disguises himself as an old newspaper salesman and watches Susuki exit the school and enter a black sedan. That expensive vehicle mirrors the capitalistic leanings of the Japanese instructor, as opposed to the altruistic slain Teacher.

The inspector again returns to the Chinese school and tells Tien that he must surrender Chen or the school will be shuttered. Tien says he knows that Chen will immediately be found guilty, because members of the Chinese minority have no chance in the system. The inspector, who is either naive or dishonest, disagrees with the prediction.

Chen stuns the Russian Petrov (Robert Baker) with a kick.

To infiltrate the Japanese facility, Chen impersonates a telephone repairman by wearing a pair of thick glasses, which makes the actor resemble Jerry Lewis during one of his racist Japanese routines. Interestingly, Lee's taste in movies included a particular fondness for Lewis' pictures, and, while living in Seattle, he did impressions of a buffoonish telephone repairman.[140]

In the dojo, the Russian—the symbol of a world superpower—performs various tests of strength, such as allowing two students to hang from his arms and two others to jump him from behind, driving nails through boards with the palms of his hands, twisting a metal bar around his arm, and bending a pipe with his hands. (The scene resembles the footage of Bob Wall performing similar feats early in *Enter the Dragon*.)

The Japanese plan calls for everyone at the Chinese school to be murdered, a grisly activity that unfolds as Chen arrives at the school to seek his revenge. (In *Fists of Fury*, Lee's cousins are massacred when his character travels to the ice house, where he discovers evidence and battles some culprits.)

At the school, Chen offers the Japanese students a final opportunity to leave, because "this does not concern you." (In *Fists*, he issues a similar offer to the

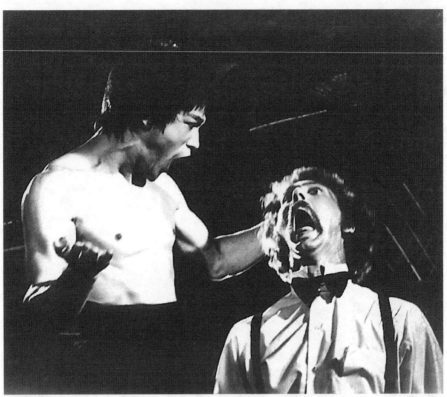
Chen delivers the death blow to Petrov.

Boss' henchmen.) After defeating the students, including a final opponent whose arms he snaps in a move later employed by aikido-expert-turned-actor Steven Seagal in a number of successful action films, Chen faces Yoshida, who uses a Samurai sword and has the weapon turned against him. The sword is kicked out of Yoshida's hands, goes into the air, and then pierces the victim's back.

The Samurai, as represented by Yoshida (and later Susuki), is a middle-class figure, while the kung fu hero is invariably a lower-class working figure who has no extended interest in society. His motives are all personal, and the tools available to him are never guns and seldom swords—which are a class above him—but his own body and perhaps a club, shaft, or crude blunt weapon.[141]

Before battling the Russian, Chen challenges three of Susuki's personal guards. As the last defeated opponent falls, Chen menacingly fixes his gaze on Susuki, with Lee using the same stare at the Japanese villain as he would before his final battle with the evil Han in *Enter the Dragon*.

In fighting Petrov—a Caucasian for the first time—Chen bites the opponent's leg, an animalistic move that literally allows him to taste the blood of his enemy, to break a hold. After dazzling him with footwork and (via camera tricks) hypnotic hand motions (fluid moves compared to the opponent's

A Chinese police official (Lo Wei) watches as Chen confronts the Japanese consul.

rigid style), Chen gives the Russian a chop to the throat with such force and intensity that Susuki, who witnesses the blow, retreats into his office to have the advantage of a sneak attack. The older Japanese leader does not meet the younger Chinese challenger face to face.

Susuki initially uses a samurai sword, which Chen blocks with street weapons—first with a staff and then with a nunchaku, which he discards right after disarming his opponent. Chen concludes the battle with a aerial jump kick, which sends Susuki through a window and to his death.

But the victory arrives too late to save most of Chen's fellow students, who have been viciously slaughtered by the Japanese students. Upon seeing the carnage, Tien, who with Yuan and a few other students, was searching for Chen, finally concedes that Chen was right. They should have fought together instead of allowing Chen to battle alone. Following the system proved their downfall. The Japanese consul, who has ordered the inspector to take action against the Chinese, demands entrance to the school and appears unmoved by the scores of bloody and beaten young bodies around him.

Chen re-enters the school through a second-story window (again coming from the outside, as in the beginning, to join the others), and agrees to surrender to prevent his friends from facing the wrath of the Japanese. On the way to the door, Chen snarls at the cowering Japanese consulate: "You just leave this school alone." A shirtless Lee dominates the center of the screen, with Lo Wei on his left and the consulate on his right.

The character's contempt for the government official parallels Lee's own dislike of police authorities. Lee said:

> "I don't like the cops and the British. Damn cops! They thought wearing those uniforms made them gods. The Chinese (cops) were worse. They were the ones that patrolled the streets. We didn't see too many Bobbies (British cops). They were usually the high-ranking officers. The cops never talked to you politely. They treated the kids, and even the Chinese, like dirt. Every time they opened their mouths, they swore at you. But if you were 'white,' they treated you completely opposite. They became so polite, bowing and smiling."[142]

Faced with the prospect of a term in prison (a penitentiary no doubt managed by the Japanese, who control the outside world), Chen commits suicide by running directly toward a small group of armed officers. Lo Wei ends *The Chinese Connection* in a freeze-frame, with Chen throwing a flying side kick and defiantly staring at his enemies.

Lee demanded that his character perish, because he was concerned with the Chinese preoccupation with violence. He said:

> "The glorification of violence is bad. That is why I insisted that the character die at the end. He had killed many people and had to pay for it."

Despite the picture's immense popularity, many Chinese resented that Lee's Chen was punished for his deeds, which his fans viewed as heroic.[143] But they were not upset enough to ignore the picture. *The Chinese Connection* caused such a sensation during its opening in Singapore that police officials ruled that showings be suspended for a week while they established new arrangements to handle the incredible amount of increased traffic the picture generated.[144]

Golden Harvest, in a press release for *The Chinese Connection*, claimed its star had "restored masculinity to the Chinese screen."[145] For more than a

Faced with the prospect of a prison term, Chen commits suicide by leaping into a group of armed officers.

century, the memories of historical defeats by Western countries fostered an inferiority complex. The combination of undue fear of anything foreign and xenophobia (fear and hatred of strangers or foreigners) created an ambivalence toward non-Chinese. They felt condescending toward foreigners, yet also felt jaded by their own culture. Lee's kung fu films clearly cashed in on this ambivalence. The blatant and exultant avocation of national identity was congenial not only to Chinese, but literally to all people—South Americans, Arabs, and Asians—who felt that they had been degraded by Western imperialism.[146]

Another important aspect of kung fu violence—particularly as seen in *The Chinese Connection*—is that it allows dignity to the small protagonist. One need not be Clint Eastwood, Fred Williamson, or Arnold Schwarzenegger, and few ghetto kids are. Bruce Lee, by his size and nationality, is a metaphor for the downtrodden. The Hong Kong Chinese laborer is unfortunately a disdained member of society from Japan to Europe and has never been considered hero material before. Elements of the possibility of such grace through violence in the person of a small, agile man can be seen in Edward G. Robinson or James

Cagney in the early 1930s. Such films and stars were popular with children of an Irish-Jewish urban lower class as the kung fu films are with poor Chinese and blacks.[147]

In *The Chinese Connection*, Bruce Lee symbolically crushed the Japanese-Western influence in his homeland. For his next picture, *Way of the Dragon* (released in the U.S. as *Return of the Dragon* because it was distributed after *Enter the Dragon*), Lee would leave the country and go to Italy to protect "his people." It was the first Mandarin production ever involved in European location shooting.[148]

Six Sequences to Watch Closely in *The Chinese Connection*

•In the pre-title sequences, Lee's character, late for the burial of his beloved Teacher, cries, jumps into the grave, and lands on top of the casket, which only has a sprinkling of dirt covering it. Study the position of Lee's body after he is knocked out by well-meaning instructor Tien. His arms go around the casket, showing him symbolically embracing death and foreshadowing the final scene with him leaping through the air in a suicidal attempt to attack the Japanese enforcers who share responsibility for Teacher's murder.

•Look closely at the entrance of the effeminate Japanese interpreter and the two Japanese students behind him when they arrive at the Ching Wu School, operated by the Chinese and founded by the murdered Teacher. Note the student in the blue gi on screen left as the interpreter explains his business. The student clearly has two protruding front teeth, the stereotypical "buck teeth" associated with racist images of the Japanese, particularly the insulting figures created by Jerry Lewis in American films. The same student is seen through much of the film, but after this introductory sequence, the false front teeth have been removed.

•At the Japanese fighting school, note the ornaments on the side walls. Antlers—symbols of death—serve as the main decorations, while at the Chinese school, pictures of the slain Teacher—the symbol of the good in life— adorn the walls and are often seen in the background as characters talk in early scenes. It's as though Teacher, now a god-like figure, is watching over the Ching Wu School, while the spirit of death surrounds the Japanese.

•During the initial Japanese school fight sequence between Lee and the students, note the use of dummies. Employing a quick-cut technique, director Lo Wei shows Lee grabbing two Japanese students and then they are replaced by costumed dummies as Lee simultaneously swings the students through the air in a circular fashion. (Sharp-eyed viewers will also notice a dummy head replaces that of Han when Lee delivers a devastating kick in the climactic mirror-room sequence of *Enter the Dragon*.) Such props, however, damage the realism of the battles, and Lee rarely used them.

94

•In the famous scene at the gate to Shanghai Park, a place off-limits to the Chinese, Lee's character is insulted by three Japanese men who offer to escort him through the park if he crawls like a dog. Note the degree of anger in Lee's face, something ignited by the prejudice he faces. He pummels these three men, a vicious attack that contrasts the comparatively minor beatings he gave to the students at the Japanese school. (Lee will display this level of total rage later in the film when he discovers the identities of the two Japanese spies who work at the Ching Wu School as chefs and poisoned Teacher.) Lee practically explodes with contempt for his enemies during this brief but extremely important Shanghai Park scene.

•In the fight between Lee and the burly Japanese instructor Yoshida, notice Lee's hand movements just before he kicks the Samurai sword out of his opponent's hands and sends the weapon high into the air. Lee quickly moves his hands in front of Yoshida and then slows them down, creating an almost hypnotic effect on his opponent. Lee's body is rock steady with just his hands traveling through space. As he slows down the movements and stops, Yoshida has a lapse in concentration, something immediately spotted by Lee, who keeps his eyes glued on the man like an animal ready to pounce. The unexpected kick is delivered with blinding speed and even catches viewers off guard, since our eyes are also locked on Lee's hypnotic hands. This ranks as a key sequence, because Lee is turning a weapon against a major opponent, as he will do with Han and the villain's razor-sharp spear in the mirror-room sequence of *Enter the Dragon*.

MAN, CAN WE USE HIM NOW!

Bruce Lee is back in the fantastic <u>all new</u> adventures
of the Super Hero from "Enter the Dragon"...

THE BATTLE OF KUNG FU KINGS: BRUCE LEE VS. AMERICA'S CHUCK NORRIS

Bruce Lee
Return of The Dragon

...his last performance is his best!

BRUCE LEE "RETURN OF THE DRAGON" Co-starring CHUCK NORRIS · Produced by RAYMOND CHOW for Golden Harvest · Written & Directed by BRUCE LEE
TECHNICOLOR® · A BRYANSTON PICTURES Release   R   **RESTRICTED**

CHAPTER 6
A *WAY*
BEHIND THE CAMERA

"I first met Bruce in 1966, when he was starring in *The Green Hornet* and appeared as a celebrity guest in a tournament I was participating in. We went back to our hotel together afterwards and spent the entire night talking about philosophies and styles. The next thing we knew, it was seven in the morning.

"We worked together for two years after that in Los Angeles, and then he left for Hong Kong to star in movies. One day, he called me and said, 'I just did two movies that were very successful. Now, I want to do one with the ultimate fight scene.' From that conversation came *Return of the Dragon*."—Personal interview with Chuck Norris by the author on March 11, 1979

Following the success of *The Chinese Connection*, Lee, in a bold (at least by Chinese motion picture industry standards) move, formed his own company, Concord Productions. In the Hong Kong film industry during the 1970s, writers, directors and dubbers earned approximately $1,250, $3,000, and $250 per movie, respectively.[149] Actors, who were signed to long-term contracts, often earned less.

With Concord Productions (which resembled Steve McQueen's Solar Productions and Clint Eastwood's Malpaso Company), Lee negotiated a contract with Raymond Chow, which called for a profit split of 50/50 between the partners. Chow said:

"After the first two pictures, there were so many offers that I told Bruce it would be difficult—impossible, in fact—for me to match the huge offers he was receiving. It would be unfair to him, and it would have been unfair to me."[150]

In 1972, Lee had effectively smashed open the Hong Kong production system and made some enemies at executive levels by demanding and receiving higher fees and better working conditions. Creative control of his project was the next obvious step, though he was far from the first star to start directing. Wang Yu had done so at least six years earlier.[151]

Lee's thoughts on directing developed much earlier. On the set of *Fists of Fury*, he studied filmmaking texts between takes, and, when an on-set interviewer asked him about becoming a director, Lee replied:

"Right. I'll be one if I have the chance.
Even if I'm not a director, reading some of
these books will still help an actor."[152]

Originally, Lee had seriously considered starring in *The Yellow Faced Tiger*, which would have been directed by Lo Wei, and Lee was even fitted for costumes. But Lee insisted that the picture's script be completed before filming commenced, while Lo Wei, who directed more than 75 features during 35 years in the film business, did not agree.[153] At that point, Lee, who felt that Chinese movies lacked "soul" and were merely run off an assembly line, decided to take control of his own career and walked off the project. Lo Wei eventually directed *The Yellow Faced Tiger* with Don Wang in the starring role.[154]

Lo Wei and Lee had been involved in a long and bitter feud since *Fists of Fury*. The martial artist resented that:

1) the director took credit for their two joint projects;
2) he called himself "the first million-dollar director."[155]

Their battle climaxed when Lee threatened the veteran filmmaker, a situation fully exploited by the headline-hungry Hong Kong newspapers. To defuse the situation, Lee signed a paper, which read: "I, Bruce Lee, will leave Lo Wei alone."

As his first project for Concord Productions, Lee selected *The Way of the Dragon*. Believing the simplistic story and cardboard characters would be ridiculed by Western audiences, Lee originally intended that distribution be limited to the Mandarin circuit. The picture was titled *Return of the Dragon* in the United States, because Bryanston Pictures released it following Lee's death and the success of *Enter the Dragon*. During its initial release in Hong Kong, *Way of the Dragon* set a new box-office record of 5,300,000 Hong Kong dollars ($1,060,000), almost a million more than *Fists of Fury*.[156] (In their original

engagements, *Fists of Fury*, *The Chinese Connection*, and *Return of the Dragon*
grossed more than $100 million worldwide.)[157]

Lee served as star, director, writer, martial arts choreographer (with Little
Unicorn, who had also been a child star),[158] and executive producer (with

Raymond Chow) on *Return of the Dragon*. (The film will be referred to by its American-release title.) He even assisted in editing the footage.[159] No other actor in Hong Kong had ever dared to challenge the studios and to assume so many duties.[160]

As a producer, Lee proved a very adept businessman. He selected Italy as the site for the picture, because of the popularity of martial arts films in that European country. *Five Fingers of Death*, for example, earned $1,500,000 in Italy alone.[161] Chow's numerous contacts in Italy for equipment, locations, and production details also made it a suitable location. And Lee was fascinated with the idea of fighting the final duel with Chuck Norris in the Colosseum.[162]

Norris, whom Lee first met in 1966 when Norris was fighting for the All-American Karate Championship, was a second choice. Lee originally wanted karate champ Joe Lewis for the pivotal role, but Lewis declined the offer. In 1969, Lewis and Lee had a "falling out" when Lewis, a native of North Carolina, won the International Karate Championship and overlooked crediting Lee for his coaching. Lewis also said that his wife at the time claimed that Lee had made "a pass at her," an accusation which "kinda ended our friendship."[163] Lewis has since starred in a handful of martial arts-oriented movies, including *Jaguar Lives* and *Force: Five*, none of which created box-office enthusiasm.

Return of the Dragon excited Lee for another reason. It would be a historic production as the first Chinese picture ever filmed in Europe.

The film opens with Lee's face dominating the screen and then cuts to Lee being curiously eyed by an older Caucasian woman in very conservative attire at an Italian airport. Again, Lee arrives from the outside. His character, Tang Lung (which means "China Dragon"), appears uncomfortable as she ignorantly stares at him, apparently not able to remove her eyes from this exotic person from Hong Kong. A bald, older man, who came to meet her, shakes the mesmerized woman before attracting her attention.

Without the ability to read the signs, Lee uses his senses (much like the fighting animal he will become at the end) to sniff out a restaurant as he waits for Chen Ching Hua (Nora Miao) to meet him. Chen, dressed stylishly in a dark pants suit, seems unimpressed with his country appearance and is annoyed because he dined instead of waiting at the gate. Tang Lung has been sent instead of Chen's sick uncle and thus he will replace the older, balanced person who would have maintained order.

Chen, who judges him by appearances (much like the Caucasian woman), immediately assumes he lacks the resources to provide any aid. He's unaware of her "problem," which he says she can tell him "later." (Being judged based on his race and appearance was long a part of Lee's life, something he deftly works into this short opening sequence.)

Chen drives a white Pontiac convertible, which the unsophisticated Tang Lung calls a BMW, then a Mustang, and finally a Rolls Royce. The feeble attempt to appear worldly simply reveals his country roots. Tang Lung learns that the syndicate (imperialistic powers) seeks ownership of the property containing Chen's Chinese restaurant, left by her father (a strong, protective figure Tang Lung will eventually represent). Tang Lung immediately says she does not have to sell, but Chen makes it clear that the law has little control over the rich and powerful, and in civilization—much like the jungle—the strong often take what they want.

To force her out, the Boss (Jon T. Benn, a Hong Kong businessman who acted as a hobby and agreed to play the villainous Caucasian),[164] sends his thugs to harass the customers and to badger the employees. As they drive by the Colosseum (where Tang Lung's final battle will occur), Chen tells him that the thugs "disappear as soon as the police arrive." Again, the established authorities prove no help to the minority members.

At her apartment, Chen informs Tang Lung that he can stay in an empty room in her living quarters (giving him a separate place from the other waiters, who live at the restaurant—much as Bruce Lee did as a young man while working his way through school as a busboy-waiter at Ruby Chow's.) "I live way out, in the new territories," Tang Lung boasts when Chen asks about his home, which is a wild, open area where his spirit can soar. He then wants to demonstrate his gung fu, but the woman stops him, containing him in the modern apartment, a stark contrast to his primitive fighting prowess, and warning him not to break anything in the apartment.

Chen wants him to deposit his money in the bank, but Tang Lung (mistrusting established institutions) balks, believing it is much safer to carry his funds. An overweight, conservatively dressed banker embraces Tang Lung in a phony show of camaraderie and says, "My friend," when he hears about the deposit. "I don't trust this weird, foreign money at all," says Tang Lung, a line that also sums up his suspicion of foreigners.

On a bench near a public fountain, Chen lectures Tang Lung on being friendly to those who are different, saying, "Just don't be so uptight." When an Italian streetwalker (Malisa Longo) sits beside him and flirts, the unsophisticated man misunderstands and, to be sociable, puts his arm around the woman, an insulting act that causes Chen to leave. (This scene was drastically cut for the American release. After Chen leaves in the original version, Tang Lung follows the prostitute back to her "office" where she plans to begin business. When she exits to another room, Tang Lung spots a full-length mirror and does kung fu poses until the hooker returns—wearing just a pair of bikini panties. Tang Lung runs from the room, much as Lee's character hurried from the brothel in *Fists of Fury*.)[165]

At Chen's apartment, Tang Lung is greeted by a portly and friendly waiter (Chin Ti), who asks, "Where did you go to just now?" The newcomer fails to answer, hinting at the embarrassment caused by the prostitute. At the

Tang Lung prepares to show the restaurant workers Chinese boxing.

restaurant, Uncle Wang (Huang Chung Hsun) complains that he has been away from Hong Kong for "ages" and longs to return (but as we later learn, he has been corrupted by the city and, at least spiritually, can never return). Tang Lung says that things have been "terrible" since he arrived in Rome and then glows with enthusiasm when he talks about the Hong Kong countryside. The first hint of Tang Lung's power is revealed in this scene as he taps Uncle Wang, who reacts with pain to the touch.

Behind the restaurant, the waiters perform rigid karate moves to pass the long wait between customers. They plan to use the stiff Japanese defense form against the local criminal element.

> **Chin Ti**: "They all started learning karate so they could deal with these damn thugs."
> **Tang Lung**: "How about you?"
> **Chin Ti**: "It's foreign. Doesn't interest me."
> **Tang Lung**: "Foreign or not, if it helps you to look after yourself when you're in a fight, then you should learn to use it. It doesn't

matter at all where it comes from, you should realize that."

Tang Lung's lines sum up Lee's fighting philosophy about taking movements from other fighting forms and adapting them to one's own style. The dialogue also slyly comments on taking self-defense techniques perfected by foreigners and then using the knowledge against them.

The waiters—with (dubbed) Americanized names such as Tony, Jimmy, Thomas, and Robert—are attired in traditional karate gis, as opposed to Tang Lung, who wears peasant garb, immediately making him stand apart from their regimented appearance. The waiters, eager to test Tang Lung's knowledge of Chinese boxing and his manhood, convince him to do a demonstration, but Uncle Wang interrupts the exhibition when customers enter the restaurant.

The middle-class patrons, who want to avoid trouble, quickly exit when the thugs, led by the skinny, swishy Ho T'ai (Wei Ping Ao, who plays a similar role in *The Chinese Connection*), begin harassments. Ho plucks out a flower and sniffs it and pinches and slaps Uncle Wang. These effeminate actions immediately stereotype Ho T'ai as a weak male and it's a disturbing homophobic image. He also wears over-sized sunglasses and gaudy clothes and stops to tuck in Tang Lung's belt when the newcomer exits the men's room and enters the dining area. No one mentions calling the police, again commenting on the lack of effectiveness of the authorities.

The four thugs—two black and two white—agree to go "out back" into an open area that better suits Tang Lung and where he will be free (as opposed to the restaurant, airport terminal, and apartment that confine him). In the restaurant, Tang Lung sits alone at a table on screen right, his eyes examining the outsiders like an animal waiting to pounce and taking in every action before making the first move.

In the alley, Jimmy (Little Unicorn), a waiter, volunteers to challenge them and performs a brief kata (art movement) before the bearded thug leader delivers one punch and knocks him out. This scene visually comments on Lee's feelings about katas. As Dan Inosanto, one of Lee's Jeet Kune Do disciples, observed:

> "Humor aside, this footage does have meaning. For in it, Bruce cleverly depicts a major premise of Jeet Kune Do, simplicity, as opposed to extraneous—and therefore useless—motion."[166]

After waving off his fellow workers (as he does to the employees before the first ice-house fight in *Fists of Fury*), Lee then allows his character to

103

dominate the center frame as he challenges the thugs who ridicule him, because they confuse the obviously ineffective Japanese karate with Chinese boxing. After Tang Lung knocks out his first opponent, the camera zooms in on Chen, who looks excited by the newcomer's awesome physical prowess. Like her late father, he can protect her, as opposed to the others—including the older Uncle Wang—who can't. For the first time, she smiles at him.

By adapting to the fighting methods of his opponents (at one point, he even bobs and weaves like a boxer), Tang Lung defeats them. Despite the victory, Uncle Wang, who obviously recognizes his "place" as a stranger in a new land, warns them: "We're all foreigners. All around us is their territory." (His words sound much like those of the older teacher Tien, who warned about the political power the Japanese possessed in *The Chinese Connection*.)

Chen smiles, purposely walks to Tang Lung, and—for the first time—takes the newcomer's arm as they exit. At the apartment, Chen offers him something to eat, the first domestic inclination shown by this businesswoman. The unsophisticated man does not recognize the woman's sudden interest and retires to bed, noting: "I want to get up early for some training." He's more obsessed with his physical training than any sexual longing. A man in love can be hurt through his lover, who can tie him down and give him long-term responsibilities, not the kind resolved by action. Romantic entanglements have no place in Lee's action-fantasy universe, one populated by pre-adolescent fantasies.

Tang Lung offhandedly asks about the possibility of purchasing a gun, but then, apparently, rejects the idea of using a modern weapon and carves wooden darts.

The next morning Chin Ti's waiter-character prepares a fancy breakfast for Tang Lung (who now receives special treatment due to his abilities) and refuses to let the other restaurant workers share in the small morning feast. When Tang Lung arrives, the waiters also crowd around and compliment his fighting.

Tang Lung, whose face visibly hardens from that of a meek country farmer to one of a focused warrior as soon as he prepares to strike the first blow, demonstrates the power of Chinese boxing. Tony then suggests that the men "all give up karate" and removes his gi. That night, a Japanese thug, holding a revolver, waits in Chen's apartment and is quickly disarmed and beaten by Tang Lung, who deposits the bruised man in the hallway and then casually goes to bed.

At his modern office, the Boss, a Caucasian leader who smokes cigars, wears expensive suits, and sits behind an oppressive black desk, expresses his credo of greed simplistically, saying: "What I like, I get, and I want that restaurant." The Boss then questions the unsuccessful Japanese thug and as he says, "kung fu," Lee jump cuts to shots of Tang Lung going through a rigorous training exercise on a balcony. The shirtless man is distracted by a 1960s psychedelic poster of a couple making love, a shot which comments on the character's

Chen Ching (Nora Miao) and Tang Lung are startled to find an armed mobster in her apartment.

view that the sex act simply gets in the way of one's goals. He then sniffs the air and finds that Chen, for the first time in a totally domestic position (as the owner of the restaurant, she is a professional businesswoman), has prepared a meal and placed flowers in the room.

> **Chen** beams: "In Rome, you won't often find such food. Is it OK?"
> **Tang Lung**: "It's better in Hong Kong."
> **Chen**: "Sure, I know that, but I cooked it myself."

In the brief interchange, Tang Lung reveals that he will never fully adjust to or remain in this new world. He is an outsider, just passing through and in a hurry to return to his native land (again avoiding long-term obligations).

At the restaurant, the thugs return with knives and guns (raising the stakes), and Lee intercuts the footage with shots of Tang Lung and Chen on a sightseeing tour. As Tang Lung exhibits his unsophistication about the "ancient Roman relics" by likening them to Hong Kong slums, Chen now smiles rather than frowns.

105

Tang Lung easily disables the armed assassin.

While at another historical site, Chen asks:

> "This garden was built by an ancient king
> for his queen. The time and money it took to
> build all of this, I think he must have really
> loved her. Are you married? How do you like
> this place?"
>
> **Tang Lung**: "It's a big waste, all of this.
> In Hong Kong, I would build on it. Make
> money."

Chen, obviously, has been moved by the romanticism of the spot and her
newfound feelings for Tang Lung, but he can only think of the practical aspects
and never appears interested—either sexually or emotionally—in the attrac-
tive, but clearly Westernized woman. Tang Lung also misinterprets the "how
do you like this place?" question, in which Chen might be wondering if he
plans to stay in Rome, not whether he cares about the historical site. (The
dialogue exchange is also reminiscent of the final talk between Lee's character
and his girlfriend in *The Chinese Connection*. Most of her lines were
questions.)

106

In a flashy display, Tang Lung uses a nunchaku to disarm the enemies.

As they re-enter the restaurant, Chen and Tang Lung are met by a gun-toting thug. The cigar-smoking Boss scoffs at Tang Lung's abilities, saying, "Chinese kung fu!" He then slaps Tang Lung twice and prepares to swing a third time when the Chinese man grabs and holds his hand. The grasp continues until a thug points an automatic revolver at Tang Lung's head. Ho T'ai, who first feels Tang Lung's "rippling muscles," gives him an airplane ticket to return home, thereby transporting the outsider to where he belongs.

In the spacious back alley (where again he is unconfined), Tang Lung easily disarms the bearded Italian thug by pretending he does not understand the language and delivering a swift blow when the culprit shakes his head in an exasperated manner, and then picks up a staff and discards the gun. In a flashy display, he also uses a nunchaku to disarm the knife-wielding enemies, much

Although Lee recognized the cinematic value of the flashy nunchaku, he found the actual weapon ineffective.

as he used the weapon to disarm the Samurai-sword-wielding Japanese opponent in *The Chinese Connection*.

Although Lee recognized the cinematic value of the flashy nunchaku, he found the actual fighting instrument ineffective. Dan Inosanto, who introduced Lee to the weapon—which can generate 1,600 pounds of pressure—while the actor was starring on *The Green Hornet*, said: "He always questioned its validity."[167] For filming, Lee had special nunchakus constructed from soft polyethylene. The chain connecting the two sticks was also plastic, allowing Lee to add realism to his films through actual contact. Had he swung the genuine hardwood sticks connected by a nylon cord or chain, he would have been unable to produce the realistic effects intended.[168] However, for rehearsals, he used regular nunchakus and practiced so hard that his arms and shoulders would be black and blue.[169]

At the end of the battle, the bearded thug, in a rare comedic moment, picks up a nunchaku, mimics Tang Lung, who glistens from perspiration and resembles a well-oiled fighting machine, and knocks himself out, proving his inability to adapt to a foreign weapon. The Italian thug is a distinct contrast to the Chinese man, who continues to adapt to and conquer the environment. Tang Lung, who briefly assumes his country-bumpkin facial expressions to fool the culprits into thinking he's harmless, uses wooden darts to disarm the gunmen in the restaurant and then tosses his nunchaku at the Boss. The weapon wraps around his wrist, symbolically binding him. The Boss is warned not to cause further trouble, but the restaurant soon receives a letter saying: "Bullets are faster than anything," threatening Tang Lung's life if he remains past midnight. "You young kids asked for this," says the weak uncle, another corrupt, greedy father figure in Lee's body of work.

Chen pleads with him to leave Rome, and a rooftop sniper, who earlier felt the sting of Tang Lung's prowess, attempts to assassinate the foreigner. Tang Lung uses cat-like movements to travel through the dark and run up stairways and wounds the armed culprit with a wooden dart, another victory of primitive weapons over modern ones.

Back at the apartment, Chen has been abducted, and Tang Lung, who can neither read nor speak Italian, grows confused while attempting to communicate with a telephone operator in order to contact the restaurant. Although a master with wooden darts and hand-to-hand combat techniques, he still fails when attempting to use Westernized technology.

At the Boss' office, Ho T'ai, a traitor to his fellow Chinese (and a character treated in a homophobic fashion, as was the actor's Japanese villain in *The Chinese Connection*), threatens to use a knife on Chen and make her face "look very ugly." He laughs when she mentions Tang Lung, who the thugs believe was slain by the sniper and say is seeking "peace with his maker." (This line provides little insight into the personal religious philosophy of Lee, who was a fatalist. When his brother, Robert, asked Lee if he believed in God, the actor replied: "I believe in sleeping.")[170]

When Tang Lung and the waiters arrive (like the cavalry) at the Boss' office, Lee's character remains fairly uninvolved in the fight until the tide turns against his friends (who cannot survive in the dangerous world) and he is hit in the face, a violent attack that inspires him to remove his shirt to communicate his rage and hints at the damage he's about to inflict. As in *The Chinese Connection* and *Fists of Fury*, Lee's character offers one of the thugs a chance to bow out of the battle. To prove his prowess, the shirtless Tang Lung—skin again glistening from perspiration—jumps in the air and kicks out a ceiling light (as Lee does in James Garner's office in *Marlowe*). The action causes the opponent to retreat, as opposed to the first two films in which the men fought even when aware of the character's superior fighting ability.

The Boss and Ho T'ai cower behind a wall as Tang Lung orders them out, tells them to "lay off," and removes any language barrier by silently communicating with the Boss by making a fist and shaking his head from side to side. The Boss nods, a recognition of the newcomer's power.

Tang Lung still proves too unsophisticated to understand the Westernized gangsters. He has disgraced them twice in battle and continues to believe they

Tang Lung removes any language barrier by making a fist and shaking his head at the Boss (Jon T. Benn).

will cease their aggression when, in fact, they plan to escalate it. Lee commented on the uncomplicated character, saying:

> "He is a simple man, but he likes to act big, you see. He really doesn't understand a metropolis like Rome... It is really a simple plot of a country boy going to a place where he cannot speak the language, but he comes out on top because he honestly and sincerely expresses himself by beating the hell out of everybody who gets in his way."[171]

The Boss contacts a European fighter (Robert Wall), a Japanese Master of Hapkido (Whang Ing Sik), and an American martial artist, Kuda Colt (Chuck Norris), described as "America's best." (Japanese actor Sonny Chiba Shinichi was approached to appear in *Return of the Dragon* but refused, because he was starring in a television series and felt that "the standard of Hong Kong movies was too low." He now says he would have accepted the role if he had known that Lee would have been his co-star. In 1975, Chiba starred in *Street Fighter*, a

Lee had special nunchakus constructed to add realism to his films.

film most famous for receiving an X rating from the Motion Picture Association of America due to its violent content.)[172]

Selecting characters from three distinct sections of the globe symbolically allows Lee to conquer the world, a fact not missed by the uneducated masses of Hong Kong, Southeast Asia, and Chinatowns throughout the world. Those fans felt that Lee single-handedly put them on the map, created a new and positive image, and reawakened people everywhere to pride in the infinite possibilities of their own bodies, being the absolute best at beating bigger people and, symbolically, countries.[173]

At a Chinese New Year celebration in the restaurant, Lee places himself in the center of the frame as the uncle distributes New Year money to the waiters. Lee's character continues to stand apart due to his traditional Chinese attire and maintains his identity and integrity even in a strange, new environment, a stark contrast to the European suits worn by the other Asian characters still struggling to fit into the landscape. A cable arrives from Tang Lung's uncle, who wants him to return home, but the newcomer vows to stay until the "whole mess" is settled with the gangsters.

Colt enters from an airplane, having literally descended from above and visually establishing that he—like Tang Lung—has come from the outside, making them symbolic equals. Lee shoots the sequence from a low angle, giving Colt a position of power. His clothes and accessories—dark glasses

Tang Lung trades blows with Kuda Colt (Chuck Norris).

(suggesting mystery, doom), a briefcase (suggesting business), and casual Westernized clothes (suggesting a positive self-image; he doesn't require a suit to impress anyone)—also help establish the tone. Attending an initial meeting with the Boss, Colt demonstrates his karate abilities by crushing the Japanese karate expert.

During the climax of *Return of the Dragon*, Uncle Wang shows that he has been corrupted by the ways of greedy Westerners when he stabs Tony and Jimmy after Tang Lung defeats the European fighter with a driving punch to the groin

Bruce Lee and Chuck Norris pose for their climatic fight to the death.

and the Master of Hapkido with a stunning kick to the head. He then pursues Ho T'ai, who leads him to Kuda Colt. Uncle Wang, who refers to the Master of Hapkido as "that Jap," had negotiated a payoff from the Boss for convincing Chen to sell the restaurant. The corrupted man planned to use the money to return—a financial, but not spiritual success—to his wife and children in Hong Kong.

At the Colosseum, Colt, again elevated in a power position, looks down as Tang Lung searches for an entrance to the fighting arena and encounters barred openings. Although a newcomer and outsider, Colt appears in total control of the environment, especially in contrast to Tang Lung, who still appears continually rejected by the new land, but in the end, fighting skill makes Lee's Tang Lung superior.

When the fighters meet face to face, no words are spoken as Colt—in a white gi—and Tang Lung—in dark peasant garb—remove their tops and perform stretching exercises in preparation for the confrontation. The Colosseum duel, certainly one of the finest hand-to-hand combat segments in motion picture history, was painstakingly planned with 20 pages of written instruction and choreographed like a dance number.[174]

Lee was the first person in Chinese cinema to make the intricate movements of battle scenes a priority. The emphasis on choreography isn't surprising, considering Lee, a good dancer, won a cha-cha contest during his teens.[175]

113

Tang Lung avoids Colt's lethal kick.

Lee even has special props, like Fred Astaire's cane and top hat. The prop can be a staff (*Return of the Dragon*), knives (*Fists of Fury*), or nunchakus (*The Chinese Connection, Return of the Dragon*, and later *Enter the Dragon*). When Lee uses these devices, they become part of a skilled performance similar to the way Astaire or Gene Kelly might twirl a cane or flip his hat. The call is, clearly, for identification, and identification depends on the myth of skill.[176]

As the one-on-one battle commences, the bulkier American fighter, with a hairy chest and back, dominates, momentarily downing his sleek opponent with kick-punch combinations. But the smaller foe appears to gain strength—not lose it—from the blows. (Lee's character gains similar strength with fighting The Boss in *Fists of Fury*.) After finding it difficult to penetrate Colt's defenses with his basic skills, the Chinese man changes his style, bobbing and weaving (like Lee's favorite boxer, Muhammad Ali). He appears to be losing to Colt, because he fights in a purely practical fashion. Only when he switches to what Dan Inosanto labels "offset" rhythm does he begin to gain the upper hand. His philosophical message: "Adapt and blend."[177]

Lee, as a filmmaker, also insisted that *Return of the Dragon* feature an original score, in contrast to most Chinese films that employ stock music.[178] He deftly uses Ku Chai Hui's music during this battle as he underscores the shots

Tang Lung lets Colt know he may retreat, but Colt refuses to lose face.

in which he begins to change his style and visually shows his body, again glistening with perspiration, as he finally inflicts damage to Colt. (Due to the strict laws concerning filming at the Colosseum, Lee had sets built, at a cost of $130,000, in Hong Kong for the final battle.)[179]

Near the battle's conclusion, Tang Lung nods to Colt, letting the injured fighter know that he may retreat. But Colt, a warrior nearly equal to Tang Lung, refuses to lose face (as most of the other opponents have done) and makes a final lunge, which his opponent counters with a head lock before snapping the American's neck (in another move Steven Seagal would adapt for his films). In a final act of respect, Tang Lung covers the dead fighter with his traditional white gi, the first and only time one of Lee's characters pays homage to a fallen opponent.

Lee overemphasizes the fight segment with too many zoom close-ups and some annoying cuts to a cat, the only creature to observe the almost mythic battle. The Hong Kong censors apparently found the final confrontation too graphic and insisted that five kicks to Chuck Norris' head be cut. The frames were added for the U.S. release.[180]

Over the last decades, the U.S. in three major wars, has been fighting various Japanese, Koreans, Chinese, and Vietnamese.[181] On most occasions, those wars have resulted in victory for Americans, which makes it easy to understand why the lower-class Chinese were so excited when Lee defeated the larger Norris in this cinematic clash of the titans.

After the battle, the Boss arrives in a Mercedes Benz (a European car and symbol of wealth) and shoots Uncle Wang and Ho T'ai. He attempts to slay Tang Lung as the police—who were summoned by Chen (a woman also alerted the authorities in *Fists of Fury*)—finally arrive, handcuff The Boss, and take him away. The Boss, who never even gets his hair messed, remains surprisingly calm, taking comfort, no doubt, in the fact that his attorneys will have him back on the street before the bodies can be transported to the morgue.

At a cemetery (which also served as the last meeting place for Lee's character and his fiancee in *The Chinese Connection*), Chen places flowers on a grave as Tang Lung says: "Now that it's all finished with, I must go." Chen takes his hand but never kisses the departing man as she asks him to "take care." Tang Lung walks away (going back to the outside, like a Western genre hero-gunfighter who uses his lethal powers to protect society and then no longer fits into it). As he leaves, Chin Ti says to Chen:

> "In this world of guns and knives,
> wherever Tang Lung must go, he will always
> travel on his own."

The last image, a long shot of Tang Lung walking away, contrasts the opening shot that showed the character, who just arrived from the air, in full close-up. The end credits continue as Tang Lung walks from the cemetery and suddenly disappears from sight, seeming to evaporate into the landscape.

Return of the Dragon also establishes a common trait in Lee's characters: an avoidance of obligations. By evading serious relationships with the opposite sex, Lee's characters are never forced to grow up emotionally, though they are physically matured to the point of perfection. The lack of emotional entanglements and family obligations (such as the responsibility for children, household chores, and bills) allows young viewers, as well as older ones who do face such pressures in their daily lives, to enjoy the fantasy of a totally free life. In addition, Lee's characters don't perform menial tasks in the films. Although playing a person of the people, Lee kept his characters on a different level, even in *Fists of Fury*, where he is hired as a factory worker. His toil consists of pushing one block of ice before springing into action. Thus another adolescent fantasy—avoiding work by being a fighting machine admired by peers and frightening to enemies—surfaces throughout his cinematic efforts.

Six Sequences to Watch Closely in *Return of the Dragon*

•During an early restaurant scene, Uncle Wang asks about things in Hong Kong, and Lee, who has clearly expressed his discomfort at being an outsider in a foreign place (Italy), broadly smiles and happily gushes about life "in the country." The conversation is one of the rare times Lee really lights up on screen with a smile, bringing an almost child-like glee to the brief but important exchange that spotlights a very different facet of the star's personality.

•In his first battle, Lee fights four opponents and sits on the chest of the second one after knocking him out. From that low position, Lee glues his eyes on the two remaining enemies as they cautiously approach. The shot ranks as an interesting choice, with Lee, who directed, playing against expectations by having the character being looked down upon but still possessing the most power in the frame. (In *Enter the Dragon*, he will also be seated—though not on top of an opponent—after the underground battle and be gazed down upon by Han, who trapped him from above. In that later film as here, Lee, his eyes focused as in this shot, still suggests total control despite that lower position.)

•In the alley scene where Lee demonstrates the power of Chinese boxing, he uses a side kick to drive Little Unicorn, who's holding a protective cushion, into a pile of stacked boxes, which fall all around him. Lee employs the same movement to kick Bob Wall's Oharra into a group of tournament fighters, who also fall around him, in *Enter the Dragon*.

•During an early day exercise sequence, Lee goes through some stretches and punches with his shirt off. He then immediately sits down to have a meal prepared by Nora Miao. The scene delivers a sexual charge because Lee enjoys the food without wearing a shirt, much to the delight of Miao's physically interested character. The scene shows that Lee understood his sex appeal and was willing to use it, though on a limited basis.

•As a director, Lee quite deftly conveys the strength of Chuck Norris' karate champion Kuda Colt through visual imagery. In the scene where Colt visits The Boss, the evil businessman and the American fighter take their seats at exactly the same moment, showing them to be of equal power. That image contrasts the way everyone but Colt hovers around The Boss, fearing to make a move—let alone act as an equal—without permission.

•Bob Wall, most famous as Oharra in *Enter the Dragon*, seems to specialize in absorbing Lee's blows to the groin. In *Enter the Dragon*, Lee initially weakens him by a foot to the groin, while in *Return of the Dragon*, he breaks the fighter's defenses by a kick to the groin. He then kills Wall's character— Kuda Colt's top student—by dropping him to the ground and delivering a driving right punch directly between the legs of the fighter. It ranks as an incredibly painful-to-watch death blow, especially for male viewers.

This comic strip-type ad appeared in the Sunday editions of metropolitan newspapers when *Enter the Dragon* was released.

CHAPTER 7
THE *DRAGON* ENTERS

"My father created the martial arts genre in the Western world. I don't think that's presumptuous to say. I just think it's true. Certainly the films of other people have grossed more money and have had larger budgets, but for my money, no one ever equaled my dad's achievement on film, especially in *Enter the Dragon*, which is my favorite."

—Brandon Lee in a personal interview with the author on August 16, 1992

After *Return (Way) of the Dragon*, Lee had planned to direct and star in *Game of Death*, a project he envisioned as the ultimate showcase for the martial arts.[182] Production actually started in 1972,[183] and some of the combat sequences were completed when Warner Bros. firmed a deal for Lee to star in *Enter the Dragon*, marking the first American-Chinese co-production[184] and the first time a Chinese performer had his name above the title of an American motion picture.[185] Because of the success of *Five Fingers of Death* (1973) in the U.S., Warner Bros. increased *Enter*'s original budget from $450,000 to $550,000.[186]

Game of Death went into hiatus until the U.S.-financed project completed filming. *Enter the Dragon*, which originally had a four-week filming schedule, began in February 1972 and was completed in April. Lee died three weeks before he was set to begin a massive U.S. publicity tour to promote *Enter the Dragon*. Warner Bros. never exploited his untimely demise in any of the advertising. The studio also intends to continue showcasing the picture, which grossed $8.4 million during its first year of U.S. release[187] and has since grossed more than $120 million worldwide.[188] Warner Bros. has decided to distribute it on laser disc and tape and re-release it to theaters as a perennial classic rather than sell it to network television.[189]

Despite the world-wide popularity of *Enter the Dragon*, the project never proved a favorite of the star's Hong Kong fans, who felt that the picture was "glossy and unrealistic," considered the fight scenes inferior, objected to the

Many of Bruce Lee's fans resented the fact John Saxon fought the villain Bolo.

rather uninspired climactic Lee-Han battle, and resented the fact that American actor John Saxon, who had studied t'ai-chi ch'uan,[190] fought the muscular villain Bolo (Yang Sze) rather than Lee.[191] Even one of Lee's strongest supporters, Chuck Norris, described his friend's government-operative character as "monotonous."[192] The fans also resented that *Enter the Dragon*, the only Lee film designed for non-Asian tastes, was released around the world before being released in Hong Kong, and that Raymond Chow raised admission prices from five to eight Hong Kong dollars ($1.60 in U.S. currency) for the film. However, it eventually earned 3.5 million Hong Kong dollars, the same amount as *Fists of Fury*.[193]

But perhaps most of all, many of his Chinese fans considered his character—named Lee—"a white man's stooge,"[194] because he worked for the British government.

Even Lee had commented on his dislike for the British, saying:

> "They (the British) were the ruling class. They were the minority, but they ran the city (Hong Kong). They lived up on the hills with big cars and beautiful homes, while the rest of the population, who lived below, struggled and sweated to make a living. You saw so much poverty among the Chinese people that eventually it was natural to hate the filthy-rich British. They made the most money and had the best jobs because the color of their skin was white."[195]

According to Lee's friend, William Cheung, Lee also resented policemen, because, as a youth, he saw officers actively supporting certain gangs to earn payoffs.[196]

Considering the tone of Lee's anti-British quotes, it is easy to understand his fans' confusion over his acceptance of a role as an agent for Her Majesty's government and their general rejection of *Enter the Dragon*. The film, however, proved surprisingly popular in Japan, where audiences embraced it.

But by this point in his career, Lee might have been truly applying what Dan Inosanto described as "Bruce's Cup Theory," which:

> "...expressed the idea that a cup is only useful when it is empty. Applying this concept to the martial arts, if you teach a man of pride, he will say that he knows everything, his mind (cup) has been filled with old ideas and prejudice. Thus, his mind is like a cup filled with water; unless he pours out his old water, he will never be able to receive new things."[197]

Perhaps Lee was ready to receive what he envisioned to be his ultimate glory: Stardom in America.

Enter the Dragon arrived on the screen as a result of the efforts of producer Fred Weintraub. In the early 1970s, Weintraub, who commissioned the original *Kung Fu* series script,[198] planned to put Lee in a Western entitled *Kelsey*,[199] but the project collapsed. After seeing *Fists of Fury*, the producer, convinced

that Lee would soon become an international star, appealed to Warner Bros. executives to finance a production but was spurned. Undaunted, Weintraub, positive that the Chinese actor should be showcased in a Hollywood production, went to Hong Kong to formulate a deal with Concord Productions and Golden Harvest.[200] The result of those negotiations was *Enter the Dragon*, which was originally titled *Blood and Steel*[201] and later *The Deadly Three*.[202]

Lee selected the project over an MGM offer, which would have had him co-starring with Elvis Presley, a martial arts enthusiast.[203] Four other major American studios also offered Lee contracts,[204] but he remained with Weintraub and *Enter the Dragon*.

The Chinese-American actor professed a vast amount of faith in the project, noting:

> "*Enter the Dragon* should make it. This is the movie that I'm proud of, because it is made for the U.S. audience as well as for Europeans and Orientals. This is definitely the biggest movie I ever made. I'm excited to see what will happen. I think it's going to gross $20 million in the U.S."[205]

Of Lee's appeal, Weintraub observed:

> "There's no question that he would have been the biggest superstar if he had lived, for he had this thing that happens to great performers on screen—it's a kind of magnetism. It's the same with guys like Clint Eastwood— just a nice guy when you meet him at a party but something unique and special when he gets on the screen."[206]

Agreeing with that assessment was Robert Clouse, who directed *Enter the Dragon* and later filmed the non-Lee sequences for *Game of Death*. Clouse, who describes himself as "the poor man's (Sam) Peckinpah,"[207] observed:

> "He was not a great actor; he had a funny voice and an accent some people thought was humorous, but his screen presence was just tremendous. He could just stand there and stare; it was with such concentration, you felt he could kill you just by staring. It came across like a bolt of electricity."[208]

The production did not begin smoothly. Lee, whom biographers have described as immensely egotistical and hotheaded,[209] walked off the set the first day, because *Enter the Dragon* was billed in a newspaper as a Golden Harvest rather than a Concord production. The film was supposed to have been a joint venture between Concord (Lee and Chow's company), Sequoia (Weintraub and co-producer Paul Heller's company), and Warner Bros. Two weeks passed before he returned, a time lapse which has been attributed more to his nervousness over headlining an American film than to his anger over the billing error.[210] Sequences were shot around the actor during those days.

In *Bruce Lee: The Man Only I Knew*, Weintraub says:

> "He was undoubtedly nervous about *Enter the Dragon*—apprehensive. A lot was riding on it—it was his first big international film. He was under tremendous pressure, he and the writer, Michael Allin, just didn't see eye to eye. In addition, he was on his home ground (the picture was shot in Hong Kong), and I think he wanted to avoid giving the impression of partiality toward Americans, of favoring them at the expense of his own ethnic group. So there was this dichotomy operating for him. And on the whole, he wanted the film to be more Chinese than American, which was very understandable."[211]

His sister-in-law, Lin Yen-ni, the wife of Bruce's older brother Peter, described Lee's loyalty to associates as:

> "If you are his friend, you will like him for most of the time and dislike him for the rest. Like other men of strong character, his loveliness and his hatefulness are equally prominent... He is a sun, everything revolves around him. When you enter his world, you will become his accessory. He will protect and command you... Basically, this ambitious man is a solitary man who comes and goes all by himself. He has valets, but he has no intimate friend. His only friends are his books, his dream, and his wife Linda."[212]

In a 1972 newspaper article, which Lee wrote for a Taiwan newspaper after completing *Fists of Fury*, the actor detailed his feelings about being Chinese. He wrote:

Enter the Dragon **provided Bruce Lee a platform on which to display his national pride.**

"I am a Chinese and I have to fulfill my duties as a Chinese. The truth is, I am an American-born Chinese. My identity as a Chinese is beyond all doubts. At least I have always looked upon myself as a Chinese during all my years in the States, and in the eyes of the Westerners, I am, of course, a Chinese. Being a Chinese, I must possess the basic requisites. By these requisites, I refer to the truthful representation of the culture and the display of the emotions of being a Chinese."[213]

In Lee's mind, this American-financed picture—a big-budget epic by Chinese filmmaking standards—probably provided him with a sparkling platform on which to display his national pride, his newfound international status, and his incredible gung fu. Decades earlier, national exclusion legislation—first of the Chinese in 1814 and later, in 1924, of the Japanese—resulted from popular

125

anti-Asian agitation, particularly in California. The agitation employed various negative stereotypes of both the Chinese and Japanese, stereotypes that revealed a deep-seated and powerful prejudice against Asians.[214]

Now, Lee had the opportunity—paid for by Hollywood—to land a blow for "his people."

Enter the Dragon (99 minutes), which plotwise borrows elements from Terence Young's *Dr. No* (1962), the first in the James Bond series, opens with Lee—his glistening body in contrast to his black shorts, shoes, and Kempo fighting gloves—in complete control of an exhibition bout with a larger, less muscular fighter (Samo Hung). The students, teachers, and Braithwaite (Geoffrey Weeks), a British special service commander, watch with obvious awe as he masterfully and efficiently defeats his opponent. He then does a flip over the monks who have raised their hands and therefore remains above all others in terms of skill and character.

Braithwaite approaches Lee about "a matter of great importance." Lee tells him it must wait until after he works with his young Chinese student, immediately establishing him in a more traditional role as a teacher—a member of the school's ruling order—and a person of perhaps international importance (considering that a British government member traveled to confer with him). During the lesson, Lee maintains a solemn mood, unlike in his actual instructing when he used jokes and stories to reinforce concepts.[215] He also stresses "emotional content, not anger" to his student, which sounds like Lee's approach to on-screen battles, which he approached with contained energy, rarely unrestrained fury.

Summing up his philosophy of life and fighting, Lee says to the student:

> "It is like a finger pointing a way to the
> moon. Do not concentrate on the finger or
> you will miss all that heavenly glory."

In his first three pictures, Lee's characters always had to prove their combat talents before earning respect, but *Enter the Dragon* immediately establishes him as a powerful force. It also marks the first of his films in which he does not enter from the outside (although he will be an outsider on Han's island). We first see him at his Shaolin Temple, at home with his fellow teachers and students. (Lee insisted that this Shaolin Temple sequence be added to the picture, and it was shot after the completion of principal photography and added as a pre-title sequence,[216] much as the 007 pictures use pre-title sequences. It marked Lee's last fight scene.)

Even though financially committed to the project, Warner Bros. executives apparently refused to believe in Lee's box-office ability. In the title sequence, Lee and John Saxon, a supporting actor but never a marquee name, share equal

Studio chiefs mistakenly believed American audiences would not accept Bruce Lee as a solo star.

pre-title billing. The studio chiefs continued to maintain the attitude that an American audience would still not accept a Chinese actor as a solo star. (William Smith was considered for the co-starring role based on his work with Clouse on the violent 1970 detective thriller *Darker Than Amber*, an adaptation of John D. MacDonald's novel and starring Rod Taylor as Florida shamus Travis McGee. But at six-foot-six, the bodybuilder-turned-actor was considered too tall to work next to the five-foot-six Lee, who liked Clouse's action footage in *Darker Than Amber* and felt he could handle the demands of *Enter the Dragon*.)

For the story, writer Michael Allin, who claimed to have used Japanese and Chinese comic books as major references, originally planned to have the three leads all be soldiers of fortune and share equal roles. In the first drafts, Lee's

Lee appears a conservative businessman as he listens to agent Braithwaite.

character was to be a "flaky poet" who spoke in parables.[217] Lee, however, objected to a majority of the script, battled with Allin, and eventually told the producers that unless the screenwriter left Hong Kong, Lee would walk off the picture.[218] Lee, who was extremely sensitive about his height, also eliminated all references to his character being "tough considering his size."

Lee's specific input to the script will be pinpointed in the following analysis of the major scenes.

According to Braithwaite, Han (61-year-old Shih Kien, who did not speak English and mouthed his lines) was a Shaolin monk (showing him to be an evil, older father figure, like the powerful Boss-villain in *Fists of Fury*, corrupted by the Westernized vices of money and lust) who now uses drugs to weaken young women (much as the villain in *Fists* created prostitutes for his brothel). He then sells the women and narcotics across the globe. This Hollywood-financed project employs an evil Chinese character who would fit right into the type of American pictures produced through the 1930s. A common theme in films during earlier decades was the widespread abuse of women by Asians, that is, white slavery and the maintenance of prostitution as a major industry of the Asian subculture in the U.S. In the 1927 film, *Old San Francisco*, the principal business of the Chinese appears to be prostitution. And from their facial expressions, the Chinese seem to relish their "business," especially when they have a white woman to buy or sell.[219]

Lee, dressed in a European suit and tie, appears a conservative businessman as he listens to Braithwaite, who has appealed to the young fighter to enter Han's Tournament, a world-famous hand-to-hand competition. The Chinese man appears comfortable in the attire, mirroring his ability to fit into the white world. But his spirit will not explode until he discards such conservative Westernized clothing, dons Chinese garb, and battles opponents.

In contrast, Braithwaite wears a loose tie, slouches in his chair, smokes a cigarette, and has glasses resting half-way down his nose. (Lee, who was nearsighted and wore contact lenses, never appeared on screen with regular eyeglasses, a sign of imperfection.)[220]

The sequence also shows film of Han's bodyguard, Oharra (Bob Wall), being hit by boards and enduring physical pain. When Braithwaite offers Lee a drink, the character firmly replies, "No thanks," showing his disdain for the need for alcohol (a weakness). Lee suggests invading the island with guns, but is informed that Han, due to a previous accident (in which he apparently lost his right hand), refuses to permit armaments on his property. (Bruce Lee, who received a 25-automatic as a birthday gift while a waiter at Ruby Chow's, was considered an excellent shot at 75 yards with a handgun.[221] In real life, he had carried a weapon in Seattle when helping some young Chinese girls who were being taken advantage of by their landlord. Extremely angered by the incident, Lee, believing the property owner was harassing the women because they were foreigners, took along a pistol to help settle the situation.)[222]

Because Han's island rests partially within British territorial waters, the official explains that the army can invade if Lee uncovers evidence of illegalities. Braithwaite also informs him that a female operative, Mei Ling (Betty Chung), was assigned to the island and may have information.

En route to Han's island, Lee flashes back to a story about his 20-year-old sister Su-Lin (Angela Mao), told to him by an old man (Ho Lee Yan) who describes Han's henchmen as "bullying and arrogant" and responsible for the young woman's suicide. Using a hidden knife, the old man sliced and scarred Oharra's face to defend Su-Lin, but the feeble companion was viciously slapped aside.

HERE COMES THE UNBREAKABLE CHINA DOLL
WHO GIVES YOU THE LICKING OF YOUR LIFE!

ANGELA MAO
"LADY KUNG FU"

Angela Mao, Lee's sister in *Enter the Dragon*, was a top Chinese star.

In the flashback, Mao, who has played fighting roles since the age of five (first in the Chinese opera and then in films)[223] and received $100 for two days' work, portrays Su-Lin, a hapkido black belt expert who runs away when Oharra

130

and a group of Asian toughs attack her. Mao, who at the time of *Enter the Dragon* was a top Chinese star and yet earning only $150 per week from Golden Harvest,[224] was so chaste that she refused to allow director Clouse to let her blouse sleeve be torn off during the battle.[225] When she uses a piece of jagged glass to commit suicide (a practice Hollywood had, in the early part of the century, ascribed to Asians as an almost common trait)[226] to avoid the inevitable rape, Mao remains fully dressed.

Lee insisted that the flashback sequence be added to give him a revenge motivation—a staple of Chinese films.[227] He knew his fans would comprehend his need to draw blood to avenge the brutal attack on his sister, but might be far less clear on his motives for aiding a foreign government in an assault on a Chinese person, even one as unrelentingly evil as Han, who was conceived by Allin as "a combination of Richard Nixon and director John Milius."[228] Unlike Emperor Ming of the *Flash Gordon* serials in the 1930s and 1940s, Fu Manchu, and Dr. No, Han was not interested in world domination, but his evil Oriental persona merely reinforces the dastardly Asian stereotype so long propagated in Hollywood.

The Mao battle, which like all the other fights was staged by Lee, is the first non-Lee fight of the film, and her punches and kicks, which lack any real authority, merely stun her opponents. Only her brother—the male symbol—will be able to use his power to topple Han, the evil influence, who, no doubt, inspired his unsavory thugs to participate in attacks on innocent women (much as the father-villain in *Fists of Fury* inspired his son to get him young "chicks"). Lee insisted that Mao, Bob Wall, and Jim Kelly—all fighters with actual martial arts experience—be hired for *Enter the Dragon* to provide a sense of realism.[229]

Before leaving for the island, Lee, in a show of traditional respect, visits the graves of his mother and sister and says:

"You will not agree with what I am going
to do. It is contrary to all that you have taught
me, and all that Su-Lin believed. I must leave.
Please try to find a way to forgive me."

The short speech hints that Lee's mother—like his character's mother in *Fists of Fury*—believed in peace and submission, which do not work in the modern world. (Interestingly, his character's parents, often referred to, are never seen in his films, and in *Enter the Dragon*, even his sister, possibly his sole living relative, is taken away, making him a warrior truly alone and allowing him to use a woman as an emotional springboard.)

The opening sequences also provide brief glimpses into the backgrounds of the two main supporting characters. Roper (John Saxon) enters the

Jim Kelly suffered food poisoning after arriving in Hong Kong but was soon back to work.

tournament to escape three thugs (Pat Johnson, Darnell Garcia, and Mike Bissell) sent to a San Francisco golf course by a mobster to collect some debts, and Williams (six-foot-two Jim Kelly, the 1971 International Middleweight Karate Champion)[230] battles two racist policemen (William Keller and Mickey Caruso) in Watts while leaving for Han's island.

Both men served in Vietnam together and have not seen each other in the six years since concluding their military service. But their relationship never evolves beyond a surface level, and their importance—except to provide a Caucasian and African-American name to the project to possibly increase its appeal—remains secondary to Lee's. Although the Lee and Williams characters seem closest in spirit (the former helps the weak on the ship; the latter decries the ghetto conditions in the harbor), they never really speak to each other.[231]

The characters' body language on the Sampans, used to transport them to the Hong Kong harbor, mirrors their personality traits. Roper, surrounded by suitcases (suggesting his vanity), glances around nervously in the small watercraft, reflecting his precarious situation with the mobsters. Williams wears a flashy red leisure suit to mirror his fiery temper, but he also exhibits a childlike side (which, as we later see, will lead to his downfall because he fails to recognize the seriousness of the situation on Han's island) by waving to some playing youngsters.

132

Lee sits calmly with his legs folded and eyes fixed straight ahead. Unlike the other two (who are fighting in the tournament for fame and fortune), he possesses a sense of purpose, a mission that can not be measured in terms of dollars or adulation.

On board the ship bound for Han's island, Parsons (Peter Archer), a fighter from New Zealand, nervously paces, and Williams offers an opinion on what he viewed during the harbor jaunt. Williams says:

> "They (the residents) don't live so big over
> there. Ghettos are the same all over the
> world—they stink!"

(Kelly suffered from food poisoning after arriving in Hong Kong and was put in the hospital. The day of his discharge, he had to shoot the boat scene and spent the day bouncing on a Chinese junk.[232] Lee, who couldn't swim, might have been equally uncomfortable during the water sequence.)[233]

During a praying mantis fight (shot from a high angle, making the characters much like Han, who will look down on the tournament competitors), Roper gambles "50 bucks on the big one," an offer accepted by Lee, who even gives him five-to-one odds, and then wins, just like Lee—the smaller competitor will win all of the upcoming battles. (Seven praying mantises had to be flown in from Hawaii for the 20 second scene.)[234] The small praying mantis wins the battle by biting the leg of the larger one, as Roper will later do to Bolo.

En route to the island, the pacing Parsons kicks a fruit basket out of the hands of a meek Chinese attendant and then kicks the young man down on the deck. The Chinese youngster cowers and hurries away.

At this point all of the major Caucasian characters—Braithwaite, Roper, Oharra, and Parsons—have established character flaws. Braithwaite enjoys liquor; Roper gambles; Oharra abuses women; and Parsons bullies.

When Parsons attempts to rile Lee, the Shaolin-trained fighter flashes a bored glance, telling him: "Don't waste yourself." Parsons then questions his style. Lee:

> "My style? You can call it the art of
> fighting without fighting."

He then tells the New Zealander that the style can be demonstrated on a nearby island, which offers more space, and tricks him into climbing down to a rowboat. Lee lets it drift out to sea, allows the cabin boys, whom Parsons bullied, to hold the rope, and threatens to drop the line if the fighter attempts to climb back. (During the filming, Archer was nearly swept overboard because of the waves that battered the small craft.)[235]

The brief Parsons-Lee confrontation, which no doubt delighted Lee's Chinese fans who could empathize with the low-paid ship's crewmen suffering under the New Zealander's cruelty, was devised and added by Lee. Of the segment, screenwriter Allin said:

> "I think that's the most human scene in the picture. That was all Bruce's idea. I wrote it, but it was Bruce's inspiration, and the words were his. That's the way I like to remember him. The best part of Bruce inspired that scene. The rest of the movie is a comic book, but that scene was from Bruce's life."[236]

The scene—in which the lifeboat with the bully in it is towed for the trip's duration—is adapted from a story in Zen literature where two men travel to an island to fight, and the one leaves the other while he rows away in the boat.[237] Lee's desire to add this scene indicates his concern with Zen philosophy. The story of the "art of fighting without fighting" first appears in legends of Tsukahara Bokuden, a famous swordsman of the 16th century. With his unsurpassed skill in swordsmanship, Bokuden is said to have been the victor in 39 duels. But Bokuden carried his art to a more spiritual realm, developing a school he termed mutekatsu ryu (swordsmanship without hands).

According to legend, a bragging swordsman accosted Bokuden while they were crossing Lake Biwa in a boat and demanded a demonstration of mutekatsu ryu. Dissatisfied with Bokuden's refusal, he insisted on a duel. Bokuden convinced the swordsman to fight on a nearby island rather than endanger the other passengers. After the small vessel was beached and the swordsman leapt ashore, Bokuden calmly picked up an oar and shoved the boat back into the lake. "This is how the mutekatsu ryu defeats the enemy," he said.

The story suggests the essence of Zen philosophy. "Striking is not to strike nor is killing to kill," said Takuan, the Zen master.[238] In his philosophical defeat over Parsons, Lee employed what might be termed gung fu without hands. It also suggests a growth of a Lee character into someone more mature and not so anxious to fight.

The arrival once again sets up the theme of Bruce Lee as an outsider entering an alien environment. But this time he has no cousins, fellow students, or even fellow employees near. Like a Western hero, he basically operates alone. Clouse observed the parallels between Lee and a traditional Western hero, noting:

> "Philosophically, the kung fu films share a lot with the American Western. They're

Like a Western hero, Lee basically operates alone.

about one man who has the ability to control his environment. In the complex society we live in, there's a feeling of helplessness against the outside world. Most people feel they can't move against the forces around them. And here, you have the single man being able to move and control his environment. As in the Western, one man goes and rights a wrong."[239]

In each of his films, Lee plays the classic mythical hero, the clean-living individual who defeats pure evil. His characters would not have been out of place in a B-Western of the Monogram era.[240]

135

At the island, Roper immediately is intrigued at the sight of Tania (Ahna Capri), saying: "A woman like that could teach you a lot about yourself." The line comments on the character's inherent weakness (he does not truly know himself) and his willingness to submit to her based on simply viewing her physical charms.

In an overview shot of the set, constructed by Chinese craftsmen in the Hong Kong harbor[241] and on the site of a Hong Kong lawyer's tennis courts, Han's warriors, all dressed in identical white gis, can be seen in regimented rows, performing rigid, standard punching exercises. At a party in Han's palace, Lee senses that Roper is "apprehensive" about the tournament and the man running it, something Roper may not even realize himself. Roper, after hearing Lee's observation and sensing its accuracy, tells Williams:

> "I have a funny feeling we're being
> fattened up for the kill."

When Han enters, he is surrounded by six white-clad young women (three on each side) and all the servants instantly freeze in position, giving the character almost god-like authority. Lee recognizes one of the personal guards as the government agent Mei Ling, and catches a Shuriken dart, which she blows in the air. (The six young women around Han establish a set pattern in all of Lee's films: older women, except as brief observers of the action, are non-existent in physical form. We never see his mother, and the women involved in the plots are always young, whether as a maternal figure in *Fists of Fury*, a girlfriend-future mother figure in *The Chinese Connection*, a young businesswoman-potential girlfriend in *Return of the Dragon*, and, finally, purely a business contact—with no hint of romance—in *Enter the Dragon*.)

These women fall into the four basic cinematic stereotypes of Asian women: the submissive wife-daughter-employee, the exotic dragon lady, the Suzy Wong-type who seeks an American savior, and the neuter built for hard work.[242]

In the history of cinema, the less violent a male has been required to be in a film, the greater has been his interest in heterosexual love.[243] Lee's cinematic world contained no room for romance. Lee comes across like Clint Eastwood's "Man With No Name" character, a pathologically isolated figure who is too masculine even to hook up with a male buddy in his films. But neither does he often have the time or inclination to sleep with a woman.[244]

In her study of male screen images, *Big Bad Wolves: Masculinity in the American Film*, Joan Mellen writes:

> "American films have not only sought to
> render men powerless by projecting male im-
> ages of fearsome strength and competence.

Bruce Lee fits squarely into the traditional hero slot.

They have also proposed consistently over the years that the real man is not a rebel but a conformist who supports God and country, right or wrong. The heroes who exhibit the most power stand for the status quo (as Lee does in *Enter the Dragon*), even as they suggest that physical action unencumbered by effeminate introspection is what characterizes the real man; thus, in the most profound sense, the bold exterior of these men on screen conceals the fact that films actually foster a sense of passivity by suggesting that such men are never rebels but can always be trusted to acquiesce in the established order."[245]

With *Enter the Dragon*, Lee fits squarely into the traditional hero slot. As an actor, however, he breaks one mold: in American films, masculinity has rarely been represented by non-Caucasian heroes, particularly by a Chinese performer.

Except for Lee's sister, who's a victim, and his fellow agent, who remains peripheral to the action, women in *Enter* serve merely as sex objects. After the party, Tania takes an assortment of ladies (Clouse used actual prostitutes for the scene)[246] to the men's quarters. Interestingly, in the Chinese class system, actors, like prostitutes, were regarded as not only low in caste but as immoral beings. The Chinese expression, "He runs with actors and actresses," connotes total profligacy.[247]

Williams selects four ladies, which reinforces the black-stud image, described in the essay, "Black Dreams: The Fantasy and Ritual of Black Films," as "walking down the street dressed to kill (Williams previously wore a flashy red outfit), sliding into a bar (in this case Han's party) to pick up some white stuff, all alludes upward to the Black Stud myth." Williams, who claims he is "tired," even apologizes to the prostitutes he turns away. As the film industry did for poor whites during the Depression, black films—and in many ways Chinese films—offer escape from gloom, roaches, and social confusion of center-city colonies.[248] Williams comments on the Hong Kong ghettos and is originally seen exiting Watts, an American inner-city area that—as a professional athlete with exploitable talents—he can vacate.

The scene between Williams, who has posters of Jimi Hendrix and a black power fist on his wall, and the prostitutes—especially considering its placement within a predominately Chinese production—marks a form of cinematic sexual liberation. In the 1920s, only blacks were feared as passionately as Asians on the sexual issue, which traditionally arouses the most violent and persistent hostility of all the various forms of prejudice.[249]

In Lee's room, Tania offers to bring more girls if he "does not see anything" that appeals to him. The woman's use of the word "anything" rather than "anyone" reinforces the picture's use of women-as-objects.

Lee requests that Mei Ling (Betty Chung, a recording artist and nightclub singer in Hong Kong) be sent to his room, and learns that women "disappear" (making them appear as almost disposable objects) from the island. Roper, a narcissist seen staring at himself in a mirror before the prostitutes enter, asks that Tania (a fellow Caucasian) return to entertain him.

In real life, Lee reportedly maintained some distrust of Asian women. After becoming a star, Lee, during a dinner at the house of Stirling Silliphant, who was dating a Vietnamese woman, reportedly told his writer friend that he should be wary of Asian women. Silliphant said:

> "It kind of made me mad to find Bruce was such a (male) chauvinist... The last time I was in Hong Kong, I met Bruce for lunch, and he had the two most beautiful Oriental girls I had ever seen with him. He said we were all set for the afternoon, but I had to leave early and go to do a television interview. Bruce ended up with both chicks, and the next day, he said to me, 'Boy, what you missed.' Which goes to show the kind of curious morality of

In the film, Lee's morning exercises show his amazing control and physical power.

the man. What made Bruce most angry with
me was that I had gone to (Japanese) karate."[250]

According to Lee's sister-in-law, Lin Yen-ni, Linda Lee in certain ways surpassed the traditional loyalties the average Chinese woman felt toward her spouse. Yen-ni said:

> "Linda loves Bruce very much and, at the
> same time, adores him like a god. We can
> hardly find another woman like Linda among
> foreign girls. She is virtuous and refined and
> actually surpasses Chinese women."[251]

Lee's friend, William Cheung, observed that Lee, who "always suspected that he had some sexual deficiency, because he was born with only one descended testicle," remained very chaste with his girlfriend, Cho Miu Yee, in 1957 and 1958, because he feared being a disappointment in bed.[252] He remains equally chaste in *Enter the Dragon*, though his physical action scenes vibrate with a force suggesting a sexual explosion.

Despite his lack of romantic screen partners, Linda Lee has quite accurately observed that her spouse had a sexual appeal that particularly attracted young Americans. She said:

> "His piercing dark eyes and handsome
> features, totally lacking that impassivity or
> inscrutability popularly associated with Chi-
> nese by some Americans, was something as
> fresh and novel in their (his American fans)
> lives as kung fu itself."

The next morning, Clouse uses an overhead shot of a shirtless Bruce Lee working out as Oharra enters and informs him of the start of the day's festivities. The real force of Lee's dynamic screen presence is felt for the first time in the film as he contains and then focuses his anger upon the sight of Oharra. At the outdoor site, Lee arrives in traditional Chinese garb, refusing to wear the white or yellow uniform Han demands for the morning ritual and tournament. Lee, with a menacing glare, brushes off the objection to his dark attire, which quite dramatically sets him apart from the others.

The matches are workmanlike, with Williams conquering Parsons and Roper defeating a previously unintroduced Chinese opponent (Tony Liu). Prior to the match, Williams and Roper devised a gambling scam in order to win a few yen from an unworldly, older Chinese observer, but the scene lacks any spark of exciting action. It merely serves to show them as men of limited vision who don't realize they are actually gambling with their lives.

That night, Tania, an international madam now exclusively employed by Han, tells Roper "a man like you belongs here," something that the American also senses. Soon after, Williams discards the advice of one of his female companions and leaves his room to exercise in the moonlight.

Lee, dressed in black, ninja-like garb, steals into the night and discovers the underground headquarters of Han's narcotics-prostitution operation.

The following morning, Bolo viciously kills the guards who allowed Lee to succeed in his clandestine operation, a lesson that appears to genuinely upset Williams and gives Roper second thoughts about Han's operation. Unlike those two outsiders, Lee has already been alerted to Han's deeds by the British government.

Lee's first opponent, Oharra, attempts to psych-out his much-smaller rival by using his fist to smash a piece of lumber. In one of his most famous lines, Lee shrugs off the needless display, saying: "Boards don't hit back." To capture Lee's quick moves, cinematographer Gilbert Hubbs cranked up an Arriflex eight volts to the 76 mark, turned down the rheostat, then brought the torque up slowly,[253] a standard procedure for slow motion start-up to prevent ripping of

Lee's first opponent in *Enter the Dragon* is the evil Oharra (Bob Wall).

the film perforations and to capture the image so that when projected it will appear in slow motion. (Interestingly, *Enter the Dragon* was banned in Singapore, because of this fight scene and others, which officials claimed contained "excessive violence" and promoted the "long-hair culture.")[254]

During a rehearsal for the Lee-Oharra fight, Bob Wall (a former U.S. professional karate champion) accidentally cut Bruce Lee while lunging at the star with two broken water bottles. Unlike American companies, which purchase harmless sugar glass, the Chinese used real glass, resulting in a serious wound to Lee and, reportedly, major problems occurring between the two fighters. Clouse said:

> "Bruce got paranoid (after the accident) and told his buddies, 'At the end of our big fight scene, I am going to kill Bob Wall.' I got a call from Raymond Chow in the middle of the night, and he said, 'Bruce is going to kill Bob Wall, you have to talk him out of it.' So I

Bruce Lee delivers another bone-breaking blow to Oharra (Bob Wall) in *Enter the Dragon*.

called him up, and he said yes, he was going to pile drive himself into Wall's chest and kill him. Finally, I told him he couldn't do that, that we still needed Bob for some scenes here and there after the big fight. He grumbled, but it gave him an out; he could tell his pals, 'I wanted to kill him, but for the sake of the picture...'"[255]

Wall also heard the death-threat rumors and, together with Weintraub, arrived at a solution. Wall visited Lee's residence, confronted him with the rumors (which the star blamed on the "Chinese" in the production company), and suggested that—in front of the entire *Enter the Dragon* company—Lee regain his pride by beating the American fighter. During the session, Wall, after opening his gi to show that he was not wearing any protective equipment, allowed Lee to kick him eight times. (The first blow sent Wall flying into an extra, breaking the onlooker's arm.) After the public incident, Lee reportedly took Wall to Hugo's, Hong Kong's finest French restaurant, and told the fighter:

One of the rare times Bruce Lee used a double was during this flip.

"Bob, that was the greatest thing anybody ever did for me."[256]

The Lee-Oharra battle ends with the Chinese fighter jumping into the air and viciously landing on his villainous opponent, literally crushing the life out of him in a primitive way. Lee's expression as he crushes Oharra has been aptly described as "more animal than human."[257] The fact that Oharra does not know Lee is Su-Lin's brother takes away some of the scene's emotional power.

In explaining his personal combat philosophy, Lee said:

> "In fighting one's enemy, one should fight with all the strength and all attention. His action in desperation will press his enemy under heavy psychological burden. Even though he loses finally, he will be regarded as an honored loser.
>
> "In strength comparison, the stronger one will certainly beat the weaker one. However, if the weaker one fights with all his efforts and finally loses, his courage can win admiration from the stronger. Thus, one of the most important factors in fighting is morale."[258]

That philosophy plays little part in *Enter the Dragon*. Defeated fighters are discarded, almost as though they have no place dwelling with the victors. Parsons, the New Zealand fighter-bully, disappears after losing to Williams. Bolo kills the guards who unsuccessfully used their efforts to stop the intruder. Oharra dies at Lee's feet, and soon, Williams pays the ultimate price for losing to Han, a fighter whom he appears to underestimate. In Lee's Chinese pictures, his friends and co-workers are often bested in battle but return to take up the fight again. That does not occur in this American production.

After the rousing Lee-Oharra confrontation, *Enter the Dragon* falls into a predictable pattern. The death of the evil Oharra—the Irish-German man responsible for Lee's sister's suicide—dissipates much of the picture's expectation, much as if Sean Connery's James Bond had dispatched Harold Sakata's muscular Oddjob in *Goldfinger* in the middle of the picture during the golf course sequence rather than at the end, in the famous Fort Knox battle.

The true motivations of Tania, who sends Williams to Han's study (where the African-American fighter is rather easily killed by the steel-fisted Chinese crime boss), remain clouded. The Tania character fits into the "malevolent woman; woman as destroyer" category as described by Molly Haskell in *From Reverence to Rape*. Such a woman, Haskell contends:

> "...can lead a man to his doom not just aggressively and violently, but passively and imperceptibly. One of the dominant images of the '60s is the somnambulist, a true sleep-walker whose very passivity allows her to become an agent of evil. She is an extension of the woman as work of art and object of pure contemplation."[259]

Capri's Tania, the story's only important female character, mysteriously dies off-camera during the final battle between Han's warriors and the prisoners from their jail cells. (Capri played a similar character—a woman involved in prostitution and crime—in her previous film, *Darker Than Amber*, also directed by Robert Clouse. She met the same fate in that contemporary thriller.) The "evil" woman has been punished for her sins, something that also occurred when the Boss' son killed the prostitute who helped Lee's character in *Fists of Fury*. (The bars for the prison cells were sanded by hand from square blocks of wood and painted black. The Chinese craftsmen used no power tools in constructing the sets.)[260]

Roper appears somewhat interested in joining Han's operation. At one point during his tour of the Museum of Torment, Roper tells Han: "A man's strength can be measured by his appetites; indeed, a man's strength flows from

When Lee confronts Han's troops *Enter the Dragon* sparkles.

his appetites." (In the original script, that line was delivered by Han, but John Saxon, who was unhappy with his character's limited dialogue, successfully requested it.)[261]

Han, Roper quickly discovers, even corrupts his daughters, allowing them to be employed as his personal guards. The female offspring, except for a few judo flips, never display their hand-to-hand prowess. The other women appear to either work as obedient servants, willing prostitutes, or drugged captives (contained in cells painted bright red). Roper, however, cannot accept the brutal murder of his friend Williams, whose body is seen bloodied and chained in what resembles a despicable murder-lynching from the deep South when racism raged.

When Lee confronts Han's troops within the underground area, *Enter the Dragon* sparkles again. Employing a variety of weapons—including Filipino double sticks (used in Kali, a secret fighting form passed down from father to son in the Philippines after the Spaniards colonized the country and declared that the three-feet-long clubs were illegal weapons),[262] staffs, and nunchakus— and a powerful physical presence, Lee, who soon removes his ripped shirt,

Lee dominates each frame as he cuts down his enemies.

dominates each frame as he cuts down his enemies. He is finally trapped in an isolated chamber by Han, who looks down from above for the last time at the proudly seated Lee (whose perspiration glistens), and verbally salutes the man's "extraordinary" abilities.

Han, who uses his martial arts tournament as a front to recruit "new talent," wants Roper to represent him in the U.S., a proposal eventually declined by the American who, at a climactic moment, decides to fight with, rather than against, Lee. In the Roper-Bolo fight, the American bites the burly Chinese enforcer in order to break a hold. That street-type move by Roper shows him to be at the same point in the martial arts mastery as Lee's character in *The Chinese Connection*, where he employed the same biting tactic. In *Enter the Dragon*, Lee's screen persona has matured far beyond that point.[263]

The evil Han (Shih Kien) prepares to retreat to his mirror room.

The Lee-Han confrontation, in which the villain screws on a claw and then a three-bladed knife hand, lacks the excitement of any of his previous final battles—particularly the Norris-Lee encounter in *Return of the Dragon*—because Han never approaches being a fitting physical equal for Lee. (Quite annoyingly, Han's personal bodyguards—his supposedly lethal daughters—are never viewed in battle. Right to the end, women in *Enter the Dragon* remain in their places of either servants or sex objects.)

The fight assumes a tone of importance when Lee tastes his blood (the result of an abdomen flesh wound from Han's knife-hand) and tells him: "You have offended my family and you have offended a Shaolin temple." But the mood, which cannot be sustained because of the unequal match-up, quickly dissolves.

Shih Kien, an important name in the martial arts films of the 1950s and '60s, was 61 when he played Han and reportedly received the role because Lee was a fan of the veteran actor's early work. Kien, a disciple of Northern and Southern styles of kung fu, appears out of his medium using karate.[264] In order to compensate for such shortcomings, Han tricks Lee into a mirrored maze-room and then attempts to use the unusual surroundings to defeat the hero. Lee kills Han with a kick that sends him through the air and impales him on a spear which had pierced the mirrored wall.

Lee had one overriding desire for *Enter the Dragon*: that it gross more than director Sam Peckinpah's *The Getaway*, which starred his former martial arts student, Steve McQueen, and prove that Lee had finally become the world's biggest superstar.[265] His wish was realized, but he never lived to see that happen or to even see the final cut of *Enter the Dragon*.

But in death, Lee fulfilled the pledge he made to himself in the late 1960s. He wrote:

> "I, Bruce Lee, will be the highest paid
> Oriental superstar in the U.S."[266]

Following the completion of *Enter the Dragon*, Lee sent a telegram to Warner Bros. board chairperson Ted Ashley. In part, it read:

> "Quality, extremely hard work, and pro-
> fessionalism is what cinema is all about. My
> 20 years of experience, both in martial arts and
> acting, has apparently led to the successful
> harmony of appropriateness of showmanship
> and genuine efficient, artful expression. In
> short, this is it and ain't nobody knows it like
> I know it."[267]

In a 1975 essay by Margaret Ronan in *Senior Scholastic*, a magazine geared to high school students, Lee's popularity with young people was accurately and succinctly summed up as a three-part appeal:

> 1. He was the best. ("A hero's business is
> to be the best, right?")
> 2. He was "high on" identity. ("Ordinary
> guys could identify with you. You made them
> believe that if they trained hard, worked out
> regularly, nobody would dare kick sand in their
> faces either.")
> 3. You were on the good side. ("In your
> movies, you righted wrongs and struck fear

into the hearts of evildoers. You didn't drink
or smoke, and dope peddlers were your
targets.")[268]

Six Sequences to Watch Closely in *Enter the Dragon*

•Lee drops his serious side and lights up only one time during *Enter the Dragon*. Lee smiles and even slaps a hard-working boat crew member on the back (a very rare shot of him in a friendly display) in a celebratory fashion during the praying mantis fight. The brief scene shows Lee's comfort level with these workers, who gather around him, speak a common language, and celebrate his presence on the ship. He never exhibits that sort of closeness with John Saxon's Roper or any other character in this film.

•Make special note of the overhead shot of Lee doing morning exercises in his room. This is one of the few scenes in Lee's body of cinematic work that shows his amazing control and dynamic physical power in a non-contact sequence. The overhead shot provides viewers with a privileged view of Lee as his workout becomes a ballet-like movement in which he appears at the center of the universe and in total control of his finely sculpted body. It's an all-too-brief sequence worthy of Fred Astaire, Gene Kelly, or Mikhail Baryshnikov. It also reinforces Lee's lone-hero image, since he exercises alone while the others perform their morning exercises with the group on the exterior tournament grounds.

•It's fascinating to study Lee's movements during his clandestine walk through Han's chamber and across the grounds to the underground fortress. Lee, wearing a dark-blue outfit, totally blends with the environment in this scene, a forerunner for future—and far inferior—sequences featuring "invisible" warriors in ninja films. Lee's screen characters have always faced battles head on, making this scene unique in his body of work. He avoids battles as he effortlessly navigates the landscape and avoids the eyes and ears of the guards while going to investigate Han's underground world. He appears almost like a breeze passing though the night. His only surprise arrives when a snarling German shepherd barks at him. Only an animal—something Lee becomes later as he fights for his life—can sense him. This sequence also contains one of the few camera tricks used in Lee's career as he jumps from the ground into a tree. The visual trick was accomplished by having Lee sitting in a tree and jumping down and then running the film backwards, making it appear that he leaps from the ground on to a high branch in one fluid movement.

•The Lee-Oharra battle remains one of the star's best screen fights, but also interesting is the brief interplay between Lee and Oharra (Bob Wall) just before the bout commences. Lee bows to Oharra, but the Caucasian fighter refuses to return the courtesy, instead staring down on his opponent and in a display of strength tossing a piece of wood in the air and smashing it. Lee's response, "Boards don't hit back," captures his theory about avoiding showy displays and doing only what's necessary to win a fight. Director Robert Clouse gives Oharra an extreme close-up, similar to the type of shots Lee gave to Chuck

Norris during their climactic battle in *Return of the Dragon*. Only the most accomplished opponents in Lee's films receive such privileged screen treatment. Also, note how Lee mirrors his total disdain for Oharra. Unlike his upcoming fight in the underground cavern and his final battle with Han, Lee keeps his shirt on and never even works up a sweat during the Oharra battle. He also wears a crisp traditional white Chinese shirt to suggest the character's pride in his background and his love for his sister, who committed suicide rather than surrender her honor to Oharra. The garb also visually reinforces the idea of a Chinese hero totally dominating a character representing the evil of the "white" world.

•In the underground cavern sequence, during which he defeats 50 enemies, Lee peels off his ripped shirt before fighting his fourth opponent. The battle beginning with that opponent is filmed in slow motion, and to destroy the seventh opponent (who wears a black headband, making him resemble a character from a Japanese samurai film), Lee jumps in the air, landing on the fighter (as he did with Oharra), viciously crushing his neck, and suggesting to the audience the lethal level of combat to follow. Clouse discontinues the slow motion after this point and shoots the rest of the sequence at regular speed. Fittingly, the final seconds of the slow-motion unfold with Lee in the center of the frame flexing his upper body and contorting his face in a primitive fashion, allowing a clear view of the deadly creature he has become.

•In the famed mirror-room sequence, note the use of blood from Lee's wounds, the result of Han's slicing the hero with tiger and knife hands. Rather than dripping from the wounds, the blood almost glows and resembles war paint. Symbolically, Lee will be able to wash it off after defeating Han, thereby ending his personal war and allowing him to return to the peaceful, civilized world, at least until his next assignment. In contrast, Han's blood (like the blood of Oharra during his bout with Lee) is smeared across his face, suggesting a mask of death.

CHAPTER 8
THE DEATH OF THE DRAGON

"My dad only made four major films, *Fists of Fury*, *The Chinese Connection*, *Enter the Dragon* and *Return of the Dragon*. The craziness that surrounded my whole family after our dad passed away in Hong Kong—including the rumors that he was still alive—is on the same level as Elvis sightings to me. That's really what it is, a kind of mania. I don't understand it."—Brandon Lee in a personal interview with the author on August 16, 1992

Lee's disturbing death on July 20, 1973 at age 32 was met with shocked disbelief and, eventually, reluctant acceptance by his fans. He died in the apartment of Hong Kong actress Betty Ting Pei, who the press romantically linked with the star and who had been promised a part in *Game of Death*.[269]

It's impossible to overstate the impact of Lee's death on Chinese communities throughout the Far East. In Hong Kong the next morning, commuters were barraged with the same screaming headline: BRUCE LEE IS DEAD. Almost every newspaper in the colony published a special memorial issue, and the Chinese-language press doubled and tripled its circulation as readers scrambled for souvenir copies.[270]

Adding to the mystery were the conflicting stories of Lee's whereabouts at the time of his demise. Producer Raymond Chow, to save the Lee family any embarrassment, originally claimed that the star had collapsed after walking with his wife Linda in the gardens of their Kowloon Tong home. But four days later, *The Star* splashed across its front page the sensational news that Lee had been taken to the hospital from the home of Betty Ting Pei, not from his Cumberland Road home.[271] Lee was introduced to Pei in April, 1972 by Chow. At the time, she was living at the Hyatt Hotel in the Tsim Sha Tsui district.[272] She was reportedly going to work on *Way of the Dragon*, but dropped out due to illness.[273]

Bruce Lee's mother and family at the airport.

According to often-repeated official reports, Lee had complained of a headache, and Pei had given him Equagesic, an aspirin-tranquilizer combination, which her physician had prescribed for menstrual distress.[274] At the hospital, doctors said his hypersensitivity to the ingredients had made his brain "swollen like a sponge."[275]

Because an autopsy uncovered traces of marijuana in Lee's stomach, rumors immediately circulated that he had died of drug-related activities, such as cocaine use[276] and involvement with "killer weed."[277] Other press-generated rumors claimed:

•That he had been the victim of a crazed fan.
•That he had been killed by martial arts masters who objected to his commercialization of their art.
•That he had been murdered by a Shaolin cult that specialized in the "delayed death touch" because he taught non-Chinese gung fu.
•That he had been assassinated by a rival business faction.
•That he was in some Hong Kong Mafia deal and had tried to get out.
•That he was not really dead at all but staged the hoax to promote his upcoming film, *Game of Death*, and went into hiding.

Because of the persistent, endless rumors, Linda Lee issued an official statement declaring that she "held no one person or group of persons responsible"

Bruce Lee's casket arrives at the Seattle airport.

for her husband's death.[278] But more than two decades later, the speculation continues.

The late Albert Goldman, who wrote detailed accounts of the drug-related deaths of Elvis Presley and Lenny Bruce in best-selling biographies (*Elvis* and *Ladies and Gentlemen Lenny Bruce!!*), claimed that Lee ate—but never smoked—hashish to help him relax and died of hashish poisoning. According to Goldman, Steve McQueen, who also sought to escape the pressures of superstardom, used the drug to relax and suggested his friend and former gung fu teacher do likewise.[279]

Prior to his Hong Kong success, Lee had always been open with the press, allowing constant interviews and photographs of him performing gung fu and posing with his family. But once he became a star, the requests for interviews and photo sessions multiplied at an incredible rate, and Lee, who after his international success suffered from sporadic paranoia and a fear of exploitation,[280] fiercely guarded his privacy.

More than 300,000 fans attended his funeral, which was the largest in Hong Kong's history.[281] Above his casket, a banner read: "A Star Sinks in the Sea of Art." He was buried in Lake View Cemetery in Lake Washington, outside of Seattle. At his U.S. funeral, Linda Lee requested that her husband's favorite song, "And When I Die" by Blood, Sweat & Tears, be played.[282]

En route to America, his $200,000 casket was damaged, an incident which his Chinese fans interpreted as meaning that Lee's spirit was not resting.[283] Certainly his celluloid image was not at rest. *Enter the Dragon*, released a month after his death, would soon turn him into one of the most popular action stars in the history of international cinema.

155

CHAPTER 9
A FINAL *GAME*

Game of Death cannot be seriously considered a Bruce Lee film, but because it marks his last screen appearance, the 102-minute, $3 million dollar production deserves brief analysis.

In Lee's original story for *Game of Death*, a national treasure is stolen and spirited away to Korea, where it is hidden on the top floor of a pagoda-style temple. This pagoda is a training school for martial artists of differing styles, and each floor contains students of various defense forms.

The first floor is ruled by a karateka guard; the second by a hapkido expert; the third by a kung-fu disciple; the fourth by the escrima (the Philippines systematic fighting art, which centers around three distinct phases: stick, blade, and empty-hand combat);[284] and the fifth and final floor by a Jeet Kune Do-type fighter, Hakim, The Master of the Unknown, played by Kareem Abdul-Jabbar. (Jabbar, who trained at Lee's house in Culver City and could kick the top of Lee's basketball rim,[285] had said he would never be "good enough" in the martial arts to topple the master.)[286]

Bruce Lee's character, accompanied by four other martial artists, travels to the island on which the pagoda stands, fights his way through the various floors, and wins back the treasure. To ensure that no guns are used and that the action relies entirely on martial expertise, metal detectors scan the island.

In addition to Jabbar, Lee's cast list included Chuck Norris and Yang Sze (Shotokan champion of South East Asia).[287]

Lee had envisioned a symbolic opening scene for *Game of Death* which mirrored his personal philosophy. As he explained it:

> "What I want to show is the necessity to adapt one's self to changing circumstances. The inability to adapt brings destruction. I already have the first scene in my mind. As the film opens, the audience sees a wide expanse of snow. Then the camera closes in on a clump of trees while the sounds of a strong gale fill the screen.
>
> "There is a huge tree in the center of the screen, and it is all covered with thick snow.

Raymond Chow's Golden Harvest Group

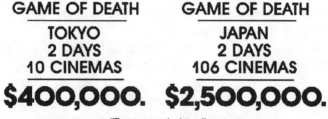
Suddenly, there is a loud snap, and a huge branch of the tree falls to the ground. It cannot yield to the force of the snow, so it breaks. Then, the camera moves to a willow tree, which is bending with the wind. Because it adapts itself to the environment, the willow survives.

Game of Death **cannot seriously be considered a Bruce Lee film.**

"It is this sort of symbolism which I think Chinese action films should seek to have. In this way, I hope to broaden the scope of action films."[288]

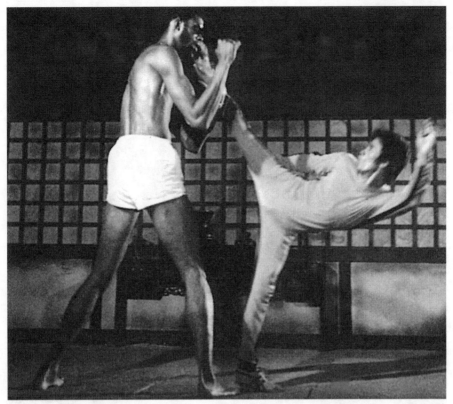

Kareem Abdul-Jabbar and Bruce Lee in a publicity shot.

Very little of Lee's original premise remains in the finished film, which was filmed in 1978 and released the next year. The story, written by Jan Spears and directed by Robert Clouse of *Enter the Dragon* fame, casts two Lee look-alikes as Billy Lo, a kung fu superstar who, along with his pop-singer girlfriend (played by Caucasian actress Colleen Camp), is being pressured by a syndicate that exploits entertainers by offering "management contracts." (The plot rather pointedly comments on the iron-fisted method employed by real Hong Kong studios in controlling their contract players.)

Dean Jagger plays Dr. Land, the syndicate head, and Hugh O'Brian plays Steiner, Dr. Land's commander of enforcement agents. Lee originally hired O'Brian for the Steiner role, and the American actor was preparing to leave for filming when he heard about the star's untimely death.[289] Also featured are Bob Wall, Mel Novak, and Dan Inosanto.

Wall was outspoken about his disappointed reaction to the final product, which he said, resulted:

> "...mainly because the director was
> shooting some scenes in one or two takes.

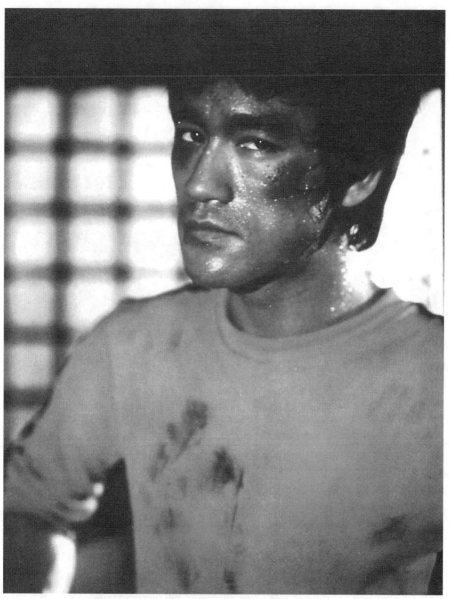

Lee stares at Abdul-Jabbar during their climactic pagoda battle.

When Bruce was alive, God rest his soul, you shot a scene 80 or 90 times until you got it right. You stayed there on that set until everything was perfect. That's part of the reason why his films were successful. You don't see a lot of bad scenes in a Bruce Lee movie."[290]

Very little of Lee's original premise remains in the finished film.

Using cut-ins of Lee's face from previous pictures and a particularly disturbing shot of Lee's body in his coffin (Steiner later digs up the coffin, pushes his cane-knife through the face, and discovers the head consists of plaster), *Game of Death* proves lifeless until the star's appearance in the final 15 minutes. Despite the roughness of some of Lee's final fight scenes (including some sloppy matching shots due to the lack of cover footage), electricity crackles off the screen as the then-deceased martial artist snaps into action.

Here are some random facts about *Game of Death*:

•Chuck Norris, who is given "featured" billing even though he only appears in *Way (Return) of the Dragon* flashbacks during the crisp credit sequence, refused to appear in *Game of Death*, because the producers insisted that he lose his fight.[291] At the time, Norris was building his own screen career, via movies such as *Good Guys Wear Black*, and sought to establish a heroic image.

•After finishing *Game of Death*, Lee planned to concentrate on pictures that stressed the philosophy of the martial arts rather than the action.[292]

•Golden Harvest hired an eight-member research group to work on the *Game of Death* script and also dispatched agents to Europe and the United States in search of a writer who understood Lee's philosophy and style. Three

162

Bruce Lee prepares for battle.

writers were ultimately sent to the research group, and one, who eventually spent six months on the project, was hired to script it.[293]

•Two actors were selected to play Lee's Billy Lo character. Tae Jeung Kim, a Korean with 11 years experience in the Korean and Chinese style martial arts, performed the action scenes, and Chinese actor Tong Lung delivered the dialogue.

•Because Abdul-Jabbar was heavily insured against injury by his NBA team, the basketball star had to perform his action sequences, which took a week to

BRUCE IS BACK

complete, in secret. To restrict reporters from the set, Lee posted a notice that he was "testing" actresses to play the film's heroine, and claimed that he did not want their pictures published to save those who were rejected embarrassment. Jabbar attended UCLA from 1965 to 1969, played with the Milwaukee Bucks from 1969 to 1975, and with the Los Angeles Lakers from 1975 to 1989.

•Gig Young, who plays a reporter who befriends Billy Lo, met Kim Schmidt, a script supervisor, on the *Game of Death* set. She became his young bride, and a few months later he killed her before committing suicide.[294]

•More extras were employed in *Game of Death* than in any other Hong Kong motion picture, and the filming marked the first time that Panavision's Panaglide (floating) camera was used in a Hong Kong-based film.[295]

On April 15, 1975, approximately 600 hopefuls showed up at Warner Bros.' Burbank studios to audition for the title role in *Bruce Lee, His Life and Legend*.[296] Producer Jon Peters, who started his career as Barbra Streisand's hairdresser, attempted to launch the project but eventually dropped it for one simple reason: No candidate could approximate the astounding cinematic prowess Lee projected.

In 1993, Universal Pictures, with the participation of Linda Lee, launched *Dragon: The Bruce Lee Story*, director Rob Cohen's print-the-legend/twist-the-facts biography of the late, great martial artist, played by Jason Scott Lee (no relation to Bruce Lee). *Dragon* did capture much of Lee's spirit and also introduced a new era of filmgoers to the subject's work. For that reason, it deserves to be celebrated by every Lee fan.

Perhaps *Dragon: The Bruce Lee Story* faced an impossible task. Lee's era is already lost to us living in the age of computers, fax machines, and E-mail. Although he starred in simple action films, Bruce Lee possessed something some performers never find: Style, one that has transformed him into a screen icon along with James Dean and Marilyn Monroe, two performers who also died before their time. That sense of style, combined with his hand-to-hand art and his driving personality, makes his films visually fascinating, emotionally uplifting, and breathtakingly timeless.

Certainly Bruce Lee has left behind a legacy for people of every race, creed, and color. His films—simple on the outside but complex once examined—show how a man can develop his body, mind, and spirit to overcome any obstacle, from armed opponents to prejudiced network chiefs.

I remember witnessing Lee overcome all challengers and challenges while watching his films in downtown Philadelphia theaters, where the majority of the audience was minority members. There was an almost worshipful silence during many portions of the films and then a frenzy when Lee snapped into action, particularly during *The Chinese Connection* in which he faces opponents from different parts of the globe and strikes winning blows for people who, like most of his characters, have never been permitted to compete on an even playing field.

Lee's original Hollywood experiences no doubt caused him pain and may have helped form some of his more cynical philosophies. In his book, *Tao of Jeet Kune Do*, Lee notes:

> "Our sense of power is more vivid when
> we break a man's spirit than when we win his
> heart, for we can win a man's heart one day
> and lose it the next. But when we break a proud
> spirit, we achieve something that is final and
> absolute."

Those words probably passed through Lee's mind in the late 1960s when he left California to carve out a career in Hong Kong. When he couldn't conquer Hollywood, Lee accepted an even bigger challenge: conquering the world. Adversity strengthened his spirit.

And if his fans walk away from his pictures with even a small percentage of that spirit, then Lee's cinematic contributions will make the world a better place.

CHAPTER 10
JUST THE FACTS ON BRUCE LEE

Here are some facts about Bruce Lee, his films and his legacy.

•Lee stood five-foot-six and weighed 140 pounds.

•Lee was forced out of the classes of Professor Yip Man, grand master of wing chun kung fu in Hong Kong, due to the jealous students who resented his abilities. After discovering Lee's mother had a part-German heritage, the students protested, claiming that the martial arts style was being taught to someone with European blood and refused to train with him. Lee left the school soon after.

•The name of Lee's Hong Kong gang was The Junction Street Eight Tigers.

•Ping Chow, who owned the Seattle restaurant, Ruby Chow's, with his wife, Ruby, had performed in the Chinese opera with Lee's father, Lee Hoi Chuen, an actor and comic who—as was the custom of the day in Hong Kong—smoked opium.

•Lee spent two hours each day practicing Jeet Kune Do, his martial arts style. He would deliver as many as 2,000 punches and 500 kicks per leg during the intense sessions.

•According to Dan Inosanto, Lee used the analogy of a sculptor when explaining the concept of Jeet Kune Do. However, instead of adding clay to create his art, the sculptor in Lee's example would chisel away until just the "essence" was revealed.

•Lee had two favorite songs: Paul Anka's "My Way," recorded by Frank Sinatra, and Laura Nyro's "And When I Die," recorded by Blood, Sweat & Tears.

•Lee liked to warm up for his arduous workout sessions while listening to the theme from CBS' *Hawaii Five-O*, recorded by The Ventures in 1969.

•*Number One Son*, the TV show for which he was approached, was originally envisioned as a James Bond-type series with realistic action. The success of *Batman* on television caused the producers to rethink their plans and instead launch *The Green Hornet* with over-the-top, comic book-type antics.

•Lee's first check from *The Green Hornet* was $400 gross pay and $313.26

after taxes. He used part of the money for a down payment on his first car, a new blue Chevy Nova worth $2,500.

•Lee was approached about opening a nationwide chain of Kato Gung-Fu Schools. He declined, believing he would not be able to control the quality of the instruction.

•In Hong Kong, *The Green Hornet* was called *The Kato Show*.

•After Lee's death, three episodes, "The Hunters and the Hunted," "The Preying Mantis," and a condensed version of "Invasion From Outer Space: Parts One and Two," of *The Green Hornet* were spliced together and released as a motion picture entitled: *Bruce Lee: The Green Hornet*. Some of Lee's fight scenes from various other *Hornet* episodes were also added to the movie. In addition, the film contained a seven-minute Hollywood black-and-white screen test of Lee, with the 24-year-old martial artist demonstrating the crane and tiger styles of gung fu.

•In his guest role on *Ironside* with Raymond Burr, Lee played a martial arts instructor named Leon Soo.

•The jumping elbow-to-the-back move the blind New Orleans insurance investigator Mike Longstreet (James Franciscus) uses to defeat the villainous dockworker on the famed *Longstreet* episode, *The Way of the Intercepting Fist*, written by Stirling Silliphant, is the same move Lee uses to bring down his second opponent during his first fight in *Fists of Fury*. Lee choreographed the *Longstreet* episode.

•Louis Gossett, Jr.—billed as Lou Gossett—plays the police detective who goes undercover and works with Lee in the *Longstreet* episode *The Way of the Intercepting Fist*.

•Lee had little respect for women as fighters, telling a Singapore reporter that females can only win a fight with a man by using their powers of "seduction," kicking the male in a "vital" area, and then running.

•Nancy Kwan, who is featured in *Dragon: The Bruce Lee Story* as Chinese restaurant owner Ruby Chow, starred with Dean Martin, Sharon Tate, and Elke Sommer in *The Wrecking Crew* (1969), a Matt Helm romp with fight choreography by Bruce Lee.

•*The Chinese Connection* and *Return of the Dragon* spoof a gay Japanese character, a homophobic approach Lee was initially exposed to in the American film *Marlowe* (1969) with James Garner. Lee's character, Winslow Wong, loses his composure and accidently jumps to his death after Marlowe teases him about the possibility of being a homosexual, saying: "You're light on your feet, Winslow. Are you a little gay?"

•Steve McQueen was Lee's most famous student, but their relationship had severe limitations. According to Rob Cohen, who directed *Dragon: The Bruce Lee Story*, Lee was unemployed after *The Green Hornet* ended and—during what the filmmaker referred to as the martial artist's "darkest time"—wrote a

Lee spent two hours each day practicing Jeet Kune Do.

script that he hoped to star in with McQueen. After perusing the screenplay, McQueen sent back a pointed note that read: "I'm in the business of being a star, not making other people stars."

•McQueen further irritated Lee by, in jest, sending him a photo with the inscription, "To Bruce Lee, my greatest fan, Steve McQueen."

•On his desk, Lee kept a sign that read, "Walk on."

Lee was dubbed for the American release of *Fists of Fury*.

•While making films in Hong Kong, Lee employed neither an agent nor a publicist.

•Robert Baker, who plays the Russian fighter Petrov in *The Chinese Connection*, was hired as Lee's bodyguard due to the Asian-American's burgeoning stardom in Hong Kong.

•The glasses Lee wears in *The Chinese Connection* were the same ones he could not afford to get repaired a few years earlier. He kept them as a reminder of his financial struggle, and they were buried with Lee, having been placed in his jacket pocket at the funeral home.

•Lee spoke both Cantonese and English, and his real voice was only heard in *Enter the Dragon*. He was dubbed for the American releases of *Fists of Fury*, *The Chinese Connection*, and *Return of the Dragon*.

•During the ice house battle in *Fists of Fury*, Lee's character buried a saw in an opponent's head. The bloody shot was considered too violent and deleted from all existing prints of the film.

•A still of the infamous *Fists of Fury* shot in which Lee buries a saw in the skull of his opponent can be seen in *Bruce Lee: The Curse of the Dragon* (Warner Home Video). The 1993 documentary on the late star was produced by Fred Weintraub, who also produced *Enter the Dragon*.

•In *Return of the Dragon*, the Lee family cat is featured during the final

Bruce Lee and producer Fred Weintraub on the set of *Enter the Dragon*.

confrontation between the director-star and Chuck Norris. The shots with the cat were filmed at the Colosseum in Rome and edited into the final cut.

•The Mercedes seen at the end of *Return of the Dragon* belonged to Lee and was his pride and joy.

•The shuffling movements seen in Lee's action scenes were adapted from fencing basics, not the martial arts.

•Lee used a video monitor to check the fight scenes in *Game of Death*.

•No formal script existed for *Game of Death* when Kareem Abdul-Jabbar arrived to film his scenes. Lee just explained his idea about the pagoda and the various fighting styles of the men inside it.

•Lee wore the yellow-and-black jumpsuit instead of traditional Chinese garb in *Game of Death* to suggest that his character had no limits when it came to the martial arts.

•Whang Ing Sik (*Return of the Dragon*), James Tien (*Fists of Fury*), Bob Wall (*Enter the Dragon*), and Jhoon Rhee (a tae Kwon do master) had been invited to participate in *Game of Death*. Lee died before their scenes were filmed.

•Lee wanted Arthur Penn, whose credits include *The Miracle Worker*, *Bonnie and Clyde*, and *Little Big Man*, to direct *Enter the Dragon* and approached him about the assignment. The film's $550,000 budget, considered low even by the

171

standards of the 1970s, ended any interest Penn might have had.

•In addition to *Blood & Steel* and *Deadly 3*, *Han's Island* was a proposed title for *Enter the Dragon*. Lee intensely disliked that title and it was discarded after he complained to executives at Warner Bros.

•Due to nervousness, Lee didn't show up on the set of *Enter the Dragon* until after the production had been underway for two weeks. To ease him into the work, his first sequence was the simple bedroom scene in which Lee's character greets his female-operative counterpart at Han's fortress. According to producer Fred Weintraub, Lee was so nervous that 25 takes were shot before they got a good one.

•Because screenwriter Michael Allin disliked Lee, he named the British government contact "Braithwaite." He knew the Asian-American star would have difficulty pronouncing the "r" in the name.

•The prostitutes used in *Enter the Dragon* earned $150 a day, making them the highest wage-earners after the stars and technical crew members. That high fee caused jealousy among the extras and secondary players. Real streetwalkers had to be employed, because Hong Kong actresses refused to portray bar girls and opium addicts.

•To make the band around its head flare out, Lee had to slap the cobra used in the underground scene. After a number of takes, the snake, which had its venom removed, bit Lee, a move that surprised and unnerved the star.

•Jackie Chan is one of the attackers during the underground fight sequence

Warner Bros. A Warner Communications Company presents
BRUCE LEE · JOHN SAXON · AHNA CAPRI in "ENTER THE DRAGON" · BOB WALL · SHIH KIEN
and Introducing JIM KELLY · Music LALO SCHIFRIN · Written by MICHAEL ALLIN · Produced by FRED WEINTRAUB and PAUL HELLER

of *Enter the Dragon*.

•The underground cells in *Enter the Dragon* were constructed by placing mud over wooden frames and chicken wire.

•Shih Kien, who plays Han, wanted to use some grappling and wrestling techniques for the final fight with Lee, and the star agreed. Director Robert Clouse, however, refused, feeling it would be more cinematic to show the villain using his claw hand.

•In the original script, Han was killed by being impaled on his metal claw hand.

•The climactic "mirror room" sequence in *Enter the Dragon* was inspired by a mirrored wall in a Hong Kong boutique visited by director Robert Clouse and his wife, Ann. The mirrored room in *Enter* was 18-by-18 foot, with a six-foot square box in the center to make it seem like "an illusion within an illusion." It required $8,000 worth of mirrors to cover all of the walls, and Clouse filmed the sequence by cutting holes that would accommodate the camera lens and then shooting with the camera totally out of view.

•In his screen career, Lee appears to have been doubled in only three shots: The backflip during his climactic fight with the evil Japanese leader Susuki in *The Chinese Connection*; the opening somersault in *Enter the Dragon*; and the backflip during the Bob Wall battle in *Enter the Dragon*.

•Cameraman Henry Wong shot five hours of behind-the-scenes footage for a 10-minute documentary on the making-of the martial arts epic *Enter the*

Dragon entitled *Location: Hong Kong With Enter the Dragon*. All of the extra footage, which included Lee choreographing fights and mixing with the cast and crew, was destroyed following the completion of the documentary.

•After seeing a rough cut of *Enter the Dragon*, Warner Bros. executives approved an additional $50,000 to hire Lalo Schifrin to upgrade the soundtrack. The Argentinian composer, whose credits include *Mission: Impossible*, completed the music in just four weeks. (Schifrin also composed the music for 1986's *Kung Fu: The Movie*, which stars David Carradine as Kwai Chang Caine and features the screen debut of Brandon Lee, who plays Caine's son.)

•*Enter the Dragon* was the third film in history to gross more than $100,000 in just one week in Pennsylvania and New Jersey. The only other films to gross that amount were *Thunderball* (1965) and *The Godfather* (1972).

•*Enter the Dragon* played at a theater in Greece for 14 years.

•*Enter the Dragon* went into profit three days after its release.

•In *Inside Kung Fu Presents Martial Arts Movies '92*, an article on the "25 All-Time Great Movie Fights" listed Lee in the first four spots. He was cited for: 1. The underground battle with the guards (which Lee also choreographed) in *Enter the Dragon*; 2. The Lee versus Chuck Norris fight in *Return of the Dragon*; 3. Lee's first battle in the Japanese karate school in *The Chinese Connection*; 4. The pagoda battle with Kareem Abdul-Jabbar, Dan Inosanto, and others in *Game of Death*.

•To avoid being recognized on the crowded streets of Hong Kong, Lee wore a disguise consisting of a beard and dark glasses.

•In Hong Kong, Lee insisted that his children be escorted to school to avoid kidnappers. He also locked the doors to rooms throughout the house, believing workers would take items as souvenirs.

•At the time of his death, Lee was negotiating with Hanna-Barbera (started by *Tom and Jerry* creators William Hanna and Joe Barbera). The cartoon studio wanted to initiate an animated series based on the martial arts star.

•In 1972, Lee was voted the worst dressed actor in Hong Kong due to his taste for silk suits.

•Metro-Goldwyn-Mayer considered a film that would team Lee and Elvis Presley, a karate enthusiast trained in the martial arts by Mike Stone, who eventually began a highly publicized affair with the singer's wife, Priscilla. Lee dismissed the offer.

•Before his death, Lee had ordered a $60,000 gold Rolls Royce Corniche convertible with a bar, refrigerator, and special plaque which read: "Specifically Built for Bruce Lee."

•When asked the reason for her son's death, his mother Grace summed up her thoughts in three words: "Too much work."

•The airline tickets Lee had been given for a trip to New York to publicize *Enter the Dragon* on *The Tonight Show* with Johnny Carson were traded for tickets to transport his casket to Seattle.

•Steve McQueen and James Coburn served as pallbearers at Lee's Seattle funeral.

•Lee (November 27, 1940-July 20, 1973) is buried in Lakeview Cemetery at the north end of 15th Avenue adjoining Volunteer Park in the Capital Hill section of Seattle. Brandon (February 1, 1965-March 31, 1993) is buried to his right.

•In 1976, Betty Ting Pei, the actress whom the star was with when he died, starred in *Bruce Lee and I*, directed by Lo Mar. The film looks at their relationship and paints Ting Pei as an innocent party. A *Variety* critic reviewed the picture during a January 10, 1976 screening at the Jade Theatre in Hong Kong. He reported the picture was met with "boos and catcalls, and comments such as, 'Clever girl, she can even make money on the dead.' The whole effort cried out for sympathy, but instead the audience seemed to be laughing at Ting Pei."

•In February, 1976, the Pennsylvania Bureau of Consumer Protection took action against the movie, *Goodbye Bruce Lee, His Last Game of Death*. It filed a lawsuit that resulted in the Philadelphia Common Pleas Court ordering Milgram Theatres, owner of the Fox Theatre, to post a box-office notice informing audiences that Bruce Lee played no acting role in the feature attraction. According to *Boxoffice* magazine, it was alleged that in its advertising, marquee, and lobby signs the Fox Theatre "created the impression that Bruce Lee of kung fu fame was back in a new martial arts feature along with basketball superstar Kareem Abdul-Jabbar." Lee appeared in the film only in a series of still photographs and a short film clip. The state attorney general's office charged that the late Bruce Lee was being used to exploit a film that "has alienated the vast majority of Lee's past and present fans." It was the first time the Pennsylvania Bureau of Consumer Protection initiated an action against a motion picture. Following the court order, the Fox Theatre posted a lobby sign stating: "Bruce Lee is not in this film. It is a tribute to his remarkable career and to his memory."

•In 1977, producer Richard St. Johns announced the launching of *The Silent Flute*, based on a idea developed by Lee and James Coburn and from a script by Stirling Silliphant. St. Johns described the $3.2 million project as "a picture about no time and no place. It's about everyman in every time in every place—a man's journey through time in visual elements that put the man through a succession of trials in the martial arts tradition. It'll be action-oriented, a very visual film." In announcing that David Carradine would star in the project (filmed in Israel and released under the title *Circle of Iron*), St. Johns cited the actor's "mysticism" and told *Boxoffice* magazine: "David is the only one who can come close to playing Bruce Lee's role." Released in 1979, *Circle of Iron*, which co-stars Christopher Lee, Roddy McDowall, and Eli Wallach, was a critical and commercial failure.

•*Game of Death 2* (1979) contains outtakes from *Enter the Dragon* but no footage from *Game of Death*.

•In 1986, Largo Toys, Ltd. produced six poseable figures for *The Legend of Bruce Lee* line, which was officially licensed from the Lee estate. The small, plastic action figures appeared briefly in stores.

•On the rap song, "Yo! Bum Rush the Show," Public Enemy salutes the martial arts superstar with the line, "Kicking like Bruce Lee's Chinese Connection."

•Brandon Lee immediately declined an offer to remake any of his father's Hong Kong films and never considered starring in *Dragon: The Bruce Lee Story*.

•In casting *Dragon: The Bruce Lee Story*, Bonnie Timmerman suggested Jason Scott Lee (no relation to the late star), a half-Chinese/half-Hawaiian actor whom she had met while casting Michael Mann's *The Last of the Mohicans* (1992). She was struck mainly by his sexuality, which reportedly was a sentiment shared by the women in her office.

•Jerry Poteet, a former Lee student, was hired to teach Jason Scott Lee the principles of Jeet Kune Do for the cinematic biography based on Linda Lee's book, *Bruce Lee: The Man Only I Knew*, and fully supported by her.

•John Cheung, who had served as Jackie Chan's stunt coordinator and had worked with Lee in 1972 and '73, was hired as the *Dragon* fight choreographer.

Jason Scott Lee starred as Bruce Lee in *Dragon: The Bruce Lee Story*.

•Lee's mother, brothers, and sisters did not cooperate with *Dragon: The Bruce Lee Story*, a failure that reportedly developed from a combination of financial demands and requests for artistic control.

•*Dragon: The Bruce Lee Story* received a budget of $15.5 million, more than triple the combined total of all of Lee's cinematic projects.

•In *Dragon*, a poster of film icon James Dean can be seen in his Hong Kong bedroom and his Seattle apartment while working at Ruby Chow's restaurant. Director Rob Cohen used the poster to draw a parallel between Dean and Lee for the audience. "He (Bruce Lee) was the James Dean of Hong Kong because he never got old and was at his peak," Cohen told the Associated Press.

•For the U.S. release of *Dragon*, Cohen had to delete some fight footage and trim a love scene to obtain a PG-13 rating rather than an R from the Motion Picture Association of America's Ratings Board. Fans were disappointed when that footage was neither reinserted nor shown as outtakes in MCA/Universal Home Video's "Signature Collection Letterboxed Edition: *Dragon: The Bruce Lee Story*," a special laser-disc presentation of the film with input from Rob Cohen and Linda Lee.

•In the "Signature Collection" laser-disc, Linda Lee provides an introduction and expresses her appreciation to Cohen's vision, saying the filmmaker "has done justice to the man" with *Dragon: The Bruce Lee Story*.

•Cohen had to cut 14 seconds of nunchaku footage from *Dragon* for the picture to be released in England, where the Asian hand weapon is outlawed. Nunchaku footage from Lee's original films also had to be deleted for their British engagements.

Ong Soo Han and Jason Scott Lee in *Dragon: The Bruce Lee Story.*

•Lee's longtime friend and Jeet Kune Do student, Dan Inosanto, said of his mentor: "As a movie actor, I feel someone will probably take his place, but as a complete martial artist, I would say no."

•In 1993, Bruce Lee finally got a star along the Hollywood Walk of Fame in Los Angeles.

•In 1994, Linda Lee sponsored an auction of numerous Bruce Lee personal items at the Superior Galleries in Beverly Hills. The event, coordinated with Linda Lee by auction consultant Mike Gutierrez, raised $337,315. The 10 items fetching the highest prices were:

1) Lee's letter titled "My Definite Chief Aim" ($29,000), which was purchased by Planet Hollywood and displayed in its New York location on 57th Street.

2) Wallet and contents ($10,250)

3) *Enter the Dragon* cat suit ($9,400)

4) Kato cap and suspenders ($8,600)

5) Premiere script for *The Green Hornet* ($7,500)

6) Hong Kong driver's license ($7,250)

7) Signed Kato photo ($7,200)

8) "Tao of Gung Fu" essay ($7,100)

9) Blue suit worn in *Enter the Dragon* ($7,000)

10) The Ultimate Source of JKD writing ($6,400)

•The auction's lowest priced item was a coffee cup given to Linda as a gift. It sold for $240.

The following is Bruce Lee's adult filmography:

1966-67: *The Green Hornet* (ABC) as Kato

1966: *Batman* (ABC) as Kato in two appearances

1968: *The Wrecking Crew* as fight coordinator

1969: *A Walk in the Spring Rain* as stunt coordinator

1969: *Marlowe* as featured villain

1969: *Ironside* (NBC) in a guest role as a martial arts instructor

1969: *Blondie* (CBS) in a guest role as a martial arts instructor

1970: *Here Come the Brides* (ABC) as a guest star in non-fighting role

1971: *Longstreet* (ABC) as featured player

1972: *Fists of Fury* as star

1972: *The Chinese Connection* as star

1972: *Return of the Dragon* as director-star-producer-writer

1973: *Enter the Dragon* as star

1979: *Game of Death* as star and director of partial footage shot in 1972

For many years, no information was available regarding Lee's appearance on "Pick on a Bully Your Own Size," an episode of the CBS-TV show, *Blondie* (1968-69), with Will Hutchins as Dagwood Bumstead and Patricia Harty as Blondie. The episode was filmed November 8 to 12, 1968 and aired on January 9, 1969.

Will Hutchins clearly remembers the filming and offered these thoughts on the episode and Lee.

The star of *Blondie* recalled:

"For my money, 'Pick on a Bully Your Own Size' was the best show we ever did on *Blondie*, and much of that was due to the presence of Bruce Lee. It was the last one we did. I didn't know diddly squat about Bruce Lee. I had never watched *The Green Hornet*, because I didn't feel they could capture the mystery and the magic of the radio show on TV, but I did know that Bruce had played Kato.

"In the episode, my son Alexander (Stuffy Singer) was being bullied by a neighborhood boy, and I went to talk to his father (played by character actor Bruce Gordon, best known as Frank Nitti on ABC's *The Untouchables*, 1959-63). My character starts to lay down the law about his bully of a son, so the bully's father starts bullying me.

"I had to learn to protect myself, so I went through a self-defense course that was taught by a martial artist played by Bruce Lee. The character taught me that when an attacker is coming at you, you assume a fighting pose and make a sound like, 'Yoosh!' I then returned to the bully's house, we got in the center of his living room floor, I assumed a position and went, 'Yoosh!' He then assumed the same position and made the same sound. The joke was that I looked into the camera and went, 'Uh-oh!' That was the end.

"Bruce was one of those magical guys around whom everything just kind of flowed. He was on a different plane than me. I first got an inkling of his greatness during a break, when he said, 'I'm going to put a penny in your hand with the palm up, I'm going to put my hand over my head, and then I'm going to try to swoop down and get that penny before you can close your fist.' He then put the penny in my palm.

"I felt kind of sorry for him, because I was pretty fast due to the quick-draw lessons I had while filming *Sugarfoot* (Hutchins played Tom 'Sugarfoot' Brewster on the ABC Western series, telecast 1957-61). Suddenly his hand swooped down like a hawk, but I still felt the penny in my hand, so it seemed like I was taking candy from a baby. When I opened my hand, a dime was there. That really got my attention, because I was a great fan of magic and I knew what he did wasn't some kind of trick. I then knew I was in the presence of someone different.

"During one of the breaks, I asked him what his (martial arts) system was. He said he developed his own style and then demonstrated a move in which he whipped his arm out in front of him. We were inside a sound stage, and it sounded just like Jack Nicklaus hitting a golf ball. I then tried the same move with my arm and hurt myself. The only sound I heard was me saying, 'Ouch.'

"My best friend asked Bruce Lee to give him a demonstration of his power. All Bruce did was rub a circle on my friend's stomach and then put all of his power into delivering a one-inch blow with just his fingertips. My buddy went shooting across the room and hit the wall. His stomach was sore for days.

"I worked with a lot of people—actors like Jack Nicholson, Clint Eastwood, Sally Field, and Richard Dreyfuss—who went on to superstardom, but the two people who stand out most for me are Bruce Lee and Elvis Presley. I starred with Elvis in two movies— *Spinout* (1966; as a cop involved with the drummer, played by Deborah Walley, in Presley's band) and *Clambake* (1967; as the singer's good buddy)—when he was a major star, and he and Bruce had something in common, a magic about them.

"When Bruce was on *Blondie*, we filmed a martial arts scene on a mat, and the show's director, Peter Baldwin, who was a wonderful guy, just let us go. We got on the mat and ad libbed. It almost felt like Zen, because our movements turned into something like a dance and I followed Bruce.

"For just a minute, it seemed like we were Fred Astaire and Ginger Rogers. As I said, he was magic."

SOURCES CITED: Personal interviews; *Bruce Lee: Fighting Spirit—A Biography* by Bruce Thomas; *Hong Kong Action Cinema* by Bey Logan; *Bruce Lee: The Biography* by Robert Clouse; *The Making of 'Enter the Dragon'* by Robert Clouse; *Entertainment Weekly*; *Premiere* magazine; *Boxoffice* magazine; *Grand Royal*; *The Modern Review*; *Karate International*; *Martial Arts Movies*; *Martial Arts Legends*; *Masters of Kung Fu*; *Fighter Illustrated*; *Black Belt*; and *Kung Fu Masters*

CHAPTER 11
THE SON SHINES

"Willing is not enough. We must do."
—Bruce Lee

No true Bruce Lee fan ever expected Brandon Lee to take his father's place.
Their lives were totally different, and Brandon, although trained in the martial arts, always made it clear that his energies would be devoted more to artistic efforts rather than physical pursuits. But the thrill came from watching the son of the Little Dragon mature into an adult with talents just starting to blossom at the time of his tragic death on March 31, 1993.

The saddest aspect of working on this book has been reading the numerous accounts of the accidental shooting of 28-year-old Brandon Lee on the set of *The Crow* at Carolco Studios in Wilmington, N.C. He died during a flashback scene—one ironically dealing with the murder of his character—when a :44-caliber bullet, which was accidentally left in the barrel of a prop gun fired by actor Michael Massee less than 20 feet away from the victim, entered his stomach and lodged near his spine. (The footage of Lee being shot was studied by authorities and then destroyed.) A crew of between 75 and 100 people were on the set, and when Brandon fell to the ground, they initially thought he was just playing through the scene.

He died 12 hours later from extensive vascular and intestinal damage at the New Hanover Regional Medical Center.

The media quickly picked up on the strange similarity between Brandon's tragedy and the plotline of his father's final film, *Game of Death*. In that picture, Bruce Lee's character (played by a double) is filming a movie-within-a-movie, and, after a mob hitman substitutes real bullets, gets shot while pretending to die of gunshot wounds.

Such stories quickly faded as authorities investigated and it became clear that the terrible incident was a tragic accident.

An obsession with death certainly gives *The Crow* a disturbing tone and haunting atmosphere. The passing of Brandon provides the R-rated film with a macabre curiosity factor, and the constant references to death throughout the story seem downright chilling in light of the on-set tragedy.

But Brandon's fine work and the dark mood created by Alex Proyas, an Australian music-video director making his big-screen debut, transform the stylish project into a visually stunning, emotionally compelling work.

Lee's mother, Linda Lee Cadwell, and his fiancee, Eliza Hutton, gave the filmmakers permission to use doubles and complete *The Crow* after Brandon's death. They knew he was proud of his work on the film and wanted the world to see it. Brandon had every right to be pleased.

Based on James O'Barr's underground comic book, *The Crow* deftly blends horror elements, stylish battles, and cutting-edge musical compositions (by groups such as My Life With the Thrill Kill Kult, the Violent Femmes, and Nine Inch Nails, performing "After the Flesh," "Color Me Once," and "Dead Souls," respectively). In the story, working-class musician Eric Draven (Lee) is murdered along with his fiancee during a pre-Halloween Devil's Night robbery, murder, and rape spree by local thugs who answer to a perverted crime lord, Top Dollar (Michael Wincott).

One year later, Draven's spirit rises from the grave with the aid of a crow, a winged creature capable of transporting souls seeking revenge from the living. Once back in the old neighborhood, Eric, whose white makeup and dark features create a nightmarish tone, stalks the drug-crazed thugs responsible for the attack.

On the surface, *The Crow* resembles a typical rape-and-revenge melodrama, a *Death Wish* variation told from a rock 'n' roll viewpoint. But thanks to eye-catching visuals and shadow-filled sets, Proyas creates a threatening world that simultaneously absorbs and repels, feelings reinforced by Brandon's carefully animated performance.

The Crow was written by O'Barr in response to a personal tragedy in which a drunk driver killed his girlfriend. (The screenplay is by David J. Schow and John Shirley.) During the painful recovery time, the Detroit comic-book writer created a character inspired by Iggy Pop (in terms of physical shape and movement), Peter Murphy of the band Bauhaus (for the accented facial features), and Edgar Allan Poe (the name Draven is a reference to *The Raven*). His work captured the frustration, rage, and gloom that so many young people feel in modern society shattering in the ugly face of crime, drug abuse, disease, divorce, and greed.

Due to the death of Brandon Lee and the state of the world, the universe O'Barr and Proyas create for *The Crow* vibrates with a brutally realistic undercurrent. It chills one right to the bone.

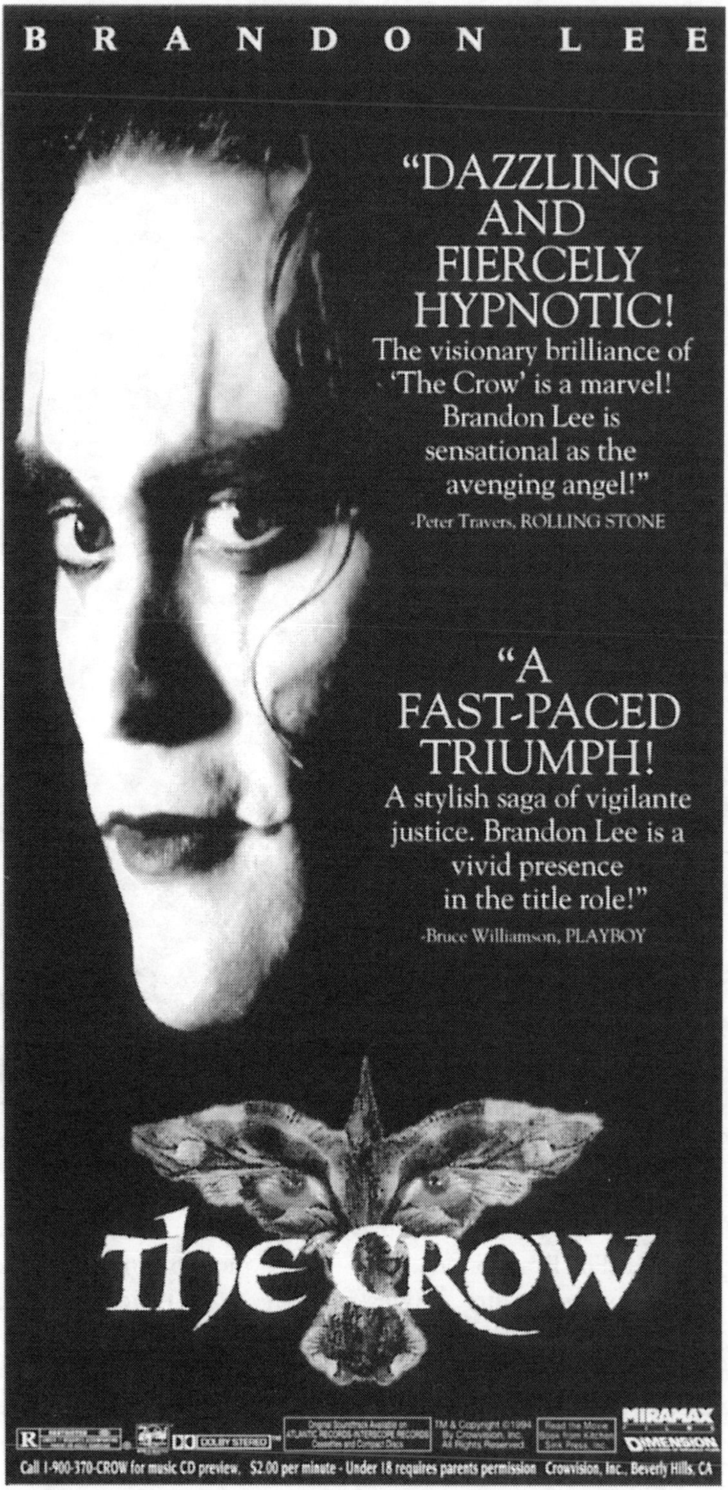

B R A N D O N L E E
"DAZZLING AND FIERCELY HYPNOTIC!
The visionary brilliance of 'The Crow' is a marvel! Brandon Lee is sensational as the avenging angel!"
-Peter Travers, ROLLING STONE
"A FAST-PACED TRIUMPH!
A stylish saga of vigilante justice. Brandon Lee is a vivid presence in the title role!"
-Bruce Williamson, PLAYBOY
The Crow
R
DOLBY STEREO
MIRAMAX
DIMENSION
Call 1-900-370-CROW for music CD preview. $2.00 per minute - Under 18 requires parents permission Crowvision, Inc., Beverly Hills, CA

Brandon Lee as he appeared in 1992's *Rapid Fire*.

The Crow was just eight days from completion when the six-foot-one, 160-pound star died. For Brandon, the dark-themed picture promised to catapult him from low-budget genre movies into big-budget pictures and, quite possibly, full-fledged stardom.

"*The Crow* was intended to be the first in a series of films with Brandon playing Eric Draven," producer Ed Pressman told me during an interview.

> "I signed Brandon to a three-picture contract, and Arnold Schwarzenegger was the only other talent with whom I had ever done that. Brandon and I saw this as a franchise character.
>
> "Brandon came into my office on the recommendation of his agent and lawyer, and I immediately responded to him. Once we met, there was never anyone else under possible consideration. He had the charm, wit, humor, and vulnerability that the character needed. He also had the strength and athleticism, which few actors possess. He actually choreographed many of his scenes."

According to Pressman, Brandon was particularly pleased that the producer wasn't awed by his father.

> "I was familiar with the name Bruce Lee but not a big fan of those martial arts films," Pressman recalled. "...one of the things Brandon liked about doing this part stemmed from the fact he wasn't getting *The Crow* because of his father.
>
> "Brandon had been trained as an actor and was ambitious. He said he someday wanted to be like Mel Gibson, and I think he had that in him."

The Crow was originally set for release by Paramount Pictures, which dropped the picture after the shooting incident. The company insuring the production gave Pressman the choice of either pulling the plug on the movie and being paid for all losses or completing the project and being reimbursed for all extra costs resulting from the use of doubles and reshoots. The distribution was picked up by Miramax/Dimension after Pressman was sure it would be completed.

> "Technically, there was no question that we could finish *The Crow*," he said. "The real question was whether we could handle it psychologically. Alex was devastated, and he

made it clear that he wouldn't even consider continuing unless Brandon's family and Eliza endorsed it, which they did. Brandon was extremely high on the picture and felt he was doing great work.

"Everyone involved felt that to bury the movie would be a crime and would prove nothing. Finishing it gave the family and the crew a sense of closure."

The cost of additional shooting (including the use of a double and digital compositing for some of Lee's unfilmed scenes) was $8 million, which increased the budget to $23 million. In Pressman's eyes, the film, which eventually opened on May 12, 1994, would have transformed Lee into an international sensation.

"I think *The Crow* would have done for Brandon what *Conan the Barbarian* (1982) did for Arnold Schwarzenegger," said the producer, whose impressive credits include Brian De Palma's *Sisters*, Wolfgang Petersen's *Das Boot*, David Byrne's *True Stories*, Oliver Stone's *Wall Street*, Barbet Schroeder's *Reversal of Fortune*, David Mamet's *Homicide*, and Abel Ferrara's *Bad Lieutenant*. "Every film is an ordeal to get made. *The Crow* was the most difficult of all."

The Crow is dedicated to Brandon and Eliza.

Rob Cohen spent four years working with Linda Lee Cadwell to develop *Dragon: The Bruce Lee Story*. (Two-and-a-half years of that time was devoted just to adapting Linda Lee's book, *Bruce Lee: The Man Only I Knew*, into a script.) During that time, he spoke with Brandon about the project.

In an interview, the director discussed his thoughts on the father and son:

"All of us involved with *Dragon* were traumatized by Brandon's death. In real life, I only spent an hour with Brandon in my office, but from filming his birth, naming, toddlerhood, and boyhood in the film, I felt like I knew him personally.

"When Linda and I talked after she got back from North Carolina (where her son was shot) and Seattle (where he was buried), we hugged and she said, 'Brandon loved your script. He cried after he read it and said, 'They honored my dad.' He then told his mother he would never be able to see *Dragon*, because it would be too painful for him to watch.

"Brandon's fiancee (Eliza Hutton) had told Linda that during the filming in North Carolina, they went to the movies and a trailer from *Dragon* came on the screen and it showed Brandon and his younger sister running into Bruce's arms (as young children). She said Brandon went from being 28 to eight as he watched and became mesmerized by the shock of remembering what it was like to be held by his father.

"I can only imagine what it was like to know Bruce Lee. My first exposure to him was in 1973, when my friend (producer) Fred Weintraub invited me to attend the Hollywood premiere of *Enter the Dragon*. I had no idea what I was going to see and thought to myself, 'What the hell am I doing here?' But then, I got so caught up in the incredible physicality of this Asian man, and when I found out that he was dead, I was stunned. I never forgot that incredible experience.

"It was the first film in which I'd ever seen an audience respond to an actor as if he were part of a live sporting event with cheering, applauding, and screaming. I'd never seen anything like that before."

"Truth can only be realized when you have discarded the untruths and the non-essentials."

—Bruce Lee

Just before *The Crow* started filming, I had the opportunity to interview Brandon Lee, who talked about his father and other topics.

Brandon Lee
Born February 1, 1965 in Oakland, California

Your father faced much prejudice in Hollywood. What is your view of what he endured and the situation today for Asian-American actors?

My dad found himself in the position to leave this country, because the people in the business of funding films couldn't see an Asian man in a leading role in an American film or television series. That was almost 30 years ago, but the fact is that in Hollywood right now, there is not a bankable Asian star. Not one.

John Lone (a respected Chinese actor who starred in 1987's *The Last Emperor*, which won nine Academy Awards, including best picture) is a very fine actor, and I like him a great deal. But he's not a bankable star. The African-American film scene has really jumped in the last decade. You've got African-American talents directing, writing, and starring in films and TV shows.

But that just hasn't happened for Asians in Hollywood. That's something I would like to see changed before the turn of the century.

What is your memory of the public reaction when your father, an international superstar, passed away?

My dad only made four films, *Fists of Fury, The Chinese Connection, Enter the Dragon,* and *Return of the Dragon*. The craziness that surrounded my whole family after our dad passed away in Hong Kong is on the same level as Elvis sightings to me. That's really what it is—a kind of mania. I don't really understand it.

My mother is a very wise woman and moved our family (Brandon and his younger sister, Shannon) back to the United States. We were away from any kind of limelight for the entire time that I was growing up. I was fortunate not to have to deal with it directly, except every once in a while when I would have an encounter with some nut, one of whom wanted me to sign his head with a penknife because I was Bruce Lee's son. I'm not making that up.

How does it feel when people compare you to your father?

I mostly put comparisons to my dad out of my mind, because that's no way to live your life. Comparisons tend to exist in the minds of other people more than in my own. I just try to do my work and don't worry how it will measure up to the work of someone else.

I honestly can't say that this is what my dad expected of me, though he started teaching me the martial arts as soon as I could walk. He never said,

"Carry on and make martial arts films, son!" My mother never tried to push me into acting. In fact, she always wanted me to be aware of what this business could be like, because she had seen it from the inside.

It's just something I've wanted to do from the time I was young. I've never wanted to do anything else.

Do you watch the films of people like Steven Seagal, Jean-Claude Van Damme, and other action stars who clearly owe a debt to your father?

My father created the martial arts genre in the Western world. I don't think that's presumptuous to say. I just think it's true. Certainly the films of other people have grossed more money and have had larger budgets, but for my money, no one has ever equaled my dad's achievement on film.

I've always found watching American films with fight scenes somewhat of a hassle. The directors do so much cutting that you don't see all the action.

Brandon Lee filmography:
1986: *Kung Fu: The Movie* (TV movie with David Carradine)
1988: *Legacy of Rage* (Hong Kong crime drama with Bolo Yeung)
1989: *Laser Mission* (a German-South African-U.S. secret agent/kung fu tale co-starring Ernest Borgnine and filmed in Namibia)
1991: *Showdown in Little Tokyo* (a Warner Bros. police drama co-starring Dolph Lundgren and set in Los Angeles' Little Tokyo)
1992: *Rapid Fire* (a Twentieth Century-Fox action-crime thriller co-starring Nick Mancuso)
1993: *The Crow* (a Miramax/Dimension release co-starring Ernie Hudson)

CHAPTER 12
THE MEN WHO WOULD BE KINGS

Filmdom's King of Kung Fu has never been replaced, though there have been many seekers to the throne.

Performers such as Chuck Norris, Steven Seagal, Jean-Claude Van Damme, and Jackie Chan have enjoyed successful careers as hard-hitting heroes, though none has approached Bruce Lee's legendary status.

Here are quotes, comments, and insights from each of these "Men Who Would Be Kings."

Chuck Norris
Born: March 10, 1940 in Ryan, Oklahoma

What led you from the martial arts to acting?

No one came up to me and said, "OK, I'm going to make you a star." I wanted to quit fighting and knew that I had to redirect my goals or I would go back to fighting and, like an old boxer who tries to return to the ring, take a chance of losing and perhaps getting hurt. I was teaching Steve McQueen at the time, and he inspired me to try acting.

Then I did *Return of the Dragon* with Bruce Lee and really became interested in film work.

What is your earliest memory of Bruce Lee?

I first met Bruce in 1966 when he was starring in *The Green Hornet* and appeared as a celebrity guest in a tournament I was participating in. We went back to our hotel together afterward and spent the entire night talking about philosophies and styles. The next thing I knew, it was seven in the morning.

We worked together for two years after that in Los Angeles, and then he left for Hong Kong to star in movies. One day, he called me and said, "I just did two movies that were very successful and now I want to do one with the ultimate fight scene." From that conversation came *Return of the Dragon*.

What is your goal as a film performer?

Chuck Norris in *Return of the Dragon*.

My whole goal as an actor is to develop a personality. I want to develop a personality like Steve McQueen, a personality that people can relate to.

You've avoided hard-core blood and guts action in most of your movies. Why?

In my films, I want to show the excellence of the kicks, not show teeth flying out. I don't want karate to dominate my films. I want them to have good characters, stories, and actors and not be like those flicks that open and end with a kick and have no story in between.

I hate to see a movie where there's blood and gore. I try to keep my fight scenes artistic, using technique as the show rather than violence and its aftermath. I think that if the quality of the fights is good, you don't have to resort to blood and guts.

There is a difference between violence and action: violence is something a kid sees and has nightmares about; action gives a kid a high while he sees it and then he never forgets about it.

Your roles have varied (from a Vietnam survivor in films like *Missing in Action* to a soft-spoken lawman in the hit TV series *Walker, Texas Ranger*) to some degree. What types of characters do you seek?

The characters that I play use their [physical] skills only as a last resort. The main thing I'm trying to demonstrate is that a person should try to avoid trouble but be able to handle it if he's pushed into a corner. I want an image like the one Gary Cooper and John Wayne gave to me when I was growing up. Since patriotism and a sense of right and wrong have always been very important to me, I decided that the first thing to do was create an image for myself and see to it that any work I did was in line with that image.

I don't want my characters to get as cynical as Clint Eastwood was when he played Dirty Harry or as funny as Burt Reynolds was (when he did the *Smokey and the Bandit* films). I'd like to hit a happy medium.

I enjoy action projects and playing a man put into a situation that he must deal with—either physically or psychologically. Those are the types of films that I like to see and the types I enjoy doing. The idea is to have the audience either excited or tense—anything but bored.

Does a common theme run through your projects?

I think the message of all of my films revolves around dealing with evil and facing a crisis in life. In my movies, I always have to be the warrior. In normal life, I want my character to be the dove, but on screen, he's forced to become the hawk and deal with situations.

That's basically Chuck Norris, anyway. In real life, I consider myself a dove, not a hawk, but when forced into situations, I become what I have to be in order to deal with them.

Do you remember a particularly offensive film?

Some films have violence for nothing more than the sake of violence, meaning there's no philosophy behind what goes on in the movie. David Lynch's *Blue Velvet* (1986) is a prime example of a film with that type of violence. To me, that was total twisted violence on the screen. Violence in a sexual way is very detrimental to kids. *Blue Velvet* was very perverted, and yet it got a lot of critical acclaim.

How did you come to the martial arts?

When I went overseas (in the Air Force), I had only heard about judo, not karate. The first time I saw people doing the martial arts I was mesmerized by their ability and agility. (He eventually studied tang soo do in Korea during the early 1960s and returned to the United States as a black belt.) It was like a dance.

I was skinny and shy as a kid. The physical ability of karate gave me the strength to crack the egg of insecurity that I had for 21 years. When I was young, I was too small for sports. The bad thing about American sports is that if you make a bad impression, you don't play. When I was a kid, I was shy, would ditch school rather than stand up in front of a class, and was completely non-athletic. I used to get into a number of fights at school, but since I learned how to fight, I've never had to. The only fights I've had since then were in the ring.

After I won the world title (Professional World Middleweight Karate Champion, which he first earned in 1968 at Madison Square Garden and held for six years until retiring undefeated in 1974), I said to myself, "Is that it?" I looked back and found that the climb to the top—not the actual winning—was the biggest thrill. The only trophy I've kept is from the Los Angeles All-Star Tournament in 1965, because that was the first competition I ever won.

In karate, you only have to impress yourself. If I could become a world champion in eight years, anyone can. If you are physically, mentally, and emotionally prepared, you'll win. This is the philosophy that makes one a great fighter, and this is the philosophy I live by.

What do you tell young people who ask about the martial arts?
When someone says, "I want to learn karate," he's really saying he wants to be a better person. Training provides a high which a person can't get from anything else. That's what I stress to kids 13, 14, and 15. They're at crossroads in their lives because of peer pressure to use drugs. I tell them that with drugs there's a high but also a low. With karate, there's just the high.

How did it feel to lose a match?
After the first couple of tournaments, I really got a swollen head. I got the idea that I could beat anyone. I especially felt that way at one small tournament that I was talked into entering. I walked in and got in the lineup. I was matched against a little guy who looked so awkward, scared, and nervous that I decided I would take it easy on him and not make him look bad in front of his friends. He beat the hell out of me. It was the first and only time I had ever been eliminated in the first round. I think I learned more from that fight than any fight or championship I ever won.

What is your approach to choreographing fight scenes?
I choreograph a fight by thinking: If I encountered this situation, how would

Lee and Norris in the final battle of *Return of the Dragon.*

I deal with it? The only criticism I get is from people who wonder if gang members would come at me one at a time instead of all at once. If they thought about gang psychology, they would realize that a person is usually in a gang because he's afraid, and the big-mouth leader is usually the worst coward of all.

How do you respond to film critics?

The critics really gave me a tough time when I started out, and my feelings were hurt. I called Steve McQueen, and he said, "Chuck, the bottom line is if the movie makes money. They can say whatever they want, but if your movies make money, you'll keep making them."

What is your definition of success?

Success can be fleeting. Success to me is working toward things I enjoy doing. The money is really just a by-product, the icing on the cake. You have to keep your life in perspective, because if my projects bomb, I could be back in the unemployment line.

Trivia Fact

Bruce Lee invited Chuck Norris to be a part of *Enter the Dragon*, but other commitments prevented the American karate champion from joining the production.

Not-to-be-missed films with Chuck Norris

—*Return of the Dragon* (1973): Norris and Bruce Lee in the greatest hand-to-hand fight ever put on celluloid. What else do you have to know?

—*The Octagon* (1980): Norris takes on ninjas in this tale where strong action compensates for a weak story.

—*Code of Silence* (1985): Andrew Davis, who went on to make *The Fugitive* and *Under Siege*, directed Norris in his best screen role. The gritty tale casts Norris as a renegade Chicago cop fighting corrupt officers, drug dealers, and gang members.

A constantly attacked film with one outstanding sequence

—*Silent Rage* (1983): Even Norris has badmouthed this film, which borrows elements from slasher films such as *Friday the 13th* and pits the star against an unstoppable foe. It's saved by an incredible barroom brawl that opens the picture and features Norris cutting through a biker gang like a chain saw through a watermelon.

A preview of a TV hero

One Riot, One Ranger (1993): The pilot for Norris' TV hit, *Walker, Texas Ranger*, provides a great way for his fans to see their hero's transition from a big-screen heavy-hitter to TV superstar. As Walker, Norris has taken John Wayne's strong, silent-type approach and become a major television personality who demonstrates his karate skills in millions of American living rooms every Saturday night.

Steven Seagal

Born: April 10, 1951 in Lansing, Michigan

What are your thoughts on Bruce Lee?

Bruce and I were not that far apart in age or (ability) level. I had my masters, and Bruce wasn't one of them. In terms of martial arts films, he made the only ones which I thought were even watchable, but even Bruce's martial arts films were exceedingly lacking in story. They were just about how many fights you can get in.

Do you respect other martial-artists-turned-actors like Chuck Norris?

I shouldn't say this, but I despise being compared with him (Norris) in any way, shape, or form. I wouldn't mind being compared to anybody but him. We're completely and absolutely different in every way.

I've met Chuck and he's a very nice guy, but the direction that I'm going is real different. I'm hoping people can look at me as Steven Seagal who has a niche of his own that has action but also has touches of smoothness and articulation for realism, story, and depth of character.

What screen star do you respect?

Clint Eastwood has found a niche, and I like that niche in the sense that he's fairly soft-spoken, not somebody who just relies on gratuitous action and violence. He usually tries to come up with a story and a memorable character. For me, an action hero is more like that.

Clint started with the (Italian) spaghetti westerns (*A Fistful of Dollars*, 1964; *For a Few Dollars More*, 1965; and *The Good, The Bad, and The Ugly*, 1966) with Sergio Leone. A lot of those were stolen or borrowed from the Akira Kurosawa classics (like *The Hidden Fortress*, *Yojimbo*, *The Seven Samurai*) that were real samurai films. All of that is endearing to me. I don't want to be compared to Eastwood, because I can't compare to him, but he's certainly more along the lines of the kind of hero to whom I can relate.

Some of your screen characters are rare because they have families, something most action stars avoid. Why is that important to you?

In my first film (*Above the Law*, 1988; directed by Chicago filmmaker Andy Davis, who also helmed *Code of Silence* with Chuck Norris and later *Under Siege*, Seagal's biggest hit), I insisted that the character be grounded with a wife (played by Sharon Stone) and child. It was my idea, because I felt it was a way to have a character who was accessible and sympathetic. Those are very important elements in creating a character whom people will care about.

I don't want to play cartoon characters like you find in films that have gratuitous violence without much of a story, like the "Commando"-type of movie (with Arnold Schwarzenegger). The *Rambo* type (with Sylvester Stallone) is also limited to me as an actor in terms of telling a story.

I try to make my films real in every way—when I get into a fistfight, when I shoot somebody, when there's a firefight. Whatever it is, I try to make it look the way it really looks. I try not to play cartoon characters.

When I shoot, I sometimes miss. I'm not Superman. I try to make sure everything is as real as the real world. That means a lot to me.

Trivia Fact

Steven Seagal worked in Los Angeles as a body guard and aikido instructor. One of his students, legendary agent Mike Ovitz, suggested that Seagal consider a movie career and helped him land his first film, *Above the Law* (1988).

Not-to-be-missed films with Steven Seagal

—*Marked for Death* (1990): Seagal joins forces with a high school athletic coach (Keith David) to fight Jamaican narcotics dealers introducing dope and voodoo to suburbia.

—*Under Siege* (1992): Everything came together for Seagal with this box-office smash that cast him as a Navy SEAL challenging mercenaries (led by Tommy Lee Jones and Gary Busey) who commandeer a battleship with nuclear weapons.

Take a chance on this Seagal film

—*On Deadly Ground* (1994): Seagal made his directing debut with this *Billy Jack*-like tale that has the action hero saving Native Americans and the environment. The often-outrageous project took on some aspects of a vanity production, but Seagal still delivers the goods, particularly in an opening saloon brawl in which the action star challenges some racist oil riggers and teaches them the meaning of respect.

Jean-Claude Van Damme
Born: October 18, 1960 in Brussels, Belgium

What is your impression of Bruce Lee in motion pictures?

The guy was fantastic on the screen, and he was exploited for years with low, low, low budget films. But he finally made one film, again low budget, *Enter the Dragon*, that was incredible. If Bruce Lee were alive, I don't know if Arnold Schwarzenegger, Sylvester Stallone, or even myself would be in business right now. Bruce was wonderful. He was an artist. He was 100 percent dedicated to the film. You could see that. He was writing the scripts, he was in front of and in back of the cameras.

Bruce knew the martial arts, but he also knew the camera very well. He came in with a new style. The way he talked and screamed in fight scenes. Lee was pure.

I mean, Robert Clouse, who directed *Enter the Dragon* with Bruce, and after Bruce Lee, what has he done that's been successful? And believe me, if an

200

Jean-Claude Van Damme in *Hard Target*.

actor is very good and very sensitive, he can write scripts, he can direct movies, he can do everything. But that can also kill you, because it's difficult.

What types of movies do you want to be involved with?

I want to make movies about relationships and passion, movies like *Rocky*, *Kramer vs. Kramer*, and *The Godfather*. I came a long way from those low-budget karate movies (*Bloodsport*, *Cyborg*, *Kickboxer*, *Death Warrant*, and *Lionheart*), but that was the only way for me to introduce myself fast into the business. I took advantage of my physical skills to establish a relationship between myself and the public.

Because you're a foreigner like Arnold Schwarzenegger, some people have compared your careers. How do you feel about that?

So many people compare me to Arnold, and it's an honor, because the guy is Number One. I'm only the shadow of his shadow. I'm a long way behind him. We're doing the same types of movies, but each of us has something special in life. Me, Arnold, Sylvester Stallone. We all have something different. I try to go my own way.

Steven Seagal has expressed some unkind sentiments about you and your films. What is your reaction to his criticism?

This business isn't going to change me. I made a promise to myself when I came from Belgium to Hollywood that I would not change my way of life to become successful. I'm going to try to be very honest and stay the way I was in Belgium. I feel good that way. You don't have to speak bad about people to try to go above those people (in terms of popularity). If you have talent and passion for what you're doing, you can make it without that (negative talk). I think Steven has something special. He has a good face, knows how to dress, and has charisma. I wish him good luck.

When you came to the U.S. from Belgium, you spoke barely a word of English and had no industry contacts. To what do you attribute your success?

Two things saved me: my passion for film and my charm. I'm a happy person, so every time I talk, I'm full of enthusiasm. I know I was naive (when arriving in America), because people looked at me and thought, "Nice kid, but what a dreamer! Look at him. He thinks he's going to make it!!" But I was always dreaming of going from a small part to a big part. If you asked me to do it again, I could not, because I suffered too much. Los Angeles is not like most of America. It's a very difficult city. When I got to the Midwest and cities like Boston and Philadelphia, people are so nice, like the people in Belgium. But in LA., there seems to be a trap on every street.

Soon after starting out in the business, you turned down some huge salaries, such as rejecting $3 million to star in *Kickboxer 2*. Was it hard to hold out for the right screen project?

In Europe (where he operated profitable karate schools and health clubs), I was making a lot of money and viewed as very successful. Everything was doing well. I was making more money than my father ever saw in his life, and I dropped everything. I was making money, but so what? I'm not that attracted to money. If I wanted to be rich today, I could do nothing but karate movies. Studios know with my name on a picture they can make a big profit. But I want to make good movies, which is why I take less salary to leave more (money) for the movie.

But you feel money is important, don't you?

Money is power, and power is like everything. In general, people with money—lots of money—are often not too legal, so they have the last word (via payoffs) with judges, the courts, and lawyers. The poor guy on the street who didn't pay his taxes from three years ago may have to go into jail, even though he has a family to feed. That's injustice. Now the rich guy who never paid his taxes has so many lawyers and corporations that he can shake hands with the politicians and everything is fine.

Many of your fans are youngsters and you've said that action films won't hurt children. Why do you feel that way?

My movies are not bad for children, and I'm 1,000 percent positive of that. I'll tell you why. You can't take children, put them in a room, and say life is beautiful and there's no violence. The day they go out on the street (for the first time), they'll be hit. They have to know about real life. You have friends and enemies, and you must fight to have a position in life. Putting children in a dream world can be dangerous. I guarantee that if we have more training for sports like boxing and karate, we'll have fewer gangs on the street. Years ago, we had less violence because parents pushed their children toward sports. That gives young people physical activities.

You changed course slightly with *Street Fighter* (1994) and *The Quest* (1996), which marked your directing debut. Why did you take a softer approach?

Street Fighter was really a big commercial machine. It was my first PG-13 movie, which is something that I wanted to do because I have such a huge following of kids. Capcom (the company that owns the *Street Fighter* video game) did research tests all over the world and asked kids whom they wanted to be the lead in *Street Fighter*. Most of them gave the name Van Damme.

I was not a karate fighter in *The Quest* (also rated PG-13). *The Quest* is a story of an orphan—someone like a white Mike Tyson—who starts on the streets of Europe and is trying to achieve something (though his fighting ability). I tried to give the film a lot of heart and scope.

Trivia Fact

When Van Damme, who started studying karate at age 11, arrived in America, he changed his name to Frank Cujo. He switched it to Jean-Claude Van Damme in 1983 after the release of the film *Cujo*, based on the Stephen King novel about a rabid Saint Bernard. His real name is Jean-Claude Van Varenberg.

Don't overlook this Jean-Claude Van Damme film

—*Maximum Risk* (1996): Hong Kong action specialist Ringo Lam, whose credits include *City on Fire* (the inspiration for Quentin Tarantino's *Reservoir Dogs*) and *Full Contact*, understands Van Damme's appeal and keeps the dialogue to a minimum and the action to a maximum in this 126-minute epic. Lam moves the picture at such a brisk pace and provides so much dazzling gunplay that viewers should just sit on the edges of their seats at the beginning and remain there. In the film, which was sadly ignored at the box office, Van Damme plays a French policeman on the trail of the Russian Mafia members who murdered his identical twin.

Van Damme certainly knows how to spot talent. He jumped at the opportunity to work with Hong Kong director John Woo on *Hard Target*, the action specialist's first motion picture for an American studio. Woo, whose credits include *A Better Tomorrow*, *The Killer*, and *Hard-Boiled*, attempted to give *Hard Target* the type of rapid-paced action scenes that punctuate his Hong Kong hits. Unfortunately, *Hard Target* had to be cut six times before it could receive an R rather than an NC-17 rating from the ratings board of the Motion Picture Association of America.

With *Maximum Risk*, Van Damme simply allows Lam to run the show, and he provides Van Damme with an action showcase that shouldn't be missed.

Note: *USA Today* and *Martial Arts Movies* magazine contributed to the opening quote from Van Damme.

Jackie Chan
Born: April 4, 1954 in Hong Kong

You are often referred to as "the new Bruce Lee." How do you feel about that description?

Bruce Lee and I are very different. In his movies, his characters would always stop and fight, but my characters will walk or run away to avoid being hit.

You tried to capture the U.S. market more than a decade ago with films such as *The Big Brawl* (1980) and *The Protector* (1985) and have since become the biggest star in Hong Kong. Why did you relaunch your career here?

For every film actor, the dream is to come to Hollywood. At that time (1980), I was famous in Asia and I said to my Asian fans, "Bye, bye. I'm going to Hollywood now, I'm buying a house in L.A. and I'm going to work." Then I lost face and didn't want to go back to Hong Kong. I totally lost confidence.

You did go back and then pledged to give your Asian fans the most spectacular screen stunts imaginable. Has that taken a physical toll on you?

Every time we design a stunt, it's exciting. We'll go, "How about a motorcycle chase scene?" and everyone will think that's good. Then when it comes time to do it, I'll worry and think, "Why would I design this?" On the day of actually doing it, you're scared, really scared. You're really nervous, and then

Jackie Chan in *Wheels on Meals*.

there's 300 people on the set looking at you. By the time the camera is rolling, you know you have to jump, you have to do it. Then, you just forget.

Afterwards, you're very happy, because you know the movie will still exist years from now. I can still see what Buster Keaton did, and each time, I wonder how he did it. When I see Gene Kelly dancing, I think, "How can he do that move?" That's why I do my own stunts, because 100 years later I want people to wonder how I did them.

As Asia's highest-paid performer, you earn $3 million per film plus a percentage of the profits and retain artistic control. That's all fine, but you take great risks with your stunts, as evidenced when you had a brush with death while filming *The Armour of God* (1986) in Yugoslavia. What happened?

I fractured my skull and almost died on *The Armour of God*. I had to jump from a castle wall to a tree that had to bend to the wall of another castle. When I landed, I had to run away. We built a tree between the castles, and the first time we did it, I landed on my hip. I wanted to land on my feet and run away like a monkey, which would have made it better. So, I did it again.

Jackie Chan in *Police Story*.

As soon as I jumped, the tree broke and I went down to the ground and almost died. I know how to fall, but I still hit my head and made a hole in it, was in the hosptial for 10 days—and do you know how terrible hospitals are in Yugoslavia?

In the 1980s when you came to Hollywood, you said you wanted to learn about moviemaking. Do you feel differently now?

Before, I had a lot of things to learn, but now, I have nothing to learn from American movies. They're all done by computers. People know that Jackie Chan movies don't have special effects, and they like that. Even if you gave me a computer, I wouldn't know how to use it. I'm so proud of my stunts. Only one movie—*Jurassic Park*—beat *Rumble in the Bronx* at the box office in Asia. That's OK and makes sense. It had a big budget, great special effects, and every child wanted to see it.

Two other foreigners—Arnold Schwarzenegger and Jean-Claude Van Damme—have carved out very successful screen careers. How do you feel about what they've accomplished?

They are both clever and lucky. They came to America and worked with good directors who helped them do a lot of things. We don't have that type of situation in Hong Kong. Nobody helped me. I helped myself.

How would you fare in a hand-to-hand battle with Schwarzenegger and Van Damme?

I think both of them could beat me right away. If Arnold squeezed me, I would die. If Van Damme kicked me, I would die right away. But on the street, they could never catch me. We have totally different fighting styles.

Trivia Fact

Jackie Chan appears in the car-crash comedies *Cannonball Run* (1981) and *Cannonball Run II* (1984). Both star Burt Reynolds, Dean Martin, Sammy Davis, Jr., and Dom DeLuise and were directed by Hal Needham (*Smokey and the Bandit*).

Don't miss Jackie Chan in this one

—*Police Story* (1985): This Hong Kong epic casts Chan as a ruggedly individualistic cop going through incredible stunts while searching for a female witness who has fled rather than testify against a crime kingpin. The film, which has spawned a number of sequels, also goes by the titles *Jackie Chan's Police Story* and *Police Force*.

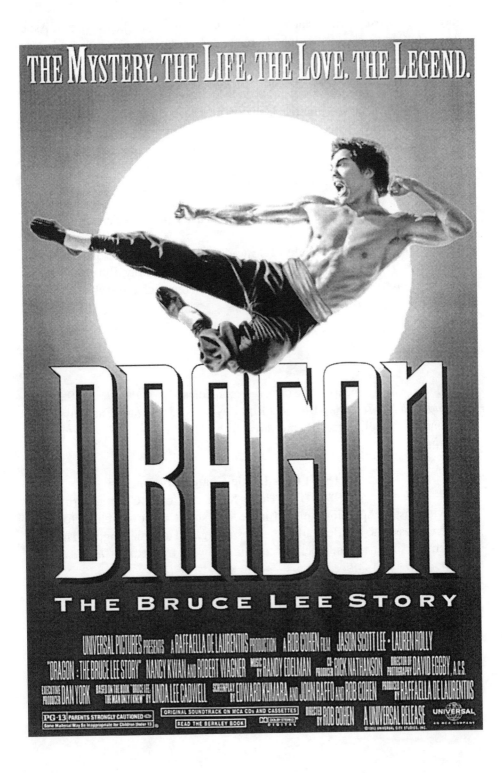

THE MYSTERY. THE LIFE. THE LOVE. THE LEGEND.

DRAGON

THE BRUCE LEE STORY

UNIVERSAL PICTURES PRESENTS A RAFFAELLA DE LAURENTIS PRODUCTION A ROB COHEN FILM JASON SCOTT LEE · LAUREN HOLLY "DRAGON : THE BRUCE LEE STORY" NANCY KWAN AND ROBERT WAGNER MUSIC BY RANDY EDELMAN CO-PRODUCER RICK NATHANSON DIRECTOR OF PHOTOGRAPHY DAVID EGGBY, A.C.S. EXECUTIVE PRODUCER DAN YORK BASED ON THE BOOK "BRUCE LEE: THE MAN ONLY I KNEW" BY LINDA LEE CADWELL SCREENPLAY BY EDWARD KHMARA AND JOHN RAFFO AND ROB COHEN PRODUCED BY RAFFAELLA DE LAURENTIS

PG-13 PARENTS STRONGLY CAUTIONED
Some Material May Be Inappropriate for Children Under 13

ORIGINAL SOUNDTRACK ON MCA CDs AND CASSETTES
READ THE BERKLEY BOOK

DOLBY STEREO
DIGITAL

DIRECTED BY ROB COHEN A UNIVERSAL RELEASE
©1993 UNIVERSAL CITY STUDIOS, INC.

UNIVERSAL
AN MCA COMPANY

CHAPTER 13
A "STAR" IS BORN
IN HOLLYWOOD

"To hell with opportunity; I create opportunity."
—Bruce Lee

A fitting way to close this book is by focusing on an event—the placing of a Bruce Lee star on the Hollywood Walk of Fame—that marked the actor/martial artist's long overdue acceptance by the motion-picture community.

The day was a celebration for Bruce Lee, and the following contains some quotes from Hollywood Mayor Johnny Grant, who served as master of ceremonies, a couple of guests, and the complete text of the speeches of two special people, director Rob Cohen and Linda Lee Cadwell, who dedicated much of their lives to the late, great actor/martial artist. Cohen and Linda Lee met when Cohen agreed to bring *Dragon: The Bruce Lee Story*, based on Linda Lee's book, *Bruce Lee: The Man Only I Knew*, to the screen for Universal Pictures.

When *Dragon* was released in May of 1993, Bruce Lee finally received his "star" along the Hollywood Walk of Fame. During the touching ceremony, held just one month after the accidental shooting death of Brandon Lee, Cohen and Linda Lee gave emotional speeches that reflected the greatness of Bruce Lee and explained to some extent how and why he touched so many people throughout his short life.

The following words are taken directly from the dedication ceremony:

Hollywood Mayor and Master of Ceremonies Johnny Grant
Welcome to this morning's Walk of Fame ceremony, sponsored by the Hollywood Historic Trust and its administrators, the Hollywood Chamber of Commerce. Today, we honor the late Bruce Lee, the master of the most dynamic art form of all—the martial arts—with his star on the Hollywood Walk of Fame.

"Bruce Lee brought to films the same drive and passion that he displayed as a fighter, writing and directing *Return of the Dragon*."—Johnny Grant

I have a short biography that I want to read here. Relentless in his pursuit of physical perfection, Bruce Lee created a revolutionary new approach to the ancient fighting forms and triumphed over the fate that pursued him from birth to become a legend for all time in both the world of motion pictures and self-defense.

Bruce was born in San Francisco on November 27th, 1940, the year of the dragon. He was raised in Hong Kong but returned to the United States when he was 18. His dreams of an America paved with gold were realized when he met the blonde American beauty Linda Emery, who would later become his wife and the mother of his two children. Bruce and Linda's relationship endured until his death and proved to be a critical guiding force in his life's work.

More of a spiritual discipline than a fighting system was Jeet Kune Do, and its founder would popularize the practice of martial arts around the world. Bruce became the best living advertisement for his new style, and Hollywood soon discovered the charismatic young fighter who would later prove to be a dynamic actor as well.

James Coburn, Steve McQueen, and Kareem Abdul-Jabbar would eventually be numbered among his pupils. Revered for breaking Hollywood's color barrier against Asian actors, Bruce enjoyed a new celebrity that revitalized his cinema career. He brought to films the same drive and passion for details that he displayed as a fighter, writing and directing *Return of the Dragon*. Its success persuaded American producers to bankroll the legendary *Enter the Dragon*.

Three weeks before the opening of the movie, Bruce Lee died of a cerebral edema at the age of 32. He was finally laid to rest in Seattle. *Enter the Dragon* went on to open to overwhelming success in the U.S. and the Far East, ensuring Bruce of a place in cinematic history.

Rob Cohen

Twenty years ago, I saw a movie here at Sid Grauman's Chinese Theater, and it starred a charismatic, young Asian-American with a fantastic screen presence, grace, beauty, and intelligence and power. As the curtain fell on *Enter the Dragon*, I was shocked to learn that this vibrant, original man, Bruce Lee, had died three weeks earlier from a cerebral edema—a swelling of the brain—at the young age of 32.

Sixteen years later, I embarked on an odyssey to learn more about him with an eye to making a movie about his life. What I learned from Linda Lee's fine biography of their life together not only cemented my commitment to make the film happen, it changed my outlook on my own life forever.

He was much more than a great martial artist. He was much more than an actor and more than the first crossover Asian movie star. He was an inspiring teacher to students of all races, a philosopher and the author of a powerful book, *The Tao of Jeet Kune Do*, a treatise on the martial arts and the art of living in harmony with the universe.

Bruce Lee was a lover, a husband, a father, and an inspiration. His life on this earth was short and intense. He burned like magnesium, brightly for a brief time, but he was a rich and a fully developed soul. He has become legendary and his effect on people around the world has never waned in these last 20 years. As Saint Augustine said: "The key to immortality is first living a life worth remembering." And that's what we're doing here today as we dedicate this star. We're remembering and celebrating his extraordinary life.

But today also means much more. By giving him this long overdue recognition, we are also honoring the things Bruce Lee has come to symbolize, the vast contributions of all Asian-American citizens, be they Chinese or Japanese, Korean, Tai, Vietnamese, Polynesian, whatever. All of these ancient and powerful cultures have merged with our own and become part of us, and we are far better off for it.

This star is for Bruce, but through him, it is also a recognition of the remarkable Asian augmentation to the weave of American life. Sometimes this kind of honor feels like a conclusion: Here's the star at last, so be it. I'm quite sure this would be the one thing that would make Bruce Lee really angry,

Lauren Holly and Jason Scott Lee in *Dragon: The Bruce Lee Story.*

because a pathfinder hacks his way through the wilderness not for himself alone but for others to follow.

Let this star commemorate not an ending but a beginning, a beginning for new and expanded opportunities for Asian-Americans, especially in our own businesses, the media, the movies, and television where our images and our self-images are so predominately constructed. We need more Asian actors and directors, writers, producers, and subject matter to be put to work. There are many more stories to be told. It is time.

Like this star for Bruce Lee, these stories are long overdue.

This then would become Bruce Lee's true legacy. This would give his star true meaning. He led the way. Now, it's time for us to help others to follow.

A year ago last spring when we started shooting *Dragon: The Bruce Lee Story*, our city was wracked by violence and racial conflict, a torturous and terrifying time. A year later as we're about to release our film, the rule of law and fairness once again marks the cohesion and potential progress of Los Angeles. A new, more compassionate president sits in the White House. A new enlightened chief of police (Willie Williams) runs our law enforcement.

Los Angeles has made the brave choice to walk out of the darkness and back into the sunlight for which it first became famous. We are paused on the brink of a new time, and as Lincoln said, "We can listen to the better angels of our nature," and (we can) remind ourselves that we live in what our Hispanic forefathers named it: The City of the Angels.

This star is for a man who believed fiercely in racial harmony, and to commemorate him properly, so must we. We must never falter from our

John Saxon and Bruce Lee discuss _Enter the Dragon_.

commitment to see brotherhood among all of our people become as tangible as this star we dedicate here today.

I'm honored to be the director who got to tell Bruce Lee's story on film. I'm honored to be here today to participate with his family and mine in placing his star on Hollywood's Walk of Fame. I'm honored to be part of a city that has chosen to live again in the golden light of moral choice.

By recognizing Bruce Lee for what he achieved, we have spread his "chi," his life force, so that it might further illuminate and fortify our own. It is truly characteristic of Bruce that any honor given to him would be transformed and come back as hope for ourselves.

That hope is his gift to us. It's a hero's gift, something transcendent and precious and enduring, pulsing with greatness, like the man himself. Thank you for sharing this day with us.

Jean-Claude Van Damme

I just came here today to pay respect to a guy who loved life like crazy. I'll talk to you soon Bruce.

John Saxon (Lee's co-star in _Enter the Dragon_)

I would just like to say that I'm very grateful to have had the opportunity to work in _Enter the Dragon_ and to get to know and to work with Bruce Lee. I'm very happy that he's being honored with a film on his life and receiving the star on the Walk of Fame. Thank you very much.

Master of Ceremonies Johnny Grant
In my way of introducing Linda, let me say that there has been a proclamation from city hall signed by (Mayor) Tom Bradley and (Councilman) Michael Woo that declares this "Bruce Lee Day" in Los Angeles.

Let me just read the last paragraph: "Now, therefore I, Tom Bradley, Mayor of the City of Los Angeles, join with Councilman Michael Woo in proclaiming Wednesday, April 28th, 1993 as Bruce Lee Day in Los Angeles in recognition of his efforts to promote multicultural understanding and harmony in his enduring achievements in the entertainment and martial arts fields."

Linda Lee
Thank you very much. I am truly delighted to be here and be representing Bruce today. Our family is greatly honored to be receiving this star on the sidewalk for Bruce. I'd like to thank the Hollywood Chamber of Commerce and Mayor Johnny Grant for recognizing the body of work that Bruce did over 20 years ago.

I'd like to thank the Jeet Kune Do Society who first made the application for the star on the sidewalk in honoring their mentor and teacher. I'd also like to thank Universal studios for actually sponsoring this star on the sidewalk and— of course—for making the picture about Bruce, *Dragon: The Bruce Lee Story*, and for this ceremony today.

Furthermore and most importantly, I'd like to thank all of the fans and friends of Bruce Lee the world over. For it is your devotion to preserving his body of work that is primarily responsible for him receiving the star on the sidewalk today. Without the fans and friends all over the world, this would not be happening. Bruce Lee could have been forgotten 20 years ago, although I doubt it.

Bruce Lee was a man of vision. He's being honored here today for his work in film and television, but he blazed trails in other areas as well. He was an avid student and teacher of philosophy and martial arts. He respected tradition; however, he was not bound by tradition. In doing that, he inspired others to search for and find their own potential in life.

Bruce Lee was also a man of action. One of his favorite quotes was: "Knowing is not enough. We must apply." By that he meant it's great to learn knowledge and study, but if you don't do anything with it, it's useless. And then he said, "Willing is not enough. We must do," by which he meant that it's fine to wish for things, to want for things, to hope and to dream, but if you don't do anything about realizing your dreams, they're not going to happen.

And so Bruce Lee envisioned his dreams and made them come true.

Linda Lee, Rob Cohen, and Raffaella De Laurentiis on the set of *Dragon: The Bruce Lee Story.*

But Bruce's greatest role in life—the one that brought him the most purpose and pleasure to his life—was being the father of his children, Brandon and Shannon. But now, four weeks ago today, the spirit of the father that shone so brightly through the son was tragically extinguished.

I feel I represent Bruce here today, and if he were here today, he would want to say to the film community that this must never happen again. So I am calling for a positive call for action to the film community—as individuals and collectively—to take measures that the safety precautions that they have on their film sets will never lead to this series of negligent acts that took the life of my son.

I say these things on behalf of Brandon's father and myself and on behalf of his sister, Shannon, and his fiancee, Eliza, and all of the extended family and friends of Bruce and Brandon Lee. We expect that a young life will not be wasted in vain, and I give the responsibility to the entertainment industry to assure us that it will not happen again.

This is, however, a joyous occasion for us to be here. We have anticipated this for 20 years, that someday there would be a star honoring Bruce's work. Brandon wanted very much to be here. He would have right now been on his honeymoon, but he wanted to come back, especially for this ceremony, because he said his father deserved it, as well he did. Brandon would say, "Bruce Lee only created a genre of film that continues to flourish to this day." And so he did.

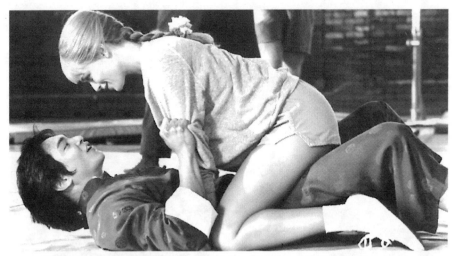

Jason Scott Lee and Lauren Holly in *Dragon: The Bruce Lee Story.*

And so, we are here today to celebrate the life of Bruce Lee and, even though our happiness is tinged with sorrow for Brandon's absence, we are doubly delighted that the movie *Dragon* will be premiering tonight. I have seen the movie. It is a beautiful, positive tribute to a man who contributed greatly in his short life.

And I would like to say thank you again to Universal studios for making the picture and especially to two particular people—Rob Cohen and (producer) Raffaella De Laurentiis—who are people of vision and action as well. Bruce would be very proud of the work that they have done in representing his life.

I thank you once again for all being here. Let's all think of today as a day of celebration of the life of Brandon and Bruce Lee.

Bruce Lee finally has his star on the Hollywood Walk of Fame. Now, it's time for an Oscar.

To have Lee considered for a special Oscar, an appeal must be forwarded to the Board of Governors of the Academy of Motion Picture Arts and Sciences. If made by a member of the academy's voting membership, the appeal is given more weight, but anyone can write and express his or her opinion on Lee's impact on Asian-Americans, multicultural efforts, and motion pictures.

Write:
Board of Governors
Academy of Motion Picture Arts and Sciences
8949 Wilshire Blvd.
Beverly Hills, California 90211

CHAPTER 14
RE-ENTER
THE DRAGON

"There are no limits. There are plateaus,
but you must not stay there, you must go
beyond them. If it kills you, it kills you."
—Bruce Lee

For Bruce Lee fans, the next few years may mark a new beginning, not an end.

A page-one story—"H'wood cyber dweebs are raising the dead"—in the November 4-10, 1996 issue of *Variety* noted that computer wizards may soon be reviving old stars.

The first one being resurrected: Bruce Lee.

"The digital age has brought seamless cinematic life to man-eating dinosaurs, rampaging pachyderms, and space aliens," Katharine Statler and Ted Johnson write in the article. "But for its next act, Hollywood may be creating a real monster: computerized resurrections of dead movie stars.

"Today's special effects wizards are at the threshold of recreating human life, if only in silicon data chips. One effects company, Kleiser-Walchzak Construction Co., has even copyrighted the term 'synthespian' to describe its computer-generated characters.

"But the launching of several ventures—including plans to re-create the late martial-arts star Bruce Lee—has raised debate on not only these Lazarus tricks, but the impact they will have on the industry."

In other words, Bruce Lee may soon be back and sharing the screen with Chuck Norris, Arnold Schwarzenegger, Steven Seagal, Jackie Chan, Jean-Claude Van Damme, and any other performer—living or dead—in a virtual-reality cinematic environment with technicians delivering movie magic.

Is it possible? *Dragon* director Rob Cohen, who experimented with digitally processed images with the sword-and-sorcery epic *Dragonheart* (1996) starring Dennis Quaid and featuring the voice of Sean Connery, thinks so. In fact, he sees such technology as being right around the corner.

"It's totally possible," Cohen said during an interview. "It is so possible that it's going to be here very soon. In the next three or four years, someone will do it.

"Right now, it would be extremely expensive (to digitally create an actor), which is the only thing that will keep it from happening. But once you have a full front and a side angle of any object, you can create its three-dimensionality in the computer. What we did with *Dragonheart* was push the technology of lip-synching and visual expression created by the computer ahead about five years.

"I think the little experiments we've seen in (1994's) *Forrest Gump* (with the character played by Tom Hanks digitally inserted into historic footage with Presidents John F. Kennedy and Richard M. Nixon) and other movies using that technique have been very primitive, but the software and hardware do exist.

"What I'm happy about is that the digital revolution—which I feel that I've been a part of and am proud of being part of it—has opened up the imagination of filmmakers and, ultimately, the whole society. It will have an effect in every area, not just the media.

"Not since the advent of sound have movies changed as much and will they change as quickly as when this digital revolution gets going. The great positive aspect of it is that anything can be done. Anything.

"It is possible that Bruce Lee will act again and probably in our lifetimes."

It's quite remarkable that both Bruce and Brandon Lee have become so linked to the digital revolution.

In order to finish *The Crow*, doubles and digital composites of Brandon Lee were employed. It was a historic accomplishment.

"The computers—Silicon Graphics workstations and Apple Macintoshes—were used in over seven different scenes comprising 52 shots literally to take the late actor from one scene and put him in others, several filmed after the actor's death..."

Variety reported in the article "'Crow' flies with computer aid" by Andy Marx:

"While some form of digital compositing has been used in feature films, it has never been used as extensively or with such sophistication as it was used in *The Crow*."

Wherever he is, Bruce Lee must be smiling.

Concepts such as digital compositing and computer cloning are as far removed from low-budget movies like *Fists of Fury* and *The Chinese Connection* as the Empire State Building is from a suburban rancher. But the question remains: Would the fans embrace Bruce Lee in such a format? If the filmmakers remained true to his cinematic spirit, they might.

The appeal of Bruce Lee films still comes down to these words: People are scared.

They always have been and perhaps always will be. The world remains a dangerous place, whether on the mean streets of Manhattan or the backroads of rural America. At any moment, survival can come down to being able to defend oneself against enemies.

While watching Bruce Lee, we can live in a fantasy of safety, if only for two hours. Watching this five-foot-six, 140-pound warrior stretches the imagination, making everyone invincible and—at least momentarily—a master of the universe.

While watching Bruce Lee, we can live in a fantasy of safety, if only for two hours.

He was far ahead of his time in so many ways, especially when one considers his multicultural approach to teaching the martial arts to those of all races, creeds, and colors and his stress on the importance of physical fitness through workouts. But nowhere was his influence greater than on filmed entertainment.

Before his breakthrough, hand-to-hand action scenes were restricted to John Wayne knockout punches. Lee wiped away that image. Forever.

His sudden cinematic impact resulted in a new way of experiencing combat on screen, and he kicked open the doors for a new generation of iron-fisted and fleet-footed stars. In addition to theaters, Lee's influence could also be felt in homes around the world. His screen exploits inspired everything from the video games *Mortal Kombat* and *Street Fighter* to comic books such as *Teenage Mutant Ninja Turtles*. Lee's success also led to the rash of ninja films, the successful installments in *The Karate Kid* series, and the coast-to-coast proliferation of martial arts schools.

After Bruce Lee, life was never the same for people across the globe, something even those who despise those Saturday afternoon *Kung Fu Theater* shows must admit, however reluctantly.

Most people know that they can never be a sports superstar due to physical shortcomings, but it was different with Bruce Lee. He was one of us.

Bruce Lee's sudden cinematic impact resulted in a new way of experiencing combat on screen.

His success resulted from a continual struggle to increase his physical prowess and mental capacities. First and foremost, Lee transformed himself into a lethal weapon, a body forged by long, demanding, and painful workouts that resulted in physical perfection.

We can imagine ourselves as this person and through his inspiration perhaps achieve our highest goals. While viewing his films, we not only watch Bruce Lee, we fight beside him and are magically transported to a higher plane by the image of a man who—through the sheer force of his will—achieved greatness despite prejudice and oppression.

Perhaps the digital revolution means that Bruce Lee won't be able to rest in peace. He probably wouldn't want it any other way.

SUGGESTED READING

For those want to learn more about the life and work of Bruce Lee, here's a suggested reading list. Some of these publications were cited in the text.

Block, Alex Ben. *The Legend of Bruce Lee.* New York: Dell, 1974

Carradine, David. *Endless Highway.* Boston: Journey Editions, 1995

Chunovic, Louis. *Bruce Lee: The Tao of the Dragon Warrior.* New York: St. Martin's Griffin, 1996

Clouse, Robert. *Bruce Lee: The Biography.* Burbank, Calif.: Unique Publications, 1988

Clouse, Robert. *The Making of 'Enter the Dragon.'* Burbank, Calif.: Unique Publications, 1987

Editors of *Black Belt Magazine. The Legendary Bruce Lee.* Burbank, Calif.: Ohara Publications, Inc., 1986

Glover, Jesse. *Bruce Lee Between Wing Chun and Jeet Kune Do.* Seattle, Washington: self-published by Glover, 1976

Inosanto, Dan. *Jeet Kune Do: The Art and Philosophy of Bruce Lee.* Los Angeles: Know Now Publishing Company, 1976

James, Clive. *Fame in the 20th Century: The Companion Volume to the PBS Series.* New York: Random House, 1993

Lee, Bruce and Uyehara, M. *Bruce Lee's Fighting Method.* Burbank, Calif.: Ohara Publications, Inc., 1978

Lee, Bruce. *Chinese Gung Fu: The Philosophical Art of Self-Defense.* Burbank, Calif.: Ohara Publications, Inc., 1987

Lee, Linda. *The Bruce Lee Story.* Santa Clarita, Calif.: Ohara Publications, Inc., 1989

Lent, John A. *The Asian Film Industry.* Austin, Texas: University of Texas Press, 1990

Logan, Bey. *Hong Kong Action Cinema.* London: Titan Books, 1995

Meyers, Richard; Harlib, Amy; Palmer, Bill and Karen. *Martial Arts Movies: From Bruce Lee to the Ninjas.* Secaucus, New Jersey, 1985

Pilato, Herbie J. *The 'Kung Fu' Book of Caine: The Complete Guide to TV's First Mystical Eastern Western.* Boston: Charles E. Tuttle Company, Inc., 1993

Thomas, Bruce. *Bruce Lee: Fighting Spirit—A Biography.* Berkeley, Calif.: Frog, Ltd., 1994

SUGGESTED VIEWING

Other than *The Green Hornet* series, the screen work of Bruce Lee is available on videotape and, in some cases, laser disc. Here's what has been released. (For those who have trouble locating any title, call 800-4-MOVIES for information on availability or to mail order.)

Fists of Fury (CBS/Fox; $14.99, tape; $39.99, letterboxed laser disc)

The Chinese Connection (CBS/Fox; $14.99, tape; $39.99, letterboxed laser disc)

Return of the Dragon (CBS/Fox; $14.99, tape; $49.99, letterboxed laser disc)

Enter the Dragon (Warner Home Video; $14.99, tape; $34.99, letterboxed laser disc)

Game of Death (CBS/Fox; $14.99, tape; $49.99, letterboxed laser disc)

Bruce Lee Four-Pack Boxed Set containing *Fists of Fury*, *The Chinese Connection*, *Return of the Dragon,* and *Game of Death* (CBS/Fox; $49.99, tape only)

Bruce Lee; The Curse of the Dragon (Warner Home Video; 1993 documentary; $19.99, tape; $34.99, laser disc)

Bruce Lee: The Legend (CBS/Fox; 1985 documentary; $14.99, tape only)

Bruce Lee: The Lost Interview (Little-Wolff Creative Group; $19.99, tape only)

Marlowe (MGM/UA Home Video; $19.99, tape only)

Dragon: The Bruce Lee Story (Universal Home Video; 1993 screen biography; $14.99, tape; $39.99, letterbox laser disc; $69.99, Signature Collection special edition laser)

Original art by Pablo Dominguez

PRODUCTION NOTES

Fists of Fury

From the National General Pictures Publicity Release
CAST: Bruce Lee (Cheng), Maria Yi (Mei); Han Ying Chieh (Mi); Tony
Liu (Mi's Son); Malalene (Prostitute); Paul Tien (Chen, Cheng's Cousin); also
featuring: Miao Ke Hsiu, Li Quin, Chin Shan, Li Hua Sze

CREDITS: Director: Lo Wei; Producer: Raymond Chow; Screenplay: Lo
Wei; Art Direction: Chien Hsin; Fighting Instructor: Han Ying Chieh; Cinematography: Chen Ching Chu; Assistant Directors: Chin Yao Chang, Chen Cho;
Assistant Producers: Liu Liang Hua, Lei Chen; A National General Pictures
release; Color; MPAA Rating: R

At the outset of the 1960s filmmakers and filmgoers alike were turned on
to the motorcycle pictures that emanated from Hollywood. These had super-
seded the beach party films and served as the antecedents for the "horror" film,
the "spaghetti western" phenomenon, and ultimately the black exploitation films.
Now a new genre is emerging. This time Hollywood has been left out and from
Hong Kong and Taiwan comes a series of Oriental films with "blood and revenge" as their themes. American-born Bruce Lee has become an Asian superstar with his first film *Fists of Fury* acquired by National General Pictures for
distribution in America.

Aside from the cost of film stock itself, the single greatest outlay in the
Chinese "karate-Kung Fu" movies goes for synthetic blood. Between 3%-5%
of the budget regularly buys innumerable half gallon plastic bottles of red sticky
liquid. "At the close of the day's shooting," a scriptwriter remarked, "a typical
set looks like a front line dressing station after a major battle. We Chinese are
a violent people—and that's what audiences want." The appeal of blood is not
limited to Chinese patrons in Taiwan, Hong Kong, and Southeast Asia. The
themes of these films have attracted wide audiences in South America, Africa,
and the Middle East.

Bruce Lee in *Fists of Fury*.

Revenge is a basic Chinese passion dating back to Confucian times. He himself warned against the passion 2,500 years ago. The vendetta was a fixture of Chinese society long before Sicilians and hillbillies adopted the blood feud. *Fists of Fury* places the emphasis on unarmed fighting (kung fu) rather than the old-fashioned sword fighting. The "spaghetti westerns" helped to launch Clint Eastwood as an international star and now these karate-kung fu films will do the same for Bruce Lee. Lee is the hottest property in the Chinese movie industry, its first superstar. He has been dubbed the "fastest fist in the East." Small boys—and some very big boys—regularly challenge him to fight when they spy him on the streets. Sometimes he accepts, for he is full of suppressed violence engendered by a singularly unhappy childhood. Bruce Lee was born in San Francisco while his Chinese opera star father was touring the States. He grew up in Hong Kong where he was regularly expelled from schools until, when he was 18, his father sent him back to the States "where all the kids are impossible." He played a few small parts in television dramas and was finally discovered on a quick trip back to Hong Kong. His first film, *Fists of Fury,* broke all attendance records.

Because most Chinese actors do not speak fluent Mandarin, the official language of China, all of the productions are shot without sound. Then a team of skilled dubbers comes in to make the soundtrack.

When the Shanghai movie community migrated en masse in 1949 just before the Communist takeover, only a few films were made in Hong Kong, and all of them were made in the Cantonese dialect. The new arrivals experienced hard times and they were able to make the only kind of films they knew; dramas of social protest or nationalistic exhortation. This new-founded prosperity is a welcome change for the Hong Kong movie community.

One of the most famous of all Chinese directors and the director of *Fists of Fury* is Lo Wei. In more than 35 years in the business, Lo Wei has supplied his deft directorial touch to 75 feature films. In addition to directing *Fists of Fury,* he also wrote the action-packed script and he is of the opinion that these karate-kung fu films are here to stay. "People want to see action," he says. "In a fast moving world, people are interested in action. They do not like sitting through dull non-action films. It is too slow." Almost half of Lo Wei's films have been action films so it was not too surprising that he was chosen to direct *Fists of Fury*. When questioned on the violence in these films, Lo Wei said, "I believe that there has to be some violence in a film of this type, but the way it is treated in *Fists of Fury* (rather tongue in cheek) is the proper way of doing it. It has been grossly exaggerated and somehow the audience rather laughs at it and realizes the futility of violence. I'm proud of *Fists of Fury* and am pleased that Western audiences will get a chance to see our work."

Fists of Fury Facts:

Fists of Fury is the highest grossing film ever to play in Hong Kong. It has outgrossed *The Sound of Music* and *Tora! Tora! Tora!,* the former record holders, by more than $600,000 American dollars.

Bruce Lee, the star of *Fists of Fury*, taught self defense to actor Lee Marvin for the latter's role in *The Professionals.*

Lo Wei, the Chinese director of *Fists of Fury*, has directed more than 30 motion pictures in his native Hong Kong.

Linda Lee, the American-born wife of Hong Kong superstar Bruce Lee, first met him while they were both students at the University of Seattle.

Bruce Lee disables a Japanese boxing student in *The Chinese Connection.*

The Chinese Connection

From the National General Pictures Publicity Release
CAST: Bruce Lee (Chen Chen); Miao Ker Hsiu (Yuan Li-erh); James Tien (Fan Chun-Hsia); Robert Baker (Russian Boxer)

CREDITS: Producer: Raymond Chow; Director: Lo Wei; Cinematographer: Chen Ching-Chu; Assistant Producer: Liu Liang Hua; Production Designer: Lo Wei; Assistant Director: Chih Yao-Ching; Screenplay: Lo Wei; Editor: Chang Ching-Chu; Music: Ku Chi-Hui; Fighting Instructor: Hen Ying Chieh; A National General Pictures Corp. Release; Color; MPAA Rating: R

The Chinese Connection was one of the most popular and successful motion pictures ever to play in Hong Kong. In dollars and cents it grossed more than *Fists of Fury*, the first of the Kung-Fu pictures to be shown to Western audiences. Bruce Lee, who starred in both, has become the first Asian super-star and it is as impossible for him to walk down the streets in China as it was for the Beatles to stroll down Carnaby Street in London during their heyday. It is Lee more than anyone else who has made Kung-Fu so popular. In Los Ange-les sales of Kung-Fu books have risen more than 50% since last January and business men are doing a brisk business in the sale of Kung-Fu uniforms. Un-like the hard, powerful style of karate, Kung-Fu involves softer, more fluid movements, all of which have philosophical meanings. It is a way of life and it is closely related to acupuncture. The same body points you use to heal a patient are the ones you use to hurt an opponent.

...It goes without saying that (these films) are the most popular mass form of entertainment in Hong Kong and Taiwan.

Bruce Lee in *Enter the Dragon.*

Enter the Dragon

From the Warner Bros. Publicity Release
CAST: Bruce Lee (Lee); John Saxon (Roper); Ahna Capri (Tania); Bob Wall (Oharra); Shih Kien (Han); Angela Mao Ying (Su-Lin); Betty Chung (Mei

231

Ling); Geoffrey Weeks (Braithwaite); Yang Sze (Bolo); Peter Archer (Parsons); Jim Kelly (Williams)

CREDITS: Producers: Fred Weintraub, Paul Heller in association with Raymond Chow; Director: Robert Clouse; Screenplay: Michael Allin; Cinematographer: Gilbert Hubbs; Editors: Kurt Hirshler, Geo. Watters; Fight Sequences: Bruce Lee; Music: Lalo Schifrin; Costume Designer: Louis Sheng; Make-up: Sheung Sun, John Hung; Warner Bros.; Panavision; Technicolor; MPAA Rating: R

Recently, screen dramas tied to the martial arts have become enormously popular around the world. *Enter the Dragon* marks the first time that a major American film company has gone to Hong Kong, birthplace of martial-arts movies, to make an international martial-arts film. The huge cast engaged by producers Weintraub and Heller unites the talents of the United States, Europe, and the Orient.

The cast of *Enter the Dragon*, the largest ever used for a movie of the martial arts, spent three months filming in and around Hong Kong and California. Locations included Kowloon, a floating sampan city, Victoria Harbor, Hong Kong Island, Los Angeles, and San Francisco.

Enter the Dragon is the first Hong Kong-American co-production, and it is the first authentic martial-arts film made by an American company. It was shot in English and will be dubbed into Mandarin, the main Chinese dialect, for simultaneous release in America and the Orient. The film was produced in association with Raymond Chow of Hong Kong's Concord Productions.

Return of the Dragon

From the Bryanston Pictures Publicity Release

CAST: Bruce Lee (Tang Lung); Nora Miao (Chen Ching Hua); Chuck Norris (Kuda); Huang Chung Hsun (Uncle Wang); Chin Ti (Ah K'ung); Jon T. Benn (Boss); Liu Yun (Ah Hung); Chu'eng Li (Ah Wei); "Little Unicorn" (Ah Jung); Robert Wall (Robert); Ch'eng Pin Chih (Ah Tung); Ho Pieh (Ah Ch'uan); Wei Ping Ao (Ho T'ai); Huang Jen Chih (Ch'ang Ku P'ing); Mali Sha (Blonde Lady)

CREDITS: Executive Producer: Raymond Chow; Associate Producers: Bruce Lee, Kuam Chih Chung, Chang-ying Peng; Director: Bruce Lee; Screenplay: Bruce Lee; Assistant Director: Chih-yao Cha'ng; Cinematographer: Ho Lang Shang; Assistant Cinematographer: Laing Hsi Ming; Music: Ku Chia Hui; Editor: Chang Yao Chang; Make-up: Hsieh Che Ming; Costume Designer:

Bruce Lee awaits another opponent in *Return of the Dragon*.

Chu Sheng Hsi; Sound Editor: Wang P'ing; Set Designer: Ch'ieng Hsin; Technical Direction and Martial Arts Choreographer: Bruce Lee; Filmed on location in Hong Kong and Rome; MPAA Rating: R

The Bruce Lee legend is back again for all local Kung Fu fans.

The man who started all the fuss with *Fists of Fury* and *Enter the Dragon*, leaps back onto the screen with *Return of the Dragon*.

Bruce Lee is already a hero in today's cinema—and strangely enough, he has had no publicity boosts or worldwide stunts to attain this position.

Perhaps his rise to power followed the vacuum for modern heroes in our cinema. Only James Bond lives—but Mr. Lee's popularity in the land of Chop Suey has even made our stiff upper lip British heroes sit up.

Despite all the spin-offs and inferior copies, Bruce Lee is still the respected King of Kung Fu—and his own particular magic sets the film apart from today's imitations.

Game of Death

From the Columbia Pictures Publicity Release
CAST: Bruce Lee (Billy Lo); Gig Young (Jim Marshall); Dean Jagger (Dr.

A poster for the falsely advertised film, *Goodbye Bruce Lee: His Last Game of Death*. Lee's appearance consisted of a series of still photos and a short film clip.

Land); Hugh O'Brian (Steiner); Colleen Camp (Ann Morris); Robert Wall (Carl Miller); Mel Novak (Stick); Kareem Abdul-Jabbar (Hakim); Chuck Norris (Fighter); Danny Inosanto (Pasqual); Billy McGill (John); Hung Kim Po (Lo Chen); Roy Chaio (Henry Lo); Tony Leung (David); Jim James (Surgeon); Russell Cawthorne (Doctor); Kim Tai Jong (Billie Lo)

CREDITS: Producer: Raymond Chow; Director: Robert Clouse; Screenplay: Jan Spears; Cinematography: Godfrey A. Godar; Editor: Alan Pattillo; Music: John Barry; Special Effects: Far East Effects; Make-up: Graham Freeborn; Martial Arts Director: Hung Kim Po; Paragon Films Ltd.; Panavision; Technicolor; 102 minutes; MPAA Rating: R

The legend of Bruce Lee reaches a new peak this year with the release of his last and most spectacular motion picture, *Game of Death* from Columbia Pictures.

Cameras had hardly stopped rolling on *Way of the Dragon* (*Return of the Dragon*) before Lee threw himself into another project, much of it his own creation. He chose the title of the film—*Game of Death,* and put every ounce of his superb dynamism, energy, and enthusiasm into his latest picture.

Perhaps the strain was too great. At the age of 32, Bruce Lee, the first Oriental superstar, idol to millions the world over, died unexpectedly, tragically—some say mysteriously. The verdict at his inquest was "death by misadventure"... but some still believe this leaves much to be answered as an aura of mystery still surrounds the legend of Bruce Lee.

To make best use of the 100 or so minutes of action Bruce had already filmed, intricate modifications were carried out to the original *Game of Death* script. Small parts were enlarged and top-class talent brought in to fill what had now become major roles all shot against the exotic Eastern backdrop of Hong Kong and Macao.

At least four local records were broken in making the film: a stadium to seat 3,000 people was built in 11 days; a 70-foot wall, strong enough to support heavy neon signs, was built in a week; more extras were used in *Game of Death* than in any other Hong Kong-based movie; and Panavision's Panaglide floating camera mechanism was used—another first for any feature film shot in Hong Kong.

The special effects team was already hard at work making 3,000 square feet of "breakaway" glass for the film, weeks before shooting began. The three-man American stunt motorcycle team that provides some hair-raising action in *Game of Death* caused anxious moments for the film's crew.

Some spectacular bike action takes place in the narrow confines of a filled warehouse. With powerful machines crashing through specially constructed windows and office walls, the riders and crew were super-tense realizing that one mistake could cause extensive damage to expensive equipment, not to mention the stars and crew themselves.

The cast and crew, respecting their director's calm insistence on the best, put up with long hours and enervating heat without complaint to ensure that Clouse got his wish. Many of those working on *Game of Death* had known Lee personally.

There were more problems. The heat, the threat of typhoons, water rationing in Hong Kong—only six hours of water a day (causing headaches for the special effects crew who had to provide monsoon rains for several scenes) and of course the language difficulties. Sets and furniture were built in record-breaking time by skilled craftsmen, and the typhoons decided to concentrate on Taiwan instead of Hong Kong.

Dragon: The Bruce Lee Story

From the Universal Studios Publicity Release

CAST: Jason Scott Lee (Bruce Lee); Lauren Holly (Linda Lee); Robert Wagner (Bill Krieger); Michael Learned (Vivian Emery); Nancy Kwan (Gussie Yang); Kay Tong Lim (Philip Tan); Ric Young (Bruce's Father); Luoyong Wang (Yip Man); Sterling Macer (Jerome Sprout); Sven-Ole Thorsen (The Demon); John Cheung (Johnny Sun); Ong Soo Han (Luke Sun); Eric Bruskotter (Joe Henderson); Aki Aleong (Principal Elder); Chao-Li Chi (Elder); Iain M. Parker (Brandon); Sam Hau (Young Bruce)

CREDITS: Producer: Raffaella De Laurentiis; Director: Rob Cohen; Screenplay: Edward Khmara, John Raffo, Rob Cohen; Based on the book *Bruce Lee: The Man Only I Knew* by Linda Lee Cadwell; Executive Producer: Dan York; Cinematograper: David Eggby; Editor: Peter Amundson: Music: Randy Edelman: Costume Designer: Carol Ramsey; Fight Choreographer: John Cheung; Universal Pictures; Panavision; Dolby Stereo; MPAA Rating: PG-13

What attracted producer Raffaella De Laurentiis (*Dune*) to the project was that: "It goes beyond being just a martial arts film, because it's told from a woman's point of view—through the eyes of his widow. In researching Bruce's life, everyone has stated that Linda was the strongest, most important influence in his life."

In addition to depicting Bruce Lee, De Laurentiis explains, "The film tells the story of this wonderfully independent woman—especially independent for those times—who fought prejudice and maintained a tremendous strength of conviction, while always keeping her femininity and knowing how to 'stand by her man.' It's a wonderful love story of a couple that fought against the odds. I know that women are going to love this film."

To transform actor Jason Lee into martial artist Bruce Lee, the filmmakers enlisted the aid of Jerry Poteet, a student of Jeet Kune Do who personally trained Bruce Lee. "I was grateful to be able to pass the art along," Poteet says. "It's like repaying my debt to Bruce, for all he gave me."

Principal photography began in Hong Kong on May 11, 1992, shooting there and on the island of Macao for six weeks.

Tsing Ling Temple was selected for the site of the opening sequence of *Dragon* partly because the area which surrounded it closely matched the Hong Kong of 40 years ago. But when the crew arrived to begin filming, they found that in the intervening six months after location scouting, fast-moving Hong Kong had already erected the most modern of skyscrapers directly behind it, forcing the crew to reorient nearly all its camera angles.

The Mongkok Kai Fong Association, where the Cha Cha dance hall sequence was filmed, serves as a welfare association for the Mongkok District of Hong Kong. Mongkok, which crushes some 120,000 people into an area of one square kilometer, is known as the most densely populated spot on Earth. Other scenes were shot at a movie theatre in the bustling heart of the Portuguese territory of Macao, and on the swarming streets of Hong Kong, finally wrapping production in Valencia, California on August 14.

FOOTNOTES

1) Bruce Lee, *Tao of Jeet Kune Do* (Burbank, Calif.: Ohara Publications 1976), p. 16.

2) Felix Dennis and Don Atyeo, *Bruce Lee: King of Kung Fu* (San Francisco: Straight Arrow Books 1974), p. 30.

3) Alex Ben Block, *The Legend of Bruce Lee* (New York: Dell Publishing Co. 1974), p. 32.

4) Albert Goldman, "The Life and Death of Bruce Lee (Part One)," *Penthouse* magazine, January, 1983, p. 214.

5) Tom Costner, "Hong Kong's answer to 007," *Village Voice*, May 17, 1973, p. 92.

6) Block, p. 13.

7) Sandra Segal, "Bruce Lee: Ten Years After," *Inside Kung Fu*, August, 1983, p. 20.

8) "The Men Behind Kung Fooey," *Time*, June 11, 1973, p. 75.

9) Kenneth Turan, "The Apotheosis of Bruce Lee," *American Film*, October, 1975, p. 67.

10) David Freeman, "Karate flicks: What it all means," *Village Voice*, May 17, 1973, p. 92.

11) Hsiung-Ping Chiao, "Bruce Lee: His Influence on the Evolution of the Kung Fu Genre," *The Journal of Popular Film and Television*, September, 1971, p. 31.

12) Kenneth Low, "Fred Weintraub: The Man Behind Two Martial Arts Movie Booms," *Martial Arts Movies*, 1980, p. 89.

13) Chiao, p. 32.

14) Goldman, p. 226.

15) John Corcoran and Emil Farkas, *The Complete Martial Arts Catalogue* (New York: Simon and Schuster 1977), p. 170.

16) Stuart Goldman, "Bruce Lee fever still running strong," *L.A. Herald-Examiner*, Nov. 29, 1979, p. 33.

17) M. Uyehara, *Bruce Lee 1940-1973* (Los Angeles: Rainbow Publications 1974), p. 12.

18) Linda Lee, *Bruce Lee: The Man Only I Knew* (New York: Warner Paperback Library 1975), p. 11.

19) Phil Ochs, "Requiem for a Dragon Departed," *Take One*, Volume 4, Number 3, p. 21.

20) Richard Hyatt, "Question: Why did Bodhidharma come from the West? Answer: To kick ass! An Introduction to Gung Fu Movies," *Take One*, Oct. 6, 1974, p. 8.

21) Michael J. Gonzalez, "Bruce Lee: His Career and Contribution," *Inside Kung Fu*, August, 1983, p. 20.

22) Turan, p. 68.

23) Linda Lee, p. 32.

24) Goldman, p. 223.

25) Dennis, p. 13.

26) Ibid., p. 12.

27) Block, p. 19.

28) Norman Borine, *The World of Bruce Lee* (Hong Kong: The World of Bruce Lee, Hong Kong Publications, 1981), p. 49.

29) Dennis, p. 13.

30) Tony Page, "My Brother, Bruce: Reminiscences by Robert Lee," *Fighting Stars*, August, 1983, p. 45.

31) Goldman, p. 214.

32) Segal, p. 21.

33) Linda Lee, p. 34.

34) Howard Reid and Michael Croucher, *The Fighting Arts: Great Masters of the Martial Arts* (New York: Simon and Schuster 1983), p. 75.

35) Dennis, p. 14.

36) Ibid. p. 33.

37) Chiao, p. 33.

38) Dennis, p. 16.

39) Linda Lee, p. 41.

40) Dennis, p. 14.

41) Paul Maslak, "The One Who Knew Bruce Best," *Inside Kung Fu*, September, 1979, p. 27.

42) Block, p. 26.

43) Verina Glaessner, *Kung Fu: Cinema of Vengeance* (Lowe & Brydone Ltd., Great Britain: Bounty Books 1974), p. 13.

44) Segal, p. 21.

45) Linda Lee, p. 48.

46) Block, p. 33.

47) Linda Lee, p. 66.

48) Dan Inosanto, *Jeet Kune Do: The Art and Philosophy of Bruce Lee* (Los Angeles: Know Now Publishing Co. 1976), p. 8.

49) Ibid., p. 19.

50) Ibid., p. 99.

51) Dennis, p. 24.

52) Turan, p. 68.

53) Linda Lee, p. 82.

54) Inosanto, p. 8.

55) Block, p. 51.

56) Linda Lee, p. 77.

57) Corcoran, p. 178.

58) Linda Lee, p. 29.

59) Linda Lee, p. 73.

60) Ibid., p. 73.

61) Jesse Glover, *Bruce Lee Between Wing Chun and Jeet Kune Do* (Seattle, Wash.: Jesse R. Glover 1976), p. 31.

62) Uyehara, p. 52.

63) Turan, p. 70.

64) Linda Lee, p. 15.

65) Glover, p. 82.

66) Block, p. 30.

67) Renardo Barden, "Kareem Abdul Jabbar: A Remembrance of Bruce Lee," *Fighting Stars*, November, 1978, p. 17.

68) Corcoran, p. 172.

69) Tim Brooks and Earle Marsh, *Complete Directory to Prime Time Network TV Shows 1946-Present* (New York: Ballantine Books, 1979), p. 301.

70) Chiao, p. 36.

71) Corcoran, p. 175.

72) Dennis, p. 33.

73) Steve Swires, "Lorenzo Semple, Jr.: The Screenwriter Fans Love to Hate (Part Two)," *Starlog*, October, 1983, p. 45./l/l

74) Chiao, p. 33.

75) Linda Lee, p. 82

76) Corcoran, p. 175.

77) Block, p. 43.

78) James Tugend, "Stirling Silliphant's World of Oscars, Emmies and Gung-Fu," *Fighting Stars*, February, 1974, p. 43.

79) Block, p. 44.

80) Dennis, p. 34.

81) John Corcoran, "Up close & personal with Stirling Silliphant," *Kick* magazine, July, 1980, p. 30.

82) Block, p. 72.

83) John Corcoran, "Up close & personal with Stirling Silliphant," *Kick* magazine, July, 1980, p. 33.

84) Uyehara, p. 11.

85) Linda Lee, p. 126.

86) Block, p. 51.

87) Tugend, p. 24.

88) Block, p. 86.

89) Stephen Farber, "Kids! Now you can chop up your old comic-book heroes with your bare hands!," *Esquire*, August, 1973, p. 74.

90) Addison Verrill, "Road to 'Dragon' & $10-Mil," *Variety*, Sept. 19, 1973, p. 3.

91) Dennis, p. 52.

92) Low, p. 86.

93) Block, p. 72.

94) Linda Lee, p. 134.

95) Glaessner, p. 91.

96) Farber, p. 74.

97) Brooks, p. 412.

98) Stuart M. Kaminsky, *Italian Westerns and Kung Fu Films: Genres of Violence, Graphic Violence on the Screen*, Thomas R. Atkins, ed. (New York: Monarch Press 1976), p. 57.

99) Linda Lee, p. 134.

100) Tony Rayns, "Threads Through the Labyrinth: Hong Kong Movies," *Sight and Sound*, Summer, 1974, p. 138.

101) Editors of *Kung-Fu Monthly, Who Killed Bruce Lee?* (Secaucus, N.J.: Castle Books 1978), p. 45.

102) A.D. Murphy, "Hong Kong Chop-Socky Pix & Cannes," *Variety*, May 30, 1973, p 3.

103) Jack Pitman, "Kung-Fu Chopping Big B.O.," *Variety*, May 2, 1973, p. 5.

104) Marilyn D. Mintz, *The Martial Arts Films* (New York: A.S. Barnes and Co. 1978), p. 219.

105) Editors of *Kung Fu Monthly*, p. 24.

106) Page, p. 47.

107) Linda Lee, p. 144.

108) Ibid., p. 145.

109) Corcoran, p. 170.

110) Ochs, p. 22.

111) Peter Homans, "Puritanism Revisited: An Analysis of the Contemporary Screen-Image Western," *Focus on the Western*, Jack Nachbar, ed. (Englewood Cliffs, N.J.: Prentice-Hall, Inc. 1974), p. 84.

112) Mintz, p. 206.

113) Block, p. 73.

114) Chiao, p. 38.

115) Kaminsky, p. 64.

116) Chiao, p. 41.

117) Glaessner, p. 24.

118) Glover, p. 48.

119) Chiao, p. 33.

120) Rayns, p. 139.

121) Alex Ben Block, "The Hong Kong Style: Part I," *Esquire*, August, 1973, p. 76.

122) Rayns, p. 140.

123) Kaminsky, p. 59.

124) Chiao, p. 40.

125) Rayns, p. 138.

126) Glaessner, p. 15.

127) Alex Ben Block, "The Hong Kong Style: Part I," *Esquire*, August, 1973, p. 146.

128) Dennis, p. 54.

129) Linda Lee, p. 36.

130) Josh Greenfeld, "A Czar Rises in the East," *Oui*, March, 1974, p. 55.

131) Mintz, p. 86.

132) Paul Simmons, *The Power of Bruce Lee* (U.S.A.: Bunch Books 1979), p. 9.

133) Page, p. 45.

134) Linda Lee, p. 151.

135) Dennis, p. 55.

136) John Scura, "The Dragon and the Franchise," *Fighting Stars*, April, 1976, p. 40.

137) Rayns, p. 139.

138) Karen Shaub, Rebecca Hall and Laurine White, "Lust, Lechery, and Laughter in Martial Arts Movies or 'Let's Go Get Some Popcorn While Nothing's Going On,'" *Martial Arts Movies*, December, 1981, p. 30.

139) Block, p. 93.

140) Glover, p. 48.

141) Kaminsky, p. 61.

142) "Bruce Lee Had To Take Kung Fu; It Was A Matter of Survival," *Fighting Stars*, Oct., 1980, p. 17.

241

143) Linda Lee, p. 151.

144) Ibid., p. 161.

145) Albert Goldman, "Part Two: The Life and Death of Bruce Lee—His Final Victim," *Penthouse* magazine, February, 1983, p. 56.

146) Chiao, p. 37.

147) Kaminsky, p. 62.

148) Chiao, p. 31.

149) Glaessner, p. 37.

150) Dennis, p. 56

151) Tony Rayns, "Enter the Dragon: Bruce Lee Lives!," *Take One*, Oct. 6, 1974, p. 34.

152) Chow Kin-men and Wong Tiak-sak, "Bruce Lee in the Production of 'Fists of Fury,'" *Bruce Lee Revenges* magazine, 1976, p. 19.

153) Linda Lee, p. 168.

154) Linda Lee, "'Way of the Dragon': From the Beginning," *Fighting Stars*, August, 1974, p. 32.

155) Block, p. 91.

156) Murphy, p. 5.

157) *Daily Variety* staff, "Bruce Lee Pix Back on Pads Via Chow's Golden Harvest," *Daily Variety*, Dec. 12, 1979, p. 10.

158) William Cheung, "The First Meeting," *Mystery of Bruce Lee* magazine, 1980, p. 12.

159) Linda Lee, "'Way of the Dragon': From the Beginning," *The Best of Bruce Lee* magazine, 1974, p. 56.

160) Linda Lee, "'Way of the Dragon': From the Beginning," *Fighting Stars*, August, 1974, p. 32.

161) Murphy, p. 5

162) Linda Lee, "'Way of the Dragon': From the Beginning," *Fighting Stars*, August, 1974, p. 35.

163) John Beasley, "Joe Lewis Fights Back," *Fighting Stars*, February, 1984, p. 33.

164) Linda Lee, "'Way of the Dragon': From the Beginning," *Fighting Stars*, August, 1974, p. 35.

165) Shaub, p. 30.

166) Inosanto, p. 96.

167) Jim Coleman, "The Myths Behind the Nunchaku," *Fighting Stars*, June, 1983, p. 30.

168) Corcoran, p. 176.

169) Dennis, p. 90.

170) Linda Lee, p. 155.

171) Dennis, p. 90.

172) Chiba Shinichi, "Bruce Lee Has Lit Up a Fire in My Heart," *Bruce Lee: The Secret of JKD and Kung Fu* magazine, 1976, p. 63.

173) Mike McGrath, "Bruce Lee: Death by Misadventure," *Concert Magazine*, November, 1975, p. 20.

174) Linda Lee, p. 169.

175) Chiao, p. 34.

176) Kaminsky, p. 57.

177) Editors of *Kung Fu Monthly*, p. 51.

178) Mintz, p. 202.

179) Masato Harada, "An Interview with Norris Opens Up A Big Secret," *Bruce Lee: His Privacy and Anecdotes* magazine, 1976, p. 16.

180) Linda Lee, p. 170.

181) Faubion Bowers, "Ah, So! Karate or Monkey Wrench?," *Esquire*, August, 1973, p. 72.

182) Editors of *Kung Fu Monthly*, p. 46.

183) Corcoran, p. 179.

184) Glaessner, p. 9.

185) Linda Lee, p. 189.

186) Verrill, p. 3.

187) Clive Hirschhorn, *The Warner Bros. Story* (New York: Crown Publishers, Inc. 1979), p. 410.

188) Kenneth Turan, "I made love to a dead man... and other true tales of the Bruce Lee cult," *New West*, July 2, 1979, p. 54.

189) Corcoran, p. 170.

190) Glaessner, p. 88.

191) Block, p. 155.

192) Harada, p. 19.

193) Block, p. 156.

194) Daniel C. Lee, "Reexaminations: 'Enter the Dragon,'" *Martial Arts Movies* magazine, July, 1981, p. 60.

195) Leslie-Ann Kerr, "Bruce Lee Had to Take Kung Fu; It Was a Matter of Survival," *Fighting Stars*, October, 1980, p. 17.

196) Cheung, p. 29.

197) Chow Kin-men and Wong Tian-sak, "Inosanto Discussed JKD, Nunchaku and Kali," *Bruce Lee in The Game of Death* magazine, 1978, p. 20.

198) Linda Lee, p. 179.

199) Uyehara, p. 19.

200) Low, p. 86.

201) Linda Lee, p. 179.

202) William B. Collins, "The Improbable Flight of Kung Fu, the New Yellow Peril," *The Philadelphia Inquirer*, June 10, 1973, p. 1-G.

203) Linda Lee, p. 177.

204) Hyatt, p. 9.

205) Mike Plane, "Superstar Bruce Lee: An Acclaimed Phenomenon," *The Best of Bruce Lee* magazine, 1974, p. 41.

206) Linda Lee, p. 187.

207) Kenneth Turan, "I made love to a dead man... and other true tales of the Bruce Lee cult," *New West*, July 2, 1979, p. 56.

208) Ibid., p. 56.

209) Kenneth Turan, "Bruce Lee: Death Machine," *Close-Ups*, Danny Peary, ed. (New York: Workman Publishing 1978), p. 243.

210) Linda Lee, p. 187.

211) Ibid., p. 186.

212) Lin Yen-ni, "The Inside World of Bruce Lee," *Bruce Lee: His Unknowns in Martial Arts Learning* magazine, 1977, p. 57.

213) Bruce Lee, "Me and Jeet-Kune-Do," *Bruce Lee: Studies on Jeet-Kune-Do*, 1976, p. 21.

214) Richard Oehling, "The Yellow Menace: Asian Images in American Films," *The Kaleidoscopic Lens: How Hollywood Views Ethnic Groups*, Randall M. Miller, ed. (Englewood, N.J.: Jerome S. Ozer, Publisher 1980), p. 182.

215) Block, p. 41.

216) Low, p. 89.

217) Sandra Segal, "'Enter the Dragon's Real Story: The Scriptwriter Speaks," *Martial Arts Movies* magazine, December, 1981, p. 19.

218) Ibid., p. 23.

219) Oehling, p. 187.

220) Chow Kin-men and Wong Tian-sak, "An Interview with the Staffs of Golden Harvest Studio," *Bruce Lee: His Privacy and Anecdotes* magazine, 1976, p. 31.

221) Glover, p. 66.

222) Yen-ni, p. 57.

223) Glasssner, p. 73.

224) Block, p. 142.

225) Shaub, p. 29

226) Oehling, p. 195.

227) Sandra Segal, "'Enter the Dragon's Real Story: The Scriptwriter Speaks," *Martial Arts Movies* magazine, December, 1981, p. 21.

228) Ibid., p. 20.

229) Editors of *Kung Fu Monthly*, p. 52.

230) Steve Jacques, "Enter the Dragon," *The Best of Bruce Lee* magazine, 1974, p. 30.

231) Kenneth Turan, "Bruce Lee: Death Machine," *Close-Ups*, Danny Peary, ed. (New York: Workman Publishing 1978), p. 85.

232) Mitch Storm, "No Business Like Show Business," *Fighting Stars*, October, 1973, p. 26.

233) Maria Yi, "A Collection of Bruce Lee's Funny Deeds," *Bruce Lee: His Privacy and Anecdotes* magazine, 1976, p. 59.

234) Linda Lee, p. 184.

235) Don McGregor, "The Dragon Has Entered!," *The Deadliest Heroes of Kung Fu* magazine,

243

Summer, 1975, p. 50.

236) Sandra Segal, "'Enter the Dragon's Real Story: The Scriptwriter Speaks," *Martial Arts Movies* magazine, December, 1981, p. 21.

237) Mintz, p. 85.

238) Sandra Segal, "'Enter the Dragon's Real Story: The Scriptwriter Speaks," *Martial Arts Movies* magazine, December, 1981, p. 22.

239) Block, p. 102.

240) Kenneth Turan, "Bruce Lee: Death Machine," *Close-Ups*, Danny Peary, ed. (New York: Workman Publishing 1978), p. 243.

241) Block, p. 102.

242) Joyce Howe, "A Nice 'Lo Fang' Boy," *Village Voice*, Dec. 6, 1983, p. 31.

243) Joan Mellen, *Big Bad Wolves: Masculinity in the American Film* (New York: Pantheon Books 1977), p. 19.

244) Ibid., p. 20.

245) Ibid., p. 5.

246) Block, p. 104.

247) Albert Goldman, "Part One: The Life and Death of Bruce Lee," *Penthouse* magazine, January, 1983, p. 230.

248) Brandon Wander, "Black Dreams: The Fantasy and Ritual of Black Films," *Film Quarterly*, Fall, 1975, p. 3.

249) Oehling, p. 183.

250) Block, p. 114.

251) Yen-ni, p. 60.

252) Cheung, p. 35.

253) Mintz, p. 180.

254) Dennis, p. 65.

255) Kenneth Turan, "I made love to a dead man... and other true tales of the Bruce Lee cult," *New West*, July 2,1979, p. 57.

256) Albert Goldman, "Part Two: The Life and Death of Bruce Lee," *Penthouse* magazine, February, 1983, p. 57.

257) Kenneth Turan, "Bruce Lee: Death Machine," *Close-Ups*, Danny Peary, ed. (New York: Workman Publishing 1978), p. 243.

258) Bruce Lee, "To Fight One's Enemy," *Bruce Lee Memorial Special* magazine, 1980, p. 4.

259) Molly Haskell, *From Reverence to Rape: The Treatment of Women in the Movies* (New York: Holt, Rinehart and Winston 1973), p. 346.

260) Jacques, p. 32.

261) Sandra Segal, "'Enter the Dragon's Real Story: The Scriptwriter Speaks," *Martial Arts Movies*, December, 1981, p. 23.

262) Chow Kin-men and Wong Tian-sak, "A Secret and Extraordinary Weapon of the Philippines—Ka-Li," *Bruce Lee's Nunchaku in Action* magazine, 1976, p. 54.

263) Jose Emiliano Alzona, "Bruce Lee As Director: The Art of Cinematic Jeet Kune Do," *Martial Arts Movies*, April, 1982, p. 47.

264) Daniel C. Lee, p. 64.

265) Block, p. 157.

266) Editors of *Kung Fu Monthly*, "Critics Attack the Violence of Bruce Lee," *Bruce Lee in Action* magazine, 1977, p. 46.

267) McGrath, p. 34.

268) Margaret Ronan, "Bruce Lee Lives," *Senior Scholastic*, Jan. 23, 1975, p. 32.

269) Albert Goldman, "Part Two: The Life and Death of Bruce Lee," *Penthouse* magazine, February, 1983, p. 185.

270) Editors of *Kung Fu Monthly*, p. 19.

271) Hank Werba, "Kung-Fu: Instant Boxoffice," *Variety*, March 7, 1973, p. 7.

272) Hui Fai, "Bruce Lee Was Full of Mal Charm," *Bruce Lee: The Superstar from Hong Kong* magazine, 1980, p. 55.

273) Ibid., p. 57.

274) Albert Goldman, "Part Two: The Life and Death of Bruce Lee," *Penthouse* magazine, February, 1983, p. 186.

275) Turan, p. 70.

276) Ochs, p. 22.

277) Caren Golden, "Bruce Lee: The Final Screen Test," *Andy Warhol's Interview Magazine*, Vol. IV, No. 11, 1974, p. 31.

278) Glaessner, p. 83.

279) Albert Goldman, "Part One: The Life and Death of Bruce Lee," *Penthouse* magazine, January, 1983, p. 214.

280) Editors of *Kung Fu Monthly*, p. 9.

281) Chiao, p. 31.

282) Corcoran, p. 180.

283) Emil Farkas, "Inside Hollywood," *The World Journal*, Summer, 1978, p. 56.

284) John Corcoran and Emil Farkas, *The Overlook Martial Arts Dictionary* (Woodstock, N.Y.: Overlook Press 1983), p. 9.

285) Inosanto, p. 53.

286) Kareen Abdul-Jabbar, "Sports Star Recalls Bruce Lee," *New York Magazine*, July 9-16, 1979, p. 16.

287) Editors of *Kung Fu Monthly*, p. 51.

288) Ibid., p. 48.

289) John Corcoran, "Game of Death," *The World Journal,* Summer, 1978, p. 18.

290) Ibid., p. 55.

291) Ibid., p. 20.

292) Cheung, p. 20.

293) Chow Kin-men and Wong Tian-sak, "The Process of Writing Out the Script in the Making of 'The Game of Death,'" *Bruce Lee in The Game of Death* magazine, 1978, p. 49.

294) Kenneth Turan, "I made love to a dead man... and other true tales of the Bruce Lee cult," *New West*, July 2, 1979, p. 56.

295) John Corcoran, "Game of Death," *The World Journal*, Summer, 1978, p. 17.

296) Jim Harwood, "No Fuling with Kung Contenders," *Daily Variety*, April 15, 1975, p. 6.

BIBLIOGRAPHY

Alzona, Jose Emiliano, "Bruce Lee As Director: The Art of Cinematic Jeet Kune Do," *Martial Arts Movies*, April, 1982.

Barden, Renardo, "Kareem Abdul-Jabbar: A Remembrance of Bruce Lee," *Fighting Stars*, November, 1978.

Beasley, John, "Joe Lewis Fights Back," *Fighting Stars*, February, 1984.

Block, Alex Ben. *The Legend of Bruce Lee*. New York: Dell Publishing Co., 1974.

Block, Alex Ben, "The Hong Kong Style: Part I," *Esquire*, August, 1973.

Borine, Norman. *The World of Bruce Lee*. Hong Kong: The World of Bruce Lee Hong Kong Publications, 1981.

Bowers, Faubion, "Ah, So! Karate or Monkey Wrench?," *Esquire*, August, 1973.

Brooks, Tim and Marsh, Earle. *Complete Directory to Prime Time Network TV Shows 1946-Present*. New York: Ballantine Books, 1979.

Cheung, William, "The First Meeting," *Mystery of Bruce Lee* magazine, 1980.

Chiao, Hsiung-Ping, "Bruce Lee: His Influence on the Evolution of the Kung Fu Genre," *The Journal of Popular Film and Television*, September, 1971.

Coleman, Jim, "The Myths Behind the Nunchaku," *Fighting Stars*, June, 1983.

Collins, William B., "The Improbable Flight of Kung Fu, the New Yellow Menace," *The Philadelphia Inquirer*, June 10, 1973.

Corcoran, John and Farkas, Emil. *The Complete Martial Arts Catalogue*. New York: Simon and Schuster, 1977.

Corcoran, John, "Up close & personal with Stirling Silliphant," *Kick*, July, 1980.

Corcoran, John and Farkas, Emil. *The Overlook Martial Arts Dictionary*. Woodstock, N.Y.: Overlook Press, 1983.

Corcoran, John, "Game of Death," *The World Journal*, Summer, 1978.

Costner, Tom, "Hong Kong's answer to 007," *Village Voice*, May 17, 1973.

Daily Variety staff, "Bruce Lee Pix Back on Pads Via Chow's Golden Harvest," *Daily Variety*, Dec. 12, 1979.

Dennis, Felix, and Atyeo, Don. *Bruce Lee: King of Kung Fu*. San Francisco: Straight Arrow Books, 1974.

Editors of *Kung-Fu Monthly*. *Who Killed Bruce Lee?* Secaucus, N.J.: Castle Books, 1978.

Editors of *Kung Fu-Monthly*, "Critics Attack the Violence of Bruce Lee," *Bruce Lee in Action* magazine, 1977.

Fai, Hui, "Bruce Lee Was Full of Male Charm," *Bruce Lee: The Superstar from Hong Kong* magazine, 1980.

Farber, Stephen, "Kids! Now you can chop up your old comic-book heroes with your bare hands!," *Esquire*, August, 1973.

Farkas, Emil, "Inside Hollywood," *The World Journal*, Summer, 1978.

Freeman, David, "Karate flicks: What it all means," *Village Voice*, May 17, 1973.

Glaessner, Verina. *Kung Fu: Cinema of Vengeance*. Great Britain: Bounty Books, 1974.

Glover, Jesse. *Bruce Lee Between Wing Chun and Jeet Kune Do*. Seattle, Wash.: Jesse R. Glover, 1976.

Golden, Caren, "Bruce Lee: The Final Screen Test," *Andy Warhol's Interview Magazine*, Vol. IV, No. 11, 1974.

Goldman, Albert, "The Life and Death of Bruce Lee (Part One)," *Penthouse* magazine, January, 1983.

Goldman, Albert, "The Life and Death of Bruce Lee — His Final Victim (Part II)," *Penthouse* magazine, Feburary, 1983.

Goldman, Stuart, "Bruce Lee fever still running strong," *L.A. Herald-Examiner*, Nov. 29, 1979.

Gonzalez, Michael J., "Bruce Lee: His Career and Contribution," *Inside Kung Fu*, August, 1983.

Greenfield, Josh, "A Czar Rises in the East," *Oui*, March, 1974.

Harada, Masato, "An Interview with Norris Opens Up A Big Secret," *Bruce Lee: His Privacy and Anecdotes* magazine, 1976.

Harwood, Jim, "No Fuling with Kung Contenders," *Daily Variety*, April 15, 1975.

Haskell, Molly. *From Reverence to Rape: The Treatment of Women in the Movies*. New York: Holt, Rinehart and Winston, 1973.

Hirschhorn, Clive. *The Warner Bros. Story*. New York: Crown Publishers, Inc., 1979.

Homans, Peter. "Puritanism Revisited: An Analysis of the Contemporary Screen-Image Western," *Focus on the Western*. Englewood Cliffs, N.J.: Prentice-Hall, Inc. 1974.

Howe, Joyce, "A Nice 'Lo Fang' Boy," *Village Voice*, Dec. 6, 1983.

Hyatt, Richard, "Question: Why did Bodhidharma come from the West? Answer: To kick ass! An Introduction to Gung Fu Movies," *Take One*, Oct. 6, 1974.

Inosanto, Dan. *Jeet Kune Do: The Art and Philosophy of Bruce Lee*. Los Angeles: Know Now Publishing Co. 1976.

Jabbar, Kareem Abdul, "Sports Star Recalls Bruce Lee," *New York Magazine*, July 9-16, 1979.

Jacques, Steve, "'Enter the Dragon," *The Best of Bruce Lee* magazine, 1974.

Kaminsky, Stuart M. "Italian Westerns and Kung Fu Films: Genres of Violence," *Graphic Violence on the Screen*. New York: Monarch Press, 1976.

Kerr, Leslie-Ann, "Bruce Lee Had to Take Kung Fu; It Was a Matter of Survival," *Fighting Stars*, October, 1980.

Kin-men, Chow and Tiak-sak, Wong, "Bruce Lee in the Production of 'Fists of Fury,'" *Bruce Lee Revenges* magazine, 1976.

Kin-men, Chow and Tian-sak, Wong, "Inosanto Discussed JKD, Nunchaku and Kali," *Bruce Lee in The* (sic) *Game of Death* magazine, 1978.

Kin-men, Chow and Tian-sak, Wong, "An Interview with the Staffs of Golden Harvest Studio," *Bruce Lee: His Privacy and Anecdotes* magazine, 1976.

Kin-men, Chow and Tian-sak, Wong, "A Secret and Extraordinary Weapon of the Philippines— Ka-Li," *Bruce Lee's Nunchaku in Action* magazine, 1976.

Kin-Men, Chow and Tian-sak, Wong, "The Process of Writing Out the Script in the Making of 'The (sic) Game of Death,'" *Bruce Lee in The Game of Death magazine*, 1978.

Lee, Bruce. *Tao of Jeet Kune Do*. Burbank, Calif.: Ohara Publications, 1976.

Lee, Bruce, "Me and Jeet-Kune-Do," *Bruce Lee: Studies on Jeet-Kune-Do* magazine, 1976.

Lee, Bruce, "To Fight One's Enemy," *Bruce Lee Memorial Special* magazine, 1980.

Lee, Daniel C., "Reexaminations: 'Enter the Dragon,'" *Martial Arts Movies*, July, 1981.

Lee, Linda. *Bruce Lee: The Man Only I Knew*. New York: Warner Paperback Library, 1975.

Lee, Linda, "'Way of the Dragon': From the Beginning," *Fighting Stars*, August, 1974.

Lee, Linda, "'Way of the Dragon': From the Beginning," *The Best of Bruce Lee* magazine, 1974.

Low, Kenneth, "Close-Up: Fred Weintraub: The Man Behind Two Martial Arts Movie Booms," *Martial Arts Movies*, 1980.

McGrath, Mike, "Bruce Lee: Death of Misadventure," *Concert Magazine*, November, 1975.

McGregor, Don, "The Dragon Has Entered!," *The Deadliest Heroes of Kung Fu*, Summer, 1975.

Maslak, Paul, "The One Who Knew Bruce Best," *Inside Kung Fu*, September, 1979.

Mellen, Joan. *Big Bad Wolves: Masculinity in the American Film*. New York: Pantheon Books, 1977.

Mintz, Marilyn D. *The Martial Arts Films*. New York: A.S. Barnes and Co., 1978.

248

Murphy, A.D., "Hong Kong Chop-Socky Pix & Cannes," *Variety*, May 30, 1973.

Ochs, Phil, "Requiem for a Dragon Departed," *Take One*, Volume 4, Number 3.

Oehling, Richard, "The Yellow Menace: Asian Images in American Films," *The Kaleidoscopic Lens: How Hollywood Views Ethnic Groups*. Englewood, N.J.: Jerome S. Oler, Publisher, 1980.

Page, Tony, "My Brother, Bruce: Reminiscences by Robert Lee," *Fighting Stars*, August, 1983.

Pitman, Jack, "Kung-Fu Chopping Big B.O.," *Variety*, May 2, 1973.

Plane, Mike, "Superstar Bruce Lee: An Acclaimed Phenomenon," *The Best of Bruce Lee* magazine, 1974.

Rayns, Tony, "Threads Through the Labyrinth: Hong Kong Movies," *Sight and Sound*, Summer, 1974.

Rayns, Tony, "Enter the Dragon: Bruce Lee Lives!," *Take One*, Oct. 6, 1974.

Reid, Howard and Croucher, Michael. *The Fighting Arts: Great Masters of the Martial Arts*. New York: Simon and Schuster, 1983.

Ronan, Margaret, "Bruce Lee Lives," *Senior Scholastic*, Jan. 23, 1975.

Scura, John, "The Dragon and the Franchise," *Fighting Stars*, April, 1976.

Segal, Sandra, "Bruce Lee: Ten Years After," *Inside Kung Fu*, August, 1983.

Shaub, Karen; Hall, Rebecca; and White, Laurine, "Lust, Lechery, and Laughter in the Martial Arts Movies or 'Let's Go Get Some Popcorn While Nothing's Going On,'" *Martial Arts Movies*, December, 1981.

Shinichi, Chiba, "Bruce Lee Has Lit Up a Fire in My Heart," *Bruce Lee: The Secret of JKD and Kung Fu* magazine, 1976.

Simmons, Paul. *The Power of Bruce Lee*. U.S.A.: Bunch Books, 1979.

Storm, Mitch, "No Business Like Show Business," *Fighting Stars*, October, 1973.

Swires, Steve, "Lorenzo Semple, Jr.: The Screenwriter Fans Love to Hate (Part Two)," *Starlog*, October, 1983.

Tugend, James, "Stirling Silliphant's World of Oscars, Emmies and Gung-Fu," *Fighting Stars*, Feburary, 1974.

Turan, Kenneth, "The Apotheosis of Bruce Lee," *American Film*, October, 1975.

Turan, Kenneth, "I made love to a dead man... and other true tales of the Bruce Lee cult," *New West*, July 2, 1979.

Turan, Kenneth, "Bruce Lee: Death Machine," *Close-Ups*. New York: Workman Publishing, 1978.

Uyehara, M. *Bruce Lee 1940-1973*. Los Angeles: Rainbow Publications, 1974.

Verrill, Addison, "Road to 'Dragon' & $10-Mil," *Variety*, Sept. 19, 1973.

Wander, Brandon, "Black Dreams: The Fantasy and Ritual of Black Films," *Film Quarterly*, Fall, 1975.

Werba, Hank, "Kung-Fu: Instant Boxoffice," *Variety*, March 7, 1973.

Yi, Maria, "A Collection of Bruce Lee's Funny Deeds," *Bruce Lee: His Privacy and Anecdotes* magazine, 1976.

Yen-ni, Lin, "The Inside World of Bruce Lee," *Bruce Lee: His Unknowns in Martial Arts Learning* magazine, 1977.

INDEX

Their deadly mission: to crack the forbidden island of hell

Author Lou Gaul poses with a favorite Bruce Lee poster.

Acknowledgments and Thanks

Stan Ellis, the *Burlington County Times* (New Jersey) and Calkins Newspapers; Academy of Motion Picture Arts and Sciences; Angie Baldwin; Leon Benen; Ben Borowsky; Joseph Browne; Bryanston Pictures; Eric Caidin; Steve Carpenter; Jackie Chan; Rob Cohen; Columbia Pictures; Pablo Dominguez; Dan Eisenhuth; Jon Falk; Jerry Frebowitz; Alyson Gaul; Denny and Carol Gaul; Elmer and Mary Gaul; Andrea Gottfried; Carl and Janice Hertensteiner; Bill and Ellen Kearns; Ron Martin; MCA/Universal Home Video; Mike Machulskis; Marc Miterman; Frank Nesko; Bill Newill; Shirley Nixon; Chuck Norris; Sandy Oppenheimer; Joyce Persico; Steven Seagal; Bob Sharp; Helen and Jeff Sheard; Rose Shields; Irv Slifkin; Lori Smith; F. Gilman Spencer; John Tartaglia; Bud Umbaugh; Jean-Claude Van Damme; Linda J. Walter; Warner Bros.; Ed Weiss; Jackie White; Terry Zablin; and John F. Zanger, Jr.

Special Thanks: Mr. Marvin Ellis, for opening the door; Prof. William K. Everson, for pointing the way; Mr. William "Bill" Holland, for being an inspiration; Susan and Gary Svehla, for improving the project; Linda Lee Cadwell, for maintaining the legacy; and, of course, Bruce Lee and Brandon Lee.

About the Author

Lou Gaul has worked with the *Burlington County* (New Jersey) *Times* and Calkins Newspapers since 1973, serving as film critic for the chain. In addition, he has written for *Rolling Stone*, *Boxoffice* magazine, and *Video Business* magazine. As film critic, he interviews celebrities and reviews all major films. His profile subjects have ranged from John Wayne to Jane Fonda and from Clint Eastwood to Madonna.

A native of Philadelphia, Gaul was raised in Southern New Jersey, where he spent many, many hours watching movies at the Roxy Theater in his hometown of Maple Shade. He has a master's degree in Cinema Studies from New York University, was previously the film critic for Philadelphia radio station WDVT-AM, and is currently a film critic for Philadelphia talk station WWDB-FM. His civic activities include memberships in numerous community volunteer organizations, and he serves as a trustee of the Friends of the Burlington County Library, Inc., of which he is a founding member.

He was named the New Jersey Library Association's "1996 Library Champion" for his donations of video tapes and film-related books to Garden State libraries and for his volunteer efforts on behalf of the library system. The statewide Champion honor is the highest award the NJLA can bestow upon an individual.

Gaul lives in South Jersey with his wife and teenage daughter, both of whom have come to enjoy Bruce Lee movies.